American Education

AMERICAN STUDIES INFORMATION GUIDE SERIES

Series Editor: Donald Koster, Professor of English Emeritus, Adelphi University, Garden City, New York

Also in this series:

AFRO-AMERICAN LITERATURE AND CULTURE SINCE WORLD WAR II—*Edited by Charles D. Peavy*

AMERICAN ARCHITECTURE AND ART—*Edited by David M. Sokol*

AMERICAN LITERATURE AND LANGUAGE—*Edited by Donald N. Koster*

AMERICAN POPULAR CULTURE—*Edited by Larry N. Landrum*

THE AMERICAN PRESIDENCY—*Edited by Kenneth E. Davison**

AMERICAN RELIGION AND PHILOSOPHY—*Edited by Ernest R. Sandeen and Frederick Hale*

AMERICAN STUDIES—*Edited by David W. Marcell*

HISTORY OF THE UNITED STATES OF AMERICA—*Edited by Ernest Cassara*

JEWISH WRITERS OF NORTH AMERICA—*Edited by Ira Bruce Nadel*

THE RELATIONSHIP OF PAINTING AND LITERATURE—*Edited by Eugene L. Huddleston and Douglas A. Noverr*

SOCIOLOGY OF AMERICA—*Edited by Charles Mark*

TECHNOLOGY AND VALUES IN AMERICAN CIVILIZATION—*Edited by Stephen H. Cutcliffe, Judith A Mistichelli, and Christine M. Roysdon*

WOMAN IN AMERICA—*Edited by Virginia R. Terris*

*in preparation

The above series is part of the

GALE INFORMATION GUIDE LIBRARY

The Library consists of a number of separate series of guides covering major areas in the social sciences, humanities, and current affairs.

General Editor: Paul Wasserman, Professor and former Dean, School of Library and Information Services, University of Maryland

Managing Editor: Denise Allard Adzigian, Gale Research Company

American Education

A GUIDE TO INFORMATION SOURCES

Volume 14 in the American Studies Information Guide Series

Richard G. Durnin

*School of Education
The City College of the
City University of New York*

Gale Research Company
Book Tower, Detroit, Michigan 48226

Library of Congress Cataloging in Publication Data

Durnin, Richard G.
    American education.

    (American studies information guide series ; v. 14)
(Gale information guide library)
    Bibliography: p.
    Includes index.
    1. Education—United States—Bibliography. I. Title.
II. Series.
Z5815.U5D87   1982   [LA210]   016.37'0973   82-15387
ISBN 0-8103-1265-4

To
Professor William W. Brickman
University of Pennsylvania

VITA

Richard G. Durnin, associate professor of education at the School of Education, City College of the City University of New York, teaches social and historical foundations of education. He holds a doctorate from the University of Pennsylvania in the history of education and is the author of numerous articles and monographs on the subject.

CONTENTS

Contents

Contents

FOREWORD

Throughout the twentieth century, and particularly since the end of World War II, education has been one of America's major growth industries. As the population rapidly expanded and as the social structure became ever more complex, the need for an increasingly varied educational machinery became compelling. How to meet this need in financial, physical, and ideological terms within the framework of a democratic society operating in fifty semiautonomous states has been an ongoing problem, the solution of which appears to be more distant than it has ever been.

In view of the foregoing facts, it is not surprising that a virtual flood of books on every conceivable aspect of education has all but inundated the publishers' marketplace. In the preface to his very valuable guide, Richard G. Durnin explains in detail why this situation has come into being, and how it has affected the work of the bibliographer in the general field of education.

To have culled from the great mass of materials available the items of greatest significance, and to have organized them according to a relatively simple plan, is a tribute to Professor Durnin's skill and to his wide knowledge of the field. His book should be useful for years to come.

Donald N. Koster
Series Editor

PREFACE

This bibliography encompasses the general and specific books relating to the backgrounds (historical, biographical, philosophical, political, and sociological) of the theory, practice, and organization of the American school as viewed within the structure of the three major groupings: elementary, secondary, and higher education.

The quantity of educational writing is overwhelming. Is there a field in American studies where there has been a greater amount? The proliferation of writing in the twentieth century, especially in the 1950s and 1960s, constituted a surfeit. The factors involved in this abundance were several: large student population growth after World War II; increased federal government involvement (very significant during the administration of Lyndon Baines Johnson, "the education President"); professors eager to publish or else perish, and no less eager publishers ready to sell books and monographs; the appearance of new educational issues associated with school integration and the discovery of the "educationally disadvantaged"; the extension of professional concerns to include early childhood and adult education; and the expansion of knowledge through research. The "education industry" reached its apex in the late 1960s. Newspapers and magazines expanded their coverage of educational matters at all levels, and professional journals increased in number.

The task of the bibliographer is made more difficult by this profusion. Not only is there a problem with the great quantity of literature available, but there are also problems in classification and in determining the significant and definitive from the ephemeral. Expanded courses and an increased student population meant more textbooks. The coming-of-age of the paperbound book greatly abetted the situation. The cut-and-paste books of readings all but dominated the output in education textbooks.

The rapidly changing nature of contemporary educational theory and practice is best reported in periodicals (for which the EDUCATION INDEX and READERS' GUIDE TO PERIODICAL LITERATURE are indispensable) and in dissertations (DISSERTATION ABSTRACTS). This bibliographical work on American education deals with books. With some exceptions, highly derivative textbooks and books of readings have not been included.

Preface

As this work was prepared not many years after the Bicentennial of the United States, it might serve as a fitting assessment of the production of scholarship in education during this significant period in the nation's history. Long before the Independence of 1776, there was some indigenous writing on matters of education. Schooling in North America had its beginnings in the early seventeenth century when people in the several colonies, with their several inheritances--essentially English, Scottish, and Dutch--began to make provisions for teaching children the common branches of knowledge and the principles of religion.

Several bibliographies on American education, both in general and under specific topics, have been published. And there have been bibliographies in American studies that have included works on education. The first bibliography on America was the BIBLIOTHECAE AMERICANAE PRIMORDIA, compiled by the Anglican Bishop, White Kennett, and published in London in 1713. Bishop Kennett listed at least ten volumes that could be classified under "education." A more recent work, THE COLONIAL SCENE, 1602-1800 (Worcester: American Antiquarian Society, 1950), listed thirty-one books for the period.

The most comprehensive general bibliography of American education up to 1965 was Joe Park's THE RISE OF AMERICAN EDUCATION: AN ANNOTATED BIBLIOG-RAPHY (Evanston, Ill.: Northwestern University Press, 1965). There were areas not covered in this work, and, of course, the happenings and the publication explosion have been considerable since the mid-1960s.

The literature of American education is so vast that it naturally lends itself to discrete bibliographical treatment. Many separate bibliographies have appeared which deal with almost every educational category.

Specialized bibliographies are included in a great many books on education topics. Periodicals can also be the source of such bibliographies. For example, William W. Brickman, in 1941, prepared a "Bibliography of Recent Educational Bibliographies" that appeared in the journal, EDUCATIONAL ADMINISTRATION AND SUPERVISION (27 [October 1941]: 481-512). More recently, his "Selected Bibliography of the History of American Education in the United States" was included in PAEDAGOGICA HISTORICA (10, no. 3, Ghent, Belgium [1970]: 622-30). A "Bibliography of Educational Materials" is found in the back of the EDUCATION YEARBOOK for 1972-1973 and for subsequent years. Included in this guide, by categories ("Alternatives to Tradition," "Curriculum," etc.), are the new books for the two years of that volume.

In the present work bibliographies on education that have been published in book form are listed under either "Bibliographies of Education: General," or under the topic to which they pertain.

The bibliographical essay ties together significant developments, movements, concerns, and themes in the history of American education with important books and other sources that appeared at the time. The model for this form of presentation is "A Bibliographical Essay" in Bernard Bailyn's EDUCATION IN THE FORMING OF AMERICAN SOCIETY: NEEDS AND OPPORTUNITIES FOR STUDY (Chapel Hill: University of North Carolina Press, 1960).

All bibliographies, by their nature, are inconclusive. Of the making of books there is no end. Perusing every book written on education in America would be a task not worth the extraordinary effort. And one would run the risk of being drowned in the morass. There are significant and interesting works among those in the heap. The matter of selection is the first essential in researching the writings on American education. The next is classification.

From the surfeit, works considered definitive (not always easily agreed upon) must be listed. Then there are the volumes of interest for historical perspective. Admittedly, in some areas, the matter of selection has had to be more or less arbitrary.

The topics listed alphabetically are those presently in common usage associated with the subdivision of the larger subject of education. Although some argument could be made for a chronological listing, showing the historical development of the idea, practice, or institution, the books here are listed alphabetically by author. Making the vast output of books on American education fit into a tight classification system is indeed all but impossible.

For many of the historic educational classics, the original edition of the work is cited. Where there has been a more recent reprint this has been noted.

It is hoped that this guide to book sources on American education will be of help in providing a one-volume, quick and convenient reference for those persons seeking information on some area in the voluminous subject.

As a last note, I would like to acknowledge the very competent and generous assistance of the reference staff of the Ladd Library of Bates College, Lewiston, Maine, during the summer of 1980, which was invaluable in the completion of this undertaking.

BIBLIOGRAPHICAL ESSAY

SEVENTEENTH CENTURY

Although no known book inventory or library listing of seventeenth-century America listed Roger Ascham's THE SCHOLEMASTER (London, 1570), the work must have been known to some of the colonial Latin grammar schoolmasters of the time. One part ethical and the other part on educational method, the book was influential in the improvement of instruction in the flourishing Latin grammar schools of late Renaissance England. Ascham served King Edward VI, Queen Mary I, and Queen Elizabeth I in the capacities of tutor or Latin secretary.

John Brinsley's A CONSOLATION FOR OUR GRAMMAR SCHOOLES . . . MORE ESPECIALLY FOR ALL THOSE OF THE INFERIOR SORT, AND ALL RUDER COUNTRIES AND PLACES: NAMELY FOR IRELAND, WALES, VIRGINIA AND THE SUMMER ISLANDS (London, 1622) would probably qualify as a first in a bibliography of American works on education. It was intended for use in the British plantations, among other "ruder" places. Bishop White Kennett lists the work in his BIBLIOTHECAE AMERICANAE PRIMORDIA (London, 1713), the first bibliography of writings about America.

The first indigenous publication of an educational work was a broadside, THESES, PHILOGICAS, printed in 1642 on the first colonial press at Harvard College. This sheet was used in the college's first commencement. NEW ENGLAND'S FIRST FRUITS, a promotional pamphlet giving the first account of Harvard College, was printed in London in 1643. The work is attributed to Thomas Lechford. Requirements for admission, the curriculum, college rules, and a description of the fledgling institution were included. Charles Chauncy, Harvard's second president, authored the first book printed in America that would be considered a work on education. GOD'S MERCY, SHEWED TO HIS PEOPLE, IN GIVING THEM A FAITHFUL MINISTRY AND SCHOOLES OF LEARNING (Cambridge, Mass., 1655), a book of fifty-seven pages, was a commencement sermon wherein Chauncy stressed the importance of the college in supplying the ministry.

SPIRITUAL MILK FOR BOSTON BABES IN EITHER ENGLAND. DRAWN OUT OF THE BREASTS OF BOTH TESTAMENTS FOR THEIR SOULS NOURISHMENT (Cambridge, Mass., 1656), by John Cotton, minister of the church in Boston, was a catechism prepared especially for children. This work subsequently became a part of the many editions of the NEW ENGLAND PRIMER. Another children's catechism, written by John Fiske, entitled THE WATERING OF THE OLIVE PLANT IN CHRIST'S GARDEN. OR A SHORT CATECHISM FOR THE FIRST ENTRANCE OF OUR CHELMSFORD CHILDREN, was printed in Cambridge, Mass., in 1657.

A number of John Eliot's Indian tracts dealing with the progress of the Gospel among the Indians of New England dealt with education—religious education. His first was THE INDIAN GRAMMAR BEGUN; OR, AN ESSAY TO BRING THE INDIAN LANGUAGE INTO RULES FOR THE HELP OF SUCH AS DESIRE TO LEARN THE SAME (Cambridge, Mass., 1666), then followed THE INDIAN PRIMER; OR THE WAY OF TRAINING UP OF OUR INDIAN YOUTH IN THE GOOD KNOWLEDGE OF GOD, IN THE KNOWLEDGE OF THE SCRIPTURES AND IN AN ABILITY TO READ (Cambridge, Mass., 1669).

The NEW ENGLAND PRIMER made its first appearance toward the end of the seventeenth century. Although the earliest copy extant is dated 1727, an advertisement for the primer appeared in 1690.

It is not an easy matter to set out "education" as a discrete area of writing in the seventeenth and eighteenth centuries. The purpose of schooling was instruction in Christian piety; most of the writing that touched upon education was religious in nature.

The Harvard College library had three thousand titles by the close of the seventeenth century and many of these volumes represented the philosophy of Renaissance learning. There was access to English and continental Renaissance authors (Erasmus, More, Montaigne, Bacon, Vives) whose subjects touched upon education to a greater or lesser extent.

EIGHTEENTH CENTURY TO 1776

Cotton Mather's MAGNALIA CHRISTI AMERICANA: OR THE ECCLESIASTICAL HISTORY OF NEW ENGLAND (London, 1702) contained as Book 4 "An Account of the University of Cambridge in New England." This work brought the history of Harvard College up to the end of the seventeenth century and, with the exception of NEW ENGLAND'S FIRST FRUITS (1643), it is the first historical treatment of America's first institution of higher learning. Upon the death of the venerable Ezekiel Cheever, master of the Boston Latin School, Mather published the funeral sermon he delivered, CORDERIUS AMERICANUS. AN ESSAY UPON THE GOOD EDUCATION OF CHILDREN (Boston, 1708). This is the first biographical treatment of an American teacher. Mather, the most prolific writer in colonial America, wrote copiously on manners, morals, children, family instruction, and the care of the souls of Negroes. On this latter topic, the broadside RULES FOR THE SOCIETY OF NEGROES (Boston, 1693) and THE NEGRO CRISTIANIZED. AN ESSAY TO EXCITE AND ASSIST THAT GOOD WORK, THE INSTRUCTION OF NEGRO SERVANTS IN CHRISTIANITY (Boston, 1706) are of great value and interest as they present the views of this early clergyman-scholar concerning black Americans.

The charity schools maintained by the Society for the Propagation of the Gospel in Foreign Parts (established 1701) constituted the largest overall effort on the part of any organized group in the colonial period to provide common schooling to poor whites, Negroes, and Indians. The yearly anniversary sermon preached at a London parish, beginning as early as 1717, gave data on the status of these schools. The best eighteenth-century publication on the work of this Anglican missionary society was David Humphrey's AN HISTORICAL ACCOUNT OF THE INCORPORATED SOCIETY FOR THE PROPAGATION OF THE GOSPEL IN FOREIGN PARTS CONTAINING THEIR FOUNDATIONS, PROCEEDINGS, AND THE SUCCESS OF THEIR MISSIONARIES IN THE BRITISH COLONIES (London, 1730).

The earliest schoolbooks used by American children were those seventeenth- and eighteenth-century texts that generally came from England. Many of these were reprinted in the colonies. In arithmetic, there were books by George Fisher, John Ward, Thomas Dilworth, Edward Cocker, Thomas Simpson, and James Hodder; in Latin, by James Greenwood, William Lily, George Neville Usher, and Thomas Ruddiman; and in English, by John Walker, William Scott, Daniel Fenning, Robert Lowth, Thomas Dilworth, and Mrs. Ann Slack. Aside from the NEW ENGLAND PRIMER, which first appeared in the late seventeenth century, the work that might be considered the first native-American textbook was A SHORT INTRODUCTION TO THE LATIN TONGUE (Boston, 1709). This was the lifetime work of that famous Latin schoolmaster, Ezekiel Cheever, published posthumously. It went through seventeen editions before the Revolution.

Books for children were few in number and highly religious in nature. Reprints of English works constituted the greatest number. James Janeway's A TOKEN FOR CHILDREN was reprinted in Boston in 1702. THE HISTORY OF THE HOLY JESUS, illustrated and in verse, "being a pleasant and profitable companion for children," no doubt an indigenous work, appeared first in Boston in 1746, and reached its twenty-fourth edition by 1771. THE CHILD'S NEW PLAYTHING, OR BEST AMUSEMENT was printed in Philadelphia in 1757. The Quaker, John Woolman, was the author of A FIRST BOOK FOR CHILDREN (Philadelphia, 1769).

Sermons and treatises on the religious education of young people continued to pour from the pens of the clergy. Such titles as THE DUTY OF CHILDREN, WHOSE PARENTS HAVE PRAY'D FOR THEM (Boston, 1703), by Cotton Mather, Samuel Phillips's THE ORTHODOX CHRISTIAN: OR, A CHILD WELL INSTRUCTED IN THE PRINCIPLES OF THE CHRISTIAN RELIGION; EXHIBITED IN A DISCOURSE BY WAY OF CATECHIZING (Boston, 1738), and Samuel Moody's DISCOURSE TO LITTLE CHILDREN, AT YORK, ME., ON A CATECHIZE DAY (Boston, 1749), speak for themselves.

This was the era of many self-education books. Young George Washington used the British volume YOUNG MAN'S COMPANION as one of his models in scholarship. George Fisher's AMERICAN INSTRUCTOR, OR YOUNG MEN'S BEST COMPANION (Philadelphia, 1730) offered the common branches of knowledge along with the keeping of accounts, letter writing, gardening, and carpentering. Two reprints of English books served boys and girls of a lower social order: A PRESENT FOR AN APPRENTICE; OR A SURE GUIDE TO GAIN BOTH ESTEEM AND ESTATE FOR HIS CONDUCT TO HIS MASTER (Boston, 1747) and PRESENT FOR A SERVANT MAID, OR THE SURE MEANS OF GAINING LOVE AND ESTEEM. TO WHICH ARE ADDED DIRECTIONS FOR GOING TO MARKET, ALSO FOR DRESSING ANY COMMON DISH (Boston, 1747).

Collegiate textbooks by American scholars began to appear in 1726. Harvard's first professor of mathematics, Isaac Greenwood, was the author of the first two: AN EXPERIMENTAL COURSE ON MECHANICAL PHILOSOPHY (Boston, 1726) and ARITHMETIC, VULGAR AND DECIMAL (Boston, 1729). The Hebrew language, studied by all students in the early Harvard curriculum, had become an elective subject by 1755. Judah Monis, instructor in Hebrew at the college, was the author of the first work on that language printed in America, A GRAMMAR OF THE HEBREW TONGUE (Boston, 1735). Stephen Sewall, the Hancock Professor of Oriental Languages (a chair founded in 1764) published AN HEBREW GRAMMAR COLLECTED CHIEFLY FROM THAT OF ISRAEL LYONS, TEACHER OF HEBREW (Boston, 1763). Thomas Clap, president of Yale College from 1740 to 1766, wrote INTRODUCTION TO THE STUDY OF PHILOSOPHY (New London, 1743) and AN ESSAY ON THE NATURE AND FOUNDATION OF MORAL VIRTUE AND OBLIGATION; BEING A SHORT INTRODUCTION TO THE STUDY OF ETHICS (New Haven, 1765). AN ENGLISH AND GERMAN GRAMMAR was published in Philadelphia in 1748, and A GERMAN GRAMMAR in Germantown in 1751. Samuel Johnson, later to become the first head of King's (Columbia) College, produced a philosophic work of distinction, ELEMENTA PHILOSOPHICA: CONTAINING CHIEFLY NOETICA, OR THINGS RELATING TO THE MIND OR UNDERSTANDING; AND ETHICA, OR THINGS RELATING TO THE MORAL BEHAVIOR. The work was printed in 1752 on the press of Benjamin Franklin in Philadelphia. Myles Cooper, the young loyalist president of King's College just before the Revolution, was the author of ETHICS COMPENDIUM (New York, 1774). Treatises on educational methodology, classroom management, and school organization, generally associated with the nineteenth century, had their beginnings in America with the publication of SCHUL ORDNUNG [SCHOOL RULES] (Germantown, 1770). The author, Christopher Dock, had been a successful teacher among the German Mennonites of Pennsylvania. The work was published posthumously and went through a number of editions.

Nine colleges were established before the break with the Crown in 1776. Harvard College, established in 1636, has a rich store of early printed sources. Its CATALOGUS LIBRORUM BIBLIOTHECAE COLLEGIJ HARVARDINI (Boston, 1723) was the first institutional library catalog in the colonies. Benjamin Wadsworth's SERMON ON THE DEATH OF JOHN LEVERETT, PRESIDENT OF HARVARD COLLEGE (Boston, 1724) and Joseph Sewall's DISCOURSES UPON THE DEATH OF MR. BENJAMIN WADSWORTH, PRESIDENT OF HARVARD

COLLEGE (Boston, 1737) are good examples of the sermon as a literary form and source of historical information. Nathan Prince, a tutor, published the CONSTITUTION AND GOVERNMENT OF HARVARD COLLEGE FROM 1636 TO 1742 (Boston, 1743). The coming of George Whitefield to New England ("The Great Awakening") is represented by Whitefield's THE TESTIMONY OF THE PRESIDENT, PROFESSORS, TUTORS, AND HEBREW INSTRUCTOR OF HARVARD COLLEGE IN CAMBRIDGE AGAINST THE REV. G. WHITEFIELD AND HIS CONDUCT (Boston, 1744). The important public lectures of the college were often published. An example is TWO LECTURES ON COMETS (Boston, 1759) by John Winthrop, Hollis professor of mathematics and philosophy.

The first history of the College of William and Mary, THE PRESENT STATE OF VIRGINIA AND THE COLLEGE (London, 1727), was written by its first president, James Blair, and two other Virginians, Henry Hartwell and Edward Chilton, in 1697, but was not published until thirty years later. The college charter₁ was published in Williamsburg in 1736 as THE CHARTER AND STATUTES OF THE COLLEGE OF WILLIAM AND MARY, IN VIRGINIA. IN LATIN AND ENGLISH.

Yale's president, Thomas Clap, produced several works valuable for the institution's history: CATALOGUE OF THE LIBRARY OF YALE COLLEGE IN NEW HAVEN (New London, 1743); DECLARATION OF THE RECTOR AND TUTORS OF YALE COLLEGE AGAINST REV. GEORGE WHITEFIELD (Boston, 1745); THE RELIGIOUS CONSTITUTION OF COLLEGES, ESPECIALLY OF YALE COLLEGE, NEW HAVEN (New London, 1754); and THE ANNALS OR HISTORY OF YALE COLLEGE IN NEW HAVEN (New Haven, 1766). Two other items of Yale interest, published during this period, were Benjamin Gale's LETTER TO A MEMBER OF THE LOWER HOUSE OF ASSEMBLY, SHEWING THAT THE TAXES OF YALE COLLEGE ARE STATED HIGHER THAN IS NECESSARY (New Haven, 1759) and A COLLEGE ALMANAC BY A STUDENT OF YALE COLLEGE (New Haven, 1761). The passing of Yale's president Clap brought forth THE FAITHFUL SERVING OF GOD AND OUR GENERATION, THE ONLY WAY TO A PEACEFUL AND HAPPY DEATH: A SERMON OCCASIONED BY THE DEATH OF THE REVEREND THOMAS CLAP (New Haven, 1767) by his successor, Napthali Daggett.

Princeton's colonial presidents, Jonathan Dickinson, Aaron Burr, Jonathan Edwards, Samuel Davies, Samuel Findley, and John Witherspoon, all Calvinist divines, were prolific on the subject of religion. Very little of their writing, however, has relevance to matters of schooling; one of the exceptions being Samuel Davies's LITTLE CHILDREN INVITED TO JESUS CHRIST. A SERMON PREACHED IN HANOVER COUNTY, VIRGINIA; WITH AN ACCOUNT OF THE LATE REMARKABLE RELIGIOUS IMPRESSION AMONG THE STUDENTS IN THE COLLEGE OF NEW JERSEY (Boston, 1759). Two publications of historical significance appeared within the first two decades of the institution's founding: CATALOGUE OF BOOKS IN THE LIBRARY OF THE COLLEGE OF NEW JERSEY (Woodbridge, 1760) and AN ACCOUNT OF THE COLLEGE OF NEW JERSEY (Woodbridge, 1764). The latter item was published for the information of the public in Europe and America, and has served as the first history of the college.

The opening of King's College (Columbia) was accompanied by a number of pamphlets: SOME SERIOUS THOUGHTS ON THE DESIGN OF ERECTING A COLLEGE IN THE PROVINCE OF NEW YORK (New York, 1749), SOME THOUGHTS ON EDUCATION: WITH REASONS FOR ERECTING A COLLEGE IN THIS PROVINCE, AND FIXING THE SAME AT THE CITY OF NEW YORK (New York, 1752), THE CHARTER OF THE COLLEGE OF NEW YORK, PRINTED BY ORDER OF THE LIEUT. GOVERNOR (New York, 1754), THE QUERIST: OR A LETTER TO A MEMBER OF THE GENERAL ASSEMBLY OF THE COLONY OF NEW YORK, CONTAINING QUESTIONS OCCASIONED BY THE CHARTER GRANTED FOR THE ESTABLISHMENT OF A COLLEGE (New York, 1754), A BRIEF VINDICATION OF THE PROCEEDINGS OF THE TRUSTEES OF THE COLLEGE IN THE CITY OF NEW YORK (New York, 1754), and THE ADDITIONAL CHARTER GRANTED TO THE GOVERNORS OF THE COLLEGE OF NEW YORK IN AMERICA (New York, 1755).

The beginnings of the College, Academy, and Charitable School of Philadelphia, later to become the University of Pennsylvania, can be traced to a pamphlet written and printed by Benjamin Franklin, PROPOSALS RELATING TO THE EDUCATION OF YOUTH IN PENNSYLVANIA (Philadelphia, 1749). It appeared in what today would be called a limited edition and was aimed at a few influential citizens of Philadelphia who might be of help in getting an academy started. The university uses the date of 1740 for its origins, a date which marked the opening of a building intended for the use of the Rev. George Whitefield, the popular eighteenth-century itinerant preacher, as well as to house a charity school. The charity school, however, did not come into being until after the academy opened. Franklin followed his earlier tract with IDEA OF THE ENGLISH SCHOOL, SKETCHED OUT FOR THE CONSIDERATION OF THE TRUSTEES OF THE PHILADELPHIA ACADEMY (Philadelphia, 1751). The academy was formerly opened in 1751 with the Rev. Richard Peters delivering on the occasion a SERMON ON EDUCATION AT THE OPENING OF THE ACADEMY AT PHILADELPHIA (Philadelphia, 1751). Collegiate status was achieved by the charter of 1755. An early report of the institution was written by its first provost, William Smith, entitled "Account of the College, Academy, and Charitable School of Philadelphia," which appeared in his collection of writings entitled DISCOURSES ON PUBLIC OCCASIONS IN AMERICA (London, 1759).

Rhode- Island College, renamed Brown University in 1804, was chartered in 1764 through the efforts of a group of Baptist clergymen. Its first catalog for the years 1769 to 1775 was published in a broadside, CALOGUS EORUM QUI IN COLLEGIO RHOD. INS. ET PROV. PLANT. NOV. ANGLORUM . . . .(Providence, 1775).

Queen's College in New Brunswick, New Jersey, received its first charter in 1766 (no copy survives) and its second one in 1770. The latter document was published as CHARTER OF A COLLEGE TO BE ERECTED IN NEW JERSEY, BY THE NAME OF QUEEN'S COLLEGE, FOR THE EDUCATION OF YOUTH OF THE SAID PROVINCE AND THE NEIGHBORING COLONIES IN TRUE RELIGION AND LEARNING. . . (New York, 1770). Instruction began in 1771, under a tutor, Frederick Frelinghuysen, but the Revolution soon uprooted the work of the institution. It was not until 1785 that a president was appointed. In 1825 the name was changed to Rutgers College.

It was the work of the Rev. Eleazar Wheelock in schooling Indian youth, beginning in Lebanon, Connecticut, in 1754, that led to the establishment of Dartmouth College in 1769. Accounts of Moor's Indian Charity School, written by Wheelock, appeared as tracts over several years. The period from 1754 to 1762 was covered in A PLAIN AND FAITHFUL NARRATIVE OF THE ORIGINAL DESIGN, RISE, PROGRESS AND PRESENT STATE OF THE INDIAN CHARITY-SCHOOL AT LEBANON, IN CONNECTICUT (Boston, 1763). The years 1762 to 1765 were chronicled in A CONTINUATION OF THE STATE, & OF THE INDIAN CHARITY-SCHOOL (Boston, 1765). Other continuations followed: A CONTINUATION OF THE NARRATIVE OF THE INDIAN CHARITY-SCHOOL IN LEBANON, IN CONNECTICUT; FROM THE YEAR 1768 TO THE INCORPORATION OF IT WITH DARTMOUTH COLLEGE, AND REMOVAL AND SETTLEMENT OF IT IN HANOVER, IN THE PROVINCE OF NEW HAMPSHIRE, 1771 (Hartford, 1771); A CONTINUATION OF THE NARRATIVE OF THE INDIAN CHARITY-SCHOOL, BEGUN IN LEBANON, IN CONNECTICUT; NOW INCORPORATED WITH DARTMOUTH COLLEGE. . . .(n.p., N.H., 1773), encompassed the time from May 1771 to September 1772; A CONTINUATION OF THE NARRATIVE OF THE INDIAN CHARITY-SCHOOL, BEGUN IN LEBANON, IN CONNECTICUT; NOW INCORPORATED WITH DARTMOUTH COLLEGE, IN HANOVER, IN THE PROVINCE OF NEW HAMPSHIRE (Hartford, 1773), for the year September 1772 to September 1773; and, lastly, A CONTINUATION OF THE NARRATIVE OF THE INDIAN CHARITY-SCHOOL, BEGUN IN LEBANON, IN CONNECTICUT, NOW INCORPORATED WITH DARTMOUTH COLLEGE. . . .(Hartford, 1775), concluded the history from September 1773 to February 1775.

LAST QUARTER OF THE EIGHTEENTH CENTURY

This was the period that marked the break with the Crown, the revolutionary war, and the establishment of the new republic. For the most part, educational activity lay dormant during the war years, but it had a vigorous revival as the eighteenth century came to a close.

These years encompassed several developments and institutions that were to be even more important in the early years of the nineteenth century. American schoolbooks appeared replacing those from England. The academy movement was well established by 1800. Concerns for the schooling of females were voiced. The old colleges recovered from the aftermath of the Revolution and some new ones, not tied to religious groups, joined their numbers. Perhaps most significant in this period, plans for a national school system for the United States were put forth.

In the realm of schoolbooks, American reprints of English texts continued but gave way to the many indigenous texts that began to appear. Thomas Dilworth's A NEW GUIDE TO THE ENGLISH TONGUE was first published in England in 1740, and was frequently reprinted in America during the late colonial period. A fourteenth edition of this work was printed in New York in 1790. The first American edition of Thomas Ruddiman's THE RUDIMENTS OF THE LATIN

TONGUE, an English work, came out in Philadelphia in 1776. A New York City Latin grammar school teacher, Edward Rigg, published THE NEW AMERICAN LATIN GRAMMAR there in 1784.

Among the earliest indigenous schoolbooks published soon after Independence were three by Anthony Benezet, a Philadelphia philanthropist and teacher: A FIRST BOOK FOR CHILDREN, ABCD-XYZ (Philadelphia, 1778) was followed in 1779 by an enlarged edition known as THE PENNSYLVANIA SPELLING BOOK, and AN ESSAY TOWARDS THE MOST EASY INTRODUCTION TO THE KNOWLEDGE OF ENGLISH GRAMMAR COMPILED FOR THE PENNSYLVANIA SPELLING BOOK.

Two works on the teaching of music appeared in 1778: THE SINGING MASTER'S ASSISTANT, OR KEY TO PRACTICAL MUSIC (Boston, 1778) by William Billings, and THE COMPLETE INSTRUCTOR FOR THE VIOLIN, FLUTE, GUITAR AND HARPSICHORD (Philadelphia, 1778) by H.B. Victor.

It was Noah Webster, "Schoolmaster to America," who epitomized the movement toward American intellectual freedom, along with political independence, and the substitution of native textbooks for those of England. His ambitious GRAMMATICAL INSTITUTES OF THE ENGLISH LANGUAGE came out in three parts over a three-year period. Part 1 was the speller, published in Hartford in 1783, with a typical long title of the times: A GRAMMATICAL INSTITUTE OF THE ENGLISH LANGUAGE . . . . IN THREE PARTS. PART I. CONTAINING A NEW AND ACCURATE STANDARD OF PRONUNCIATION. This work, published subsequently under different titles, became the famous "blue back" speller which would go through 80 million copies by 1980. Then came A GRAMMATICAL INSTITUTE OF THE ENGLISH LANGUAGE . . . PART SECOND. CONTAINING A PLAIN AND COMPREHENSIVE GRAMMAR . . . (Hartford, 1784), and finally A GRAMMATICAL INSTITUTE OF THE ENGLISH LANGUAGE . . . PART III. CONTAINING THE NECESSARY RULES OF READING AND SPEAKING, AND A VARIETY OF ESSAYS, DIALOGUES, AND DECLAMATORY PIECES . . . (Hartford, 1785). These last two works were not as successful as the speller, having met competition from a number of other English grammar books and selections of readings. The reader (part 3 of the Institutes), however, was the first native schoolbook in which American history and geography were included.

America's first geographer, Jedidiah Morse, wrote his first book, GEOGRAPHY MADE EASY (New Haven, 1784), while he was a student at Yale. This work went through twenty-five editions in his lifetime.

Nicholas Pike's A NEW AND COMPLETE SYSTEM OF ARITHMETIC COMPOSED FOR THE USE OF CITIZENS OF THE UNITED STATES (Newburyport, Mass., 1788) introduced federal money in arithmetical computations. It was Chauncey Lee, in THE AMERICAN ACCOMPTANT; BEING A PLAIN, PRACTICAL AND SYSTEMATIC COMPENDIUM OF FEDERAL ARITHMETIC (Lansingburgh, N.Y., 1797), who first made use of the dollar sign ($) in a schoolbook.

An early French text was L'ABEILLE FRANCOISE (Boston, 1792), by Paul Nancrede, a teacher of that language at Harvard.

The late eighteenth century saw the increased publication of books for children. Many were still from Old World sources, but a few were indigenous. Some of the more popular works were Daniel DeFoe's THE WONDERFUL LIFE AND SURPRISING ADVENTURES OF THE RENOWNED HERO ROBINSON CRUSOE (New York, 1775); THE FABLES OF AESOP AND OTHERS (Philadelphia, 1777); THE HISTORY OF LITTLE GOODY TWO-SHOES; OTHERWISE CALLED MRS. MARGERY TWOSHOES (Philadelphia, 1776); A LITTLE LOTTERY BOOK FOR CHILDREN; CONTAINING A NEW METHOD OF PLAYING THEM INTO A KNOWLEDGE OF LETTERS, FIGURES, &C. (New York, 1778); and A PRETTY PLAYTHING FOR CHILDREN OF ALL DENOMINATIONS: CONTAINING THE ALPHABET IN VERSE . . . (New York, 1785).

These years generated an increasing interest in education and this concern manifested itself in sermons, essays, and other works. A pamphlet by the Quaker, Anthony Benezet, SOME NECESSARY REMARKS ON THE EDUCATION OF YOUTH IN THE COUNTRYPARTS OF THIS, AND THE NEIGHBORING GOVERNMENTS (Philadelphia, 1778), and one in which he was one of the signers, SOME OBSERVATIONS RELATING TO THE ESTABLISHMENT OF SCHOOLS (Philadelphia, 1778), show the efforts of the Society of Friends in the matter of schooling. A broadside, printed in Boston in 1789, addressed itself to a need that was increasingly to be voiced in the century to come: FREEHOLDERS AND OTHER INHABITANTS OF THE TOWN OF BOSTON . . . TO CONSIDER THE PROPOSALS . . . FOR THE INSTRUCTION OF THE YOUTH OF BOTH SEXES; AND FOR REFORMING THE PRESENT SYSTEM OF PUBLIC EDUCATION. A seven-page leaflet, THE SYSTEM OF PUBLIC EDUCATION ADOPTED BY THE TOWN OF BOSTON, came soon after.

The beginnings of the academy movement can be seen in the printed orations and sermons offered at the opening of these institutions. A good example is David McClure's AN ORATION ON THE ADVANTAGES OF AN EARLY EDU-CATION, DELIVERED AT EXETER, IN THE STATE OF NEW HAMPSHIRE, MAY 1, 1783, AT THE OPENING OF THE PHILLIPS EXETER ACADEMY (Exeter, 1783).

The early concern for female education can be shown by no better example than a work by Benjamin Rush, THOUGHTS UPON FEMALE EDUCATION, ACCOMMODATED TO THE PRESENT STATE OF SOCIETY, MANNERS AND GOVERNMENT IN THE UNITED STATES OF AMERICA (Philadelphia, 1787).

The output of printed sources from the colleges was varied. There were broad-sides of theses at commencements, sermons by the clergymen-presidents to the student body, catalog of books in the college libraries, student addresses at public examinations, poetry written and read publicly by students, inaugural addresses by incoming college heads, scholarly lectures by professors, college charters and statutes, and eulogies on the death of a student, faculty member, or president. There is no better way to achieve an understanding of what was happening in American higher education during the late eighteenth century than by a perusal of a selection of these sources.

The desire to have system, order, and universality in American public education was a development that had gathered momentum in the 1790s. As early as 1779, Thomas Jefferson had introduced a proposal for a system of schools in Virginia to that state's legislature, but it met defeat. Benjamin Rush wrote a set of plans for Pennsylvania and extended them to the republic at large in his A PLAN FOR THE ESTABLISHMENT OF PUBLIC SCHOOLS AND THE DIFFUSION OF KNOWLEDGE IN PENNSYLVANIA; TO WHICH ARE ADDED THOUGHTS UPON THE MODES OF EDUCATION PROPER IN A REPUBLIC (Philadelphia, 1786). In 1796 the American Philosophical Society offered a prize of one hundred dollars to the person proposing "the best system of liberal education and literary instruction adapted to the genius of the government of the United States; comprehending also a plan for instituting and conducting public schools in this country, on principles of the most extensive utility." The prize was divided between Samuel Knox, a Maryland academy headmaster, for his AN ESSAY ON THE BEST SYSTEM OF LIBERAL EDUCATION, ADAPTED TO THE GENIOUS OF THE GOVERNMENT OF THE UNITED STATES (Baltimore, 1799), and Samuel H. Smith, a Philadelphia magazine editor, for his REMARKS ON EDUCATION: ILLUSTRATING THE CLOSE CONNECTION BETWEEN VIRTUE AND WISDOM. TO WHICH IS ANNEXED, A SYSTEM OF LIBERAL EDUCATION . . . (Philadelphia, 1798).

NINETEENTH CENTURY: 1800 TO 1825

The first years of the nineteenth century saw the publication of many American textbooks. The intellectual independence from England was well underway. Nathan Daboll, a self-educated Connecticut almanac maker, wrote DABOLL'S SCHOOLMASTER'S ASSISTANT. BEING A PLAIN PRACTICAL SYSTEM OF ARITHMETIC (New London, 1800). Daniel Adams's THE SCHOLAR'S ARITHMETIC, OR FEDERAL ACCOUNTANT (Leominster, 1801) had a wide circulation through the first half of the century. John Pierpont's THE AMERICAN FIRST CLASS BOOK (Boston, 1823) was compiled with the express intent of making it a truly American text. Warren Colburn's FIRST LESSONS IN ARITHMETIC ON THE PLAN OF PESTALOZZI (Boston, 1822) was the first textbook to show the influence of the prominent Swiss educator in America. Elijah Parish's A COMPENDIOUS SYSTEM OF UNIVERSAL GEOGRAPHY (Newburyport, Mass., 1807) began to displace the earlier popular work by Morse. Joseph E. Worcester contributed ELEMENTS OF GEOGRAPHY (Boston, 1819) and ELEMENTS OF HISTORY (Boston, 1826), the latter being the first comprehensive history book for schools.

The New York Free School Society was incorporated in 1805, and the earliest account of its organization and charity schools is found in AN ACCOUNT OF THE FREE-SCHOOL SOCIETY OF NEW YORK (New York, 1814). The influence of Joseph Lancaster, English promoter of the monitorial system, which was widely practiced during the first half of the century, was incorporated into another early work of this society, MANUAL OF THE LANCASTRIAN SYSTEM OF TEACHING READING, WRITING, ARITHMETIC, AND NEEDLE-WORK, AS PRACTICED IN THE SCHOOLS OF THE FREE-SCHOOL SOCIETY OF NEW YORK (New York, 1820).

The teachings of Johann Pestalozzi were brought to America by Joseph Neef, who came to Philadelphia from France in 1806. Neef did much to introduce the thought and practice of the Swiss educator through his SKETCH OF A PLAN AND METHOD OF EDUCATION (Philadelphia, 1808). This volume is often considered the first pedagogical work published in English in the United States.

Noah Webster's first dictionary was published in New Haven in 1806, entitled A COMPENDIOUS DICTIONARY OF THE ENGLISH LANGUAGE. In 1807, his second dictionary, A DICTIONARY OF THE ENGLISH LANGUAGE; COMPILED FOR THE USE OF COMMON SCHOOLS IN THE UNITED STATES, appeared. These two works led to the 1828 publication of Webster's great work, the two-volume AN AMERICAN DICTIONARY OF THE ENGLISH LANGUAGE.

Educational journals had their beginnings during this period. THE JUVENILE MIRROR, OR EDUCATIONAL MAGAZINE (New York, 1811) was the first educational periodical and was directed both to teacher and pupil. It was followed by THE ACADEMICIAN (New York, 1818), published by Albert Picket, a self-educated schoolmaster and textbook writer in New York City. Both of these publications were short-lived.

It was in 1818 that Thomas Jefferson prepared his recommendations for a university in Virginia. The legislature of the state chartered the University of Virginia in 1819. Jefferson's report is contained in Gordon Lee's CRUSADE AGAINST IGNORANCE: THOMAS JEFFERSON ON EDUCATION (New York, 1961).

The Boston English Classical School is credited with being the first public high school. A report of the city's school committee in 1820 led to the opening of the school in 1821. Ellwood P. Cubberley's READINGS IN PUBLIC EDUCATION IN THE UNITED STATES (Boston, 1934) reprints the report of 1820.

NINETEENTH CENTURY: 1826 TO 1850

The belief in man's perfectibility through schooling and the concept of self-education flourished during this period of the nineteenth century. Libraries, mechanics' institutes, female education, public lectures, and the movement toward public-supported common schools are all manifestations of the movement.

Almira Hart Lincoln Phelps, a teacher at Emma Willard's Troy Female Seminary, wrote LECTURES TO YOUNG LADIES, COMPRISING OUTLINES AND APPLICATIONS OF THE DIFFERENT BRANCHES OF FEMALE EDUCATION (Boston, 1833), and Catherine E. Beecher's A TREATISE ON DOMESTIC ECONOMY, FOR THE USE OF YOUNG LADIES AT HOME, AND AT SCHOOL (Boston, 1841) were two of many works on the education of women that appeared.

Josiah Holbrook is credited with establishing the lyceum, that early adult education movement which popularized knowledge by means of lectures, often by prominent people, in towns and villages, as early as 1826. The basic work on this movement is his AMERICAN LYCEUM OR SOCIETY FOR THE IMPROVEMENT OF SCHOOLS AND DIFFUSION OF USEFUL KNOWLEDGE (Boston, 1829). William Hosmer's SELF-EDUCATION, OR THE PHILOSOPHY OF MENTAL IMPROVEMENT (Geneva, N.Y., 1847) is an example of the genre of self-improvement books.

Several significant books on schoolkeeping and methodology appeared during this second quarter of the nineteenth century. Samuel R. Hall's LECTURES ON SCHOOL-KEEPING (Boston, 1829) is a classic and constitutes the first American treatise on that subject written in English. Bronson Alcott, an educational radical of the times, wrote OBSERVATIONS ON THE PRINCIPLES AND METHODS OF INFANT INSTRUCTION (Boston, 1830). Thomas Palmer's THE TEACHER'S MANUAL: BEING AN EXPOSITION OF AN EFFICIENT AND ECONOMICAL SYSTEM OF EDUCATION SUITED TO THE WANTS OF THE PEOPLE (Boston, 1840) was awarded a prize by the American Institute of Instruction. THE SCHOOL AND THE SCHOOLMASTER (New York, 1842), by Alonzo Potter and George B. Emerson, was one of the most popular teacher's manuals of the century. Among other items, it discussed ventilation, heating, and lighting of schools. David P. Page's THEORY AND PRACTICE OF TEACHING: OR, THE MOTIVES AND METHODS OF GOOD SCHOOL-KEEPING (Syracuse, 1847) was for many years the authoritative work on the subject. An early work on the blackboard, an instructional device dating from this period, is John Goldsbury's THE BLACK-BOARD. EXERCISES AND ILLUSTRATIONS ON THE BLACK-BOARD; FURNISHING AN EASY AND EXPEDITIOUS METHOD OF GIVING INSTRUCTION (Keene, 1847).

Textbooks proliferated, especially in American history. Significant books included Charles A. Goodrich's A HISTORY OF THE UNITED STATES OF AMERICA (Hartford, 1822), Emma Willard's HISTORY OF THE UNITED STATES (New Haven, 1828), Noah Webster's HISTORY OF THE UNITED STATES (New Haven, 1832) (he had been the first to include American history in his 1785 reader), and Samuel G. Goodrich's THE FIRST BOOK OF HISTORY. FOR CHILDREN AND YOUTH (Boston, 1831). The latter Goodrich was the author of the popular "Peter Parley's Tales" and of A NATIONAL GEOGRAPHY FOR SCHOOLS (New York, 1845). Most of these books were illustrated with engravings, and the text revealed the progress of the United States in righteousness.

William Holmes McGuffey, whose readers set the moral tone of virtue for children's literature during the remainder of the century, published his FIRST ECLECTIC READER (Cincinnati) in 1836. By 1920, 122 million of McGuffey's readers had been sold.

The American Institute of Instruction, the first professional organization of educators, was established in 1830 and it continued to about 1908. The discourses delivered before the annual conventions of this society were generally by prominent educators. The lectures and proceedings of these annual meetings of the institute were published in Boston from 1831 on.

The AMERICAN JOURNAL OF EDUCATION, begun in Boston in 1826 by William Russell, was the first successful professional journal for educators. It was continued after August of 1830 as the AMERICAN ANNALS OF EDUCATION AND INSTRUCTION, under the editorship of William C. Woodbridge. The ANNALS continued to 1839. Horace Mann began the COMMON SCHOOL JOURNAL in 1838 and continued as its editor to 1848. The periodical continued to 1852.

This was the epoch of Horace Mann. In his twelve reports as secretary of the Massachusetts Board of Education (1837-48), he discussed the needs of common schools, discipline, methodology, teacher training, and European practices. All the reports are contained in the five-volume LIFE AND WORK OF HORACE MANN (Boston, 1865-68), edited by Mary Peabody Mann.

Teacher training in teachers' institutes and normal schools is reflected in William B. Fowle's THE TEACHERS' INSTITUTE; OR, FAMILIAR HINTS FOR YOUNG TEACHERS (Boston, 1847), and Henry Barnard's NORMAL SCHOOLS, AND OTHER INSTITUTIONS, AGENCIES, AND MEANS DESIGNED FOR THE PROFESSIONAL EDUCATION OF TEACHERS (Hartford, 1851). The latter work reports upon all of the normal schools established up through 1850.

A number of commentaries on education in the form of essays were published during the first half of the nineteenth century. James G. Carter, one of the promoters of the idea of normal school training for prospective teachers, and one of the founders of the American Institute of Instruction, was the author of ESSAYS ON POPULAR EDUCATION (Boston, 1826), an early support for public schools over private ones. Caleb Atwater's AN ESSAY ON EDUCATION (Cincinnati, 1841) dealt with females, moral and mental education, and schooling in the western states. An early work on higher education was THOUGHTS ON THE PRESENT COLLEGIATE SYSTEM IN THE UNITED STATES (Boston, 1842), wherein Francis Wayland, president of Brown University, urged an expansion of the college curriculum and the addition of new degrees.

The first work on American Negro education was published in New York in 1830. It was THE HISTORY OF THE NEW YORK AFRICAN FREE SCHOOLS FROM THEIR ESTABLISHMENT IN 1787 TO THE PRESENT TIME, by Charles C. Andrews.

NINETEENTH CENTURY: 1851 TO 1875

The desire to have American universities built on the German model with a
dedication to scientific inquiry was realized in the inception of Johns Hopkins
University, which opened in 1876. Henry P. Tappan, president of the University of Michigan, and one of the founders of the American Association for the
Advancement of Education, put forth the idea of this new research emphasis
in his UNIVERSITY EDUCATION (New York, 1851).

In educational journalism, there were two developments of note. Henry
Barnard, whose life and work dominate this period of the century, as did
Horace Mann's in the second quarter, was the founder and editor of the
AMERICAN JOURNAL OF EDUCATION, which began publication in 1855.
This journal was not related to the one by the same name that appeared earlier
in the century. Barnard poured his financial resources and his intellectual
energy into the magazine, which he continued to edit until 1882. The thirty-
two volumes of this journal are among the most valuable sources of educational history for the nineteenth century. A children's school magazine, THE
SCHOOLMATE: A READER FOR YOUTH, appeared in New York in 1852.
This was probably the first of many such periodicals for children which have
been written as a supplement to school work.

Methods of teaching school endured as a topic of concern and as a subject
for books for teachers. Charles Northend's THE TEACHER AND THE PARENT:
A TREATISE UPON COMMON-SCHOOL EDUCATION (Boston, 1853) was
somewhat unique in that, in addition to practical suggestions for teachers, it
had a message for parents. Northend was a Massachusetts academy teacher,
principal, and school superintendent.

The National Teachers Association had its beginnings in 1857. This oldest of
professional education organizations became the National Education Association
in 1870. Edgar B. Wesley's NEA: THE FIRST HUNDRED YEARS (New York,
1957) gives a detailed account of the early years.

The kindergarten came to America from Germany in 1856 through the efforts
of Mrs. Carl Schurz. Elizabeth Peabody, of Boston, is said to have opened
the first English-speaking kindergarten in 1860. An important early work is
MORAL CULTURE OF INFANCY, AND KINDERGARTEN GUIDE (Boston, 1863)
by Mary P. Mann and Elizabeth P. Peabody.

President Lincoln signed the Land Grant College Act (known as the Morrill
Act) in 1862. The subsequent rapid growth of state colleges devoted to agri-
culture and mechanic arts was the consequence. READINGS IN AMERICAN
EDUCATIONAL HISTORY (New York, 1951), edited by Edgar W. Knight and
Clifton L. Hall, contains the pertinent legislation.

Federal involvement with education, albeit very limited, became legitimate
with the creation of the Department of Education in 1867. Despite the term

"department," it was not a cabinet post, and the name was soon changed to "Office of Education." A return to the "Office of Education" came in 1929, and the elevation to cabinet level as the "Department of Education" in 1979. THE UNITED STATES OFFICE OF EDUCATION: A CENTURY OF SERVICE (New York, 1955), by Harry Kursch, is the best source.

The 1874 Kalamazoo decision in Michigan, concerning the right to use local tax money to establish free public high schools, encouraged many state legislatures to establish provisions for such schools. I.L. Kandel's HISTORY OF SECONDARY EDUCATION (Boston, 1930) treats the development, and the decision is in READINGS IN AMERICAN EDUCATION HISTORY (New York, 1951) by Edgar W. Knight and Clifton L. Hall.

The popular historian Benson J. Lossing wrote a PICTORIAL HISTORY OF THE UNITED STATES. FOR SCHOOLS AND FAMILIES (New York, 1854) which was well illustrated and widely used into the 1870s. Benjamin Greenleaf, a schoolmaster and mathematician, who published his first NATIONAL ARITH-METIC, in Boston in 1836, is generally associated with the second half of the nineteenth century. His ARITHMETIC went through many reprintings and sold over a million copies. His ELEMENTS OF GEOMETRY, WITH PRACTICAL APPLICATIONS TO MENSURATION (Boston, 1858) and NEW ELEMENTARY ALGEBRA (Boston, 1862) were widely used to the end of the century. Daniel Fish's AN INTERMEDIATE ARITHMETIC, COMBINING ORAL AND WRITTEN (New York, 1874) enjoyed popularity through the century. The most prolific of textbook writers at this time was William Swinton. After a varied life of theological study, teaching, reporting, literary criticism, and a short-time professorship at the University of California, he spent the remaining years as a financially successful textbook writer. SWINTON'S PRIMARY UNITED STATES. FIRST LESSONS IN OUR COUNTRY'S HISTORY (New York, 1872), WORLD-BOOK OF ENGLISH SPELLING. ORAL AND WRITTEN (New York, 1872), LANGUAGE LESSONS: AN INTRODUCTORY GRAMMAR AND COM-POSITION FOR PRIMARY AND INTERMEDIATE GRADES (New York, 1873), OUT-LINES OF THE WORLD'S HISTORY (New York, 1874), and A COMPLETE COURSE IN GEOGRAPHY (New York, 1875) all went through many editions and had wide and long use.

NINETEENTH CENTURY: 1876 TO 1899

The centennial of the independence of the United States was celebrated in 1876. The Philadelphia Centennial Exposition demonstrated the relationship of education to the nation's progress. The country was well on its way to educational independence. There had been, of course, influences from European thought and practice along the way: the monitorial schools of Lancaster, Pestalozzian methods, the kindergarten, and the idea of research in graduate education. Now the Americans were to learn further at the ex-position: it was the Russian exhibit of a Moscow technical school. Manual and industrial education in American schools had their beginnings here.

Indeed, Lawrence Cremin, in THE TRANSFORMATION OF THE SCHOOL (New York, 1961), has traced the origin of the progressive education movement to this event. Calvin Woodward, a critic of the schools, promoted the industrial arts curriculum, and his book, THE MANUAL TRAINING SCHOOL (Boston, 1887), serves as a good historical source for the beginnings of the "new education."

Joseph M. Rice, a physician, psychologist, and advocate of the scientific method in educational study and practice, wrote THE PUBLIC SCHOOL SYSTEM OF THE UNITED STATES (New York, 1893), an account of the failure of the common schools in nineteenth-century America. This was the first critical report based upon scientific methods in educational research.

The state of secondary education and admission to college were issues of such importance that a Committee of Ten on Secondary School Studies, with Charles Eliot of Harvard as chairman, was created by the National Education Association in 1892. The report of this commission had far-reaching and long-lasting influences upon both the secondary schools and the colleges. The REPORT OF THE COMMITTEE OF TEN ON SECONDARY SCHOOLS (Washington, D.C., U.S. Bureau of Education, 1893) and Edward A. Krug CHARLES W. ELIOT AND PUBLIC EDUCATION (New York, 1961) are sources for the report and its influence.

Four significant works on higher education by four prominent leaders in that field serve to delineate some concerns and issues during the last quarter of the nineteenth century. Noah Porter's AMERICAN COLLEGES AND THE AMERICAN PUBLIC (New York, 1878), a revision of an earlier work by the Yale president, presents a conservative view of the nature and purpose of collegiate education. James B. Angell's THE HIGHER EDUCATION: A PLEA FOR MAKING IT ACCESSIBLE TO ALL (Ann Arbor, 1897) was a commencement address by the long-time president of the University of Michigan, who was a strong advocate of public education. Daniel C. Gilman's UNIVERSITY PROBLEMS IN THE UNITED STATES (New York, 1898), by the first president of Johns Hopkins, reflects upon the mission of the American University with Johns Hopkins as a model. Charles F. Thwing, president of Western Reserve and a prolific writer on education and related subjects, wrote THE AMERICAN COLLEGE IN AMERICAN LIFE (New York, 1897) wherein he examined the purposes of a liberal education.

Two school history texts, both by distinguished American historians, are worthy of special mention among those that appeared in the last years of the nineteenth century. John Fiske was the most popular historian of the period. He wrote with great style and his "critical period" (the early years of the republic) is still an accepted historical term. His HISTORY OF THE UNITED STATES FOR SCHOOLS (Boston, 1894) was still in use well into the twentieth century. John B. McMaster's A SCHOOL HISTORY OF THE UNITED STATES (New York, 1897) was a standard text into the 1930s. His viewpoint, which was less than favorable toward the new immigrants, and his proexpansionism, reflected the feelings of many of his fellow Americans at the time.

Francis W. Parker's NOTES OF TALKS ON TEACHING (New York, 1883) stressed the cultivation of freedom and informality in classroom method. These were themes that were to be prominent in the new education of the twentieth century.

The considerable impact of Harvard's Charles W. Eliot on every level of American education in the late nineteenth and early twentieth centuries can be appreciated from his EDUCATIONAL REFORM: ESSAYS AND ADDRESSES (New York, 1898).

John Dewey, who also belongs to both the nineteenth and twentieth centuries, wrote his first significant educational treatise, THE SCHOOL AND SOCIETY (Chicago, 1899), while a professor at the University of Chicago. The theme, learning by doing, was one he emphasized throughout his long and productive life in education.

TWENTIETH CENTURY: 1900 TO 1920

Events in higher education crowd the early years of the new century. The establishment in 1900 of the College Entrance Examination Board gave uniformity to the process of entry to America's colleges. THE COLLEGE BOARD: ITS FIRST FIFTY YEARS (New York: Columbia University Press, 1950), by Claude Fuess, is a comprehensive treatment of the board's story.

Abraham Flexner is remembered for his THE AMERICAN COLLEGE (New York: Century Co., 1908), the first wide-scale survey of the strengths and problems of higher education at the outset of the twentieth century, and for his MEDICAL EDUCATION IN THE UNITED STATES AND CANADA (New York: Carnegie Foundation for the Advancement of Teaching, 1910), the famous "Flexner Report" which brought about fundamental changes in medical education.

Four national educational organizations were founded in the first twenty years of the century. The National Society for the Study of Education was established in 1901 with Nicholas M. Butler, John Dewey, and Charles H. Judd among the leaders. The annual yearbooks of the society, over the years, have brought current viewpoints to a wide variety of education topics. The Carnegie Foundation for the Advancement of Teaching was founded in 1905 with an endowment of $10 million. The most important of its early reports was the 1910 Flexner Report mentioned above. The American Council on Education dates from 1918. It is a coordinating organization of higher education and its many commission reports are important sources of education policy (e.g., Committee on Religion and Education, THE RELATION OF RELIGION TO PUBLIC EDUCATION, Washington, D.C., 1947). The Association for the Advancement of Progressive Education held its first meeting in 1919. The organization grew out of the child-study movement of the 1890s and the writings of John Dewey on education. The 1919 platform is contained in the Progressive Education Association's PROGRESSIVE EDUCATION ADVANCES

(New York, 1938), and the most complete treatment of the association and the movement of progressive education is Lawrence A. Cremin's THE TRANSFORMATION OF THE SCHOOL: PROGRESSIVISM IN AMERICAN EDUCATION, 1876-1957 (New York: Alfred Knopf, 1961).

A major development in vocational education came in 1917 with the signing by President Woodrow Wilson of the Smith-Hughes Act for Vocational Education. Federal funds went to the states for the training of teachers in agriculture, home economics, and industrial subjects. The text of the act is contained in Hawkins, Prosser, and Wright's DEVELOPMENT OF VOCATIONAL EDUCATION (Chicago, 1951).

The "Seven Cardinal Principles of Secondary Education" were familar to teachers and teachers-in-training until recent years. These emphases on what the high schools should be doing was the result of a 1918 report of the Commission on Secondary Education of the National Education Association. The report appears in the Commission on Reorganization of Secondary Education's CARDINAL PRINCIPLES OF SECONDARY EDUCATION (Washington, D.C.: U.S. Bureau of Education, Bulletin 35, 1918).

Psychology, child study, and educational measurements, all in their infancy, were represented by two giants of scholarship. Edward L. Thorndike, the founder of American educational psychology, was the author of EDUCATIONAL PSYCHOLOGY (New York: Lemcke and Buechner, 1903) and AN INTRODUCTION TO THE THEORY OF MENTAL AND SOCIAL MEASUREMENTS (New York: Science Press, 1904). The old theory of mental discipline was eclipsed by new laws of learning. Measurement and statistics became the chief tools in the science of education. G. Stanley Hall adopted the methods of science and research scholarship in gathering empirical data on children, and produced the massive, two-volume ADOLESCENCE; ITS PSYCHOLOGY AND ITS RELATION TO PHYSIOLOGY, ANTHROPOLOGY, SEX, CRIME, RELIGION, AND EDUCATION (New York: D. Appleton, 1904). This was the definitive work on this age group for thirty years, and it has served as the model for many subsequent studies.

Ellwood P. Cubberley's classic and much-used textbook, PUBLIC EDUCATION IN THE UNITED STATES (Boston: Houghton Mifflin, 1919), dominated the scene into the 1950s. It was a narrow view, which tended to restrict the story of American education to public schooling.

TWENTIETH CENTURY: 1921 TO 1940

The post-World War I years were marked by a number of social revolutions: a rise of secularism, the spread of science and technology, and the belief in universal education to promote socially desirable behavior. The education revolution challenged earlier concepts of the child versus the curriculum: the child-centered curriculum versus the subject-centered curriculum. The 1920s and 1930 were the heyday of progressive education.

There were many protagonists for the new education movement, and they were prolific in their writings. William H. Kilpatrick's EDUCATION FOR A CHANGING CIVILIZATION (New York: Macmillan, 1926) stressed the need for the school curriculum and methods of teaching to be dynamic rather than static, in the light of changing economic and social conditions. Boyd H. Bode, in MODERN EDUCATIONAL THEORIES (New York: Macmillan, 1927), was very supportive of the newer practices. Harold Rugg and Ann Shumaker's THE CHILD-CENTERED SCHOOL: AN APPRAISAL OF THE NEW EDUCATION (New York: World Book, 1928) presented an early evaluation of progressive education: the proof of its value rests in the cultivation of creativity. Harold Benjamin's THE SABER-TOOTH CURRICULUM (New York: McGraw-Hill, 1939), an allegory upholding child-centered education, received wide national attention.

The Progressive Education Association created a Commission on the Relation of School and College. Essentially, its purpose was to explore how progressive education might be extended into secondary schools. The commission's work, known as the "Eight-Year Study," continued to 1940. The conclusions and recommendations are in THE STORY OF THE EIGHT-YEAR STUDY (New York: Harper and Brothers, 1942), by Wilford M. Aikin.

Educational action generally generates reaction. Although it can be said that the American school was inherently "essentialist" (the three R's as the basis) from the outset, essentialism as a philosophy of education is usually thought of as a reaction, beginning in the 1930s, to the extremist tendencies in progressive education. William C. Bagley was an exponent of this reaction. He believed that tested and ordered experiences should be the basis of school instruction. EDUCATION AND EMERGENT MAN: A THEORY OF EDUCATION WITH PARTICULAR APPLICATION TO PUBLIC EDUCATION IN THE UNTIED STATES (New York: T. Nelson and Sons, 1934) is a statement of his essentialist views.

The junior high school movement had its roots in the early 1900s and the establishment of such a school in Berkeley, California, in 1910 is regarded as the historic first. But it was in the 1920s and 1930s that these three-year schools had their greatest growth. Thomas H. Briggs was one of those most influential in their development, and his THE JUNIOR HIGH SCHOOL (New York: Houghton Mifflin, 1920) is one of the earliest books on the subject.

The idea of the junior college can be traced to late-nineteenth century discussions (especially by Harvard's Eliot and Columbia's Butler), and in an 1892 action at the University of Chicago, separating the first two years (the academic college) from the last two years (the university college). The public, two-year college had its model in the 1902 institution opened in Joliet, Illinois. By the 1920s, especially in the West and mid-West, these colleges grew rapidly in number and were serving an important function in American higher education. Leonard V. Koos was one of the early leaders in the community and junior college movement, and its early history is chronicled in his THE JUNIOR COLLEGE MOVEMENT (Boston: Ginn, 1925).

Horace Mann Bond's THE EDUCATION OF THE NEGRO IN THE AMERICAN
SOCIAL ORDER (New York: Prentice-Hall, 1934) is a landmark in the educational sociology of black people. The coverage is of the post-Civil War
period.

Robert M. Hutchins appeared on the scene in the 1930s as the youthful and
innovative president of the University of Chicago. One of his earliest statements on higher education, wherein he presented the causes of confusion with
recommendations for solution, was THE HIGHER LEARNING IN AMERICA (New
Haven: Yale University Press, 1936).

A significant report of the American Historical Association in 1936 was addressed
to the education establishment. ARE AMERICAN TEACHERS FREE? (New
York: Charles Scribner's Sons, 1936), by Howard K. Beale, was an analysis
of restraints felt at that time concerning the freedom of teaching in the nation's
classrooms.

The rapid growth in the school population during these years of the twentieth
century resulted in an explosion of textbook publishing. THE ELSON BASIC
READERS, written by William H. Elson and William S. Gray, and published
in Chicago by Scott, Foresman, beginning in 1930, are good examples of the
well-illustrated, graded schoolbooks of the period. These books were among
the most popular of the reading series of the 1930s and their use in thirty-four
countries showed the international spread of American textbooks. In content
the books portrayed essentially a bucolic, nonurban, and nonminority America,
with stories of heroes from the Old World.

TWENTIETH CENTURY: 1941 TO 1981

There has not been a more volatile, revolutionary, and exciting period in
American education than the years from World War II to the present. There
were many new developments, epochs, and themes within these years. The
first significant happening was the impact of the conclusion of the war on the
education establishment. Higher education was the first to feel a transition
with the return (to college) of veterans in large numbers.

The term "life adjustment education" came into vogue in 1945 after a U.S.
Office of Education conference on vocational education. A report of the
movement is contained in the Commission on Life Adjustment Education's,
VITALIZING SECONDARY EDUCATION (Washington, D.C.: U.S. Office of
Education, Bulletin no. 3, 1951). The impact of the success of the Russians
with their earth satellite in 1957 caused the life adjustment movement to lose
its force. Americans were urged to get back to the basics.

In higher education during the late 1940s there were two developments worthy
of historical note. The publication of GENERAL EDUCATION IN A FREE
SOCIETY: THE REPORT OF THE HARVARD COMMITTEE (Cambridge: Harvard

University Press, 1945) set forth a rationale and program for achieving a "general education," and it had considerable influence upon college curriculums for over a decade. President Truman appointed a commission to study all aspects of higher education in America, and its work was the most comprehensive study of its kind to that date. It came at a time when colleges and universities were expanding greatly in order to cater to the hordes of returning veterans. The report, HIGHER EDUCATION FOR AMERICAN DEMOCRACY: A REPORT OF THE PRESIDENT'S COMMISSION ON HIGHER EDUCATION (Washington, D.C., 1947) was in six volumes.

The 1950s felt the first wave of severe criticism and profound commentary on public schooling. Robert M. Hutchins, in his THE CONFLICT IN EDUCATION IN A DEMOCRATIC SOCIETY (New York: Harper, 1953), found much of the educational doctrine then in general acceptance (adjustment, immediate needs, etc.) very much wanting. Paul Woodring's LET'S TALK SENSE ABOUT OUR SCHOOLS (New York: McGraw-Hill, 1953) was a moderate's answer to much of the shrill criticism heard. Arthur E. Bestor, a historian, deplored the declining standards and placed much of the blame on the educational establishment itself. His EDUCATIONAL WASTELANDS: THE RETREAT FROM LEARNING IN OUR PUBLIC SCHOOLS (Urbana: University of Illinois, 1953) was widely read and heatedly discussed. Mortimer B. Smith's THE DIMINISHED MIND: A STUDY OF PLANNED MEDIOCRITY IN OUR PUBLIC SCHOOLS (Chicago: H. Regner, 1954) especially criticized the high schools for "nursemaiding" their students. Hyman G. Rickover, an admiral associated with the atomic submarine, in EDUCATION AND FREEDOM (New York: Dutton, 1959), urged an educational system that would be able to meet the challenge of the atomic era. Needless to say, he very much opposed life adjustment education.

Theodore Brameld's PATTERNS OF EDUCATIONAL PHILOSOPHY: A DEMOCRATIC INTERPRETATION (Yonkers, 1950) presented the educational philosophy of reconstructionism, an advocacy of fundamental change in school and society through social consensus.

The 1954 Supreme Court decision, Brown v. Board of Education of Topeka, declaring racial segregation of schools unconstitutional, was the most significant court decision affecting public education in the nation's history. The decision is included in THE SUPREME COURT AND EDUCATION (New York: Teachers College, Columbia University, 1962) by David Fellman, editor.

The National Defense Education Act of 1958, in the Eisenhower administration, was an aftereffect of the challenge thrust forward by the success of the Russian satellite in 1957. The result of the legislation was the encourgement and improvement of the study of science and foreign languages. A source of the impact of the NDEA is Sidney C. Sufrin's ADMINISTERING THE NATIONAL DEFENSE EDUCATION ACT (Syracuse: Syracuse University Press, 1963).

Prayers and Bible reading in public schools have a heritage going back to the earliest schooling in the colonies. The Supreme Court decision of Abington

v. Schempp, in 1963, declared such practices unconstitutional. Portions of the Schempp decision appear in Sam Duker's RELIGION AND THE PUBLIC SCHOOLS (New York: Harper and Row, 1965).

The 1960s and 1970s brought forth a wave of school commentary and criticism, much of it more shrill and revolutionary than the outpouring of earlier years. Myron Lieberman, in his THE FUTURE OF PUBLIC EDUCATION (Chicago: University of Chicago Press, 1960), criticized local control of education and called for a professional, managerial, and economic revolution in the school establishment. Martin Mayer spent over two years in school visits for his THE SCHOOLS (New York: Harper, 1961) and found much to deplore, the junior high school being in need of most improvement. James B. Conant's SLUMS AND SUBURBS (New York: McGraw-Hill, 1961) was one of the earliest works on the problems of urban education. There was a surfeit of books (not all of them serious studies) on this topic during the 1960s and 1970s. Paul Goodman offered some radical alternatives to public schools (farm as a school, city as a school, etc.) in his COMPULSORY MISEDUCATION (New York: Vintage Books, 1964). Charles Silberman painted a grim picture of the public schools in his CRISIS IN THE CLASSROOM: THE REMAKING OF AMERICAN EDUCATION (New York: Random House, 1970). The open classroom concept was suggested for elementary grades as an improvement on conventional teaching.

The most radical of the books on school reform was DESCHOOLING SOCIETY (New York: Harper Row, 1971) by Ivan Illich. This was a call for a cultural revolution where, among other things, there would be an abandonment of compulsory education. Skill centers, under a variety of teachers, would replace most instruction given in the schools. John Holt's FREEDOM AND BEYOND (New York: E.P. Dutton, 1972) envisioned a deschooled society where free schools and open education would be offered as alternatives to conventional schooling. Harry Broudy's THE REAL WORLD OF THE PUBLIC SCHOOLS (New York: Harcourt Brace Jovanovich, 1972) was a well-reasoned response to the extreme educational criticism of the 1960s. He presented a down-to-earth (real world) treatment of school problems.

Diane Ravitch took on the radical revisionists in THE REVISIONISTS REVISED: A CRITIQUE OF THE RADICAL ATTACK ON THE SCHOOLS (New York: Basic Books, 1978). It was her contention that public education was the institution that had helped the immigrants, the poor, and the racial minorities economically and socially.

The period saw the publication of a number of significant scholarly works on the historical foundations of American education. Bernard Bailyn's EDUCATION IN THE FORMING OF AMERICAN SOCIETY (Chapel Hill: University of North Carolina Press, 1960) changed the focus of the study of the history of education from essentially an institutional and legal one to a broad view of the history of learning with many areas of study included. Lawrence A. Cremin produced two volumes, AMERICAN EDUCATION: THE COLONIAL EXPERIENCE, 1607-1783 (New York, 1970) and AMERICAN EDUCATION: THE NA-

TIONAL EXPERIENCE, 1783-1876 (New York: Harper and Row, 1980), the latter having been awarded the 1981 Pulitzer Prize for a work in history, the first to be awarded for a book on education. These volumes comprise the most complete treatment of the history of American education to 1876 published to date.

Lyndon B. Johnson was indeed the education president. More important legislation concerning schools was passed during his administration than in all previous ones combined. The 1964 Economic Opportunity Act brought forth the Teachers Corps, the Job Corps, and the concept of community-action programs. The 1965 Elementary and Secondary Education Act, with its several subtitles, was the most comprehensive package of federal school legislation.

The publication of the BANK STREET READERS (New York: Macmillan, 1965) marked a turning point in textbook writing. This reading series portrayed American children in an urban, multicultural, and multiracial environment. Soon after, other publishers followed the pattern.

Three important studies are worthy of mention. James Coleman's EQUALITY OF EDUCATIONAL OPPORTUNITY (Washington, D.C.: Government Printing Office, 1966), the "Coleman Report," attempted to evaluate the equality of schooling available to black and white students. Christopher Jencks's INEQUALITY: A REASSESSMENT OF THE EFFECT OF FAMILY AND SCHOOLING IN AMERICA (New York: Basic Books, 1972) showed the close relationship between the social and economic status of the family and success in schooling. The Carnegie Commission on Higher Education published PRIORITIES FOR ACTION: FINAL REPORT OF THE CARNEGIE COMMISSION ON HIGHER EDUCATION (New York, 1973) which was the final report of the commission that had been at work since 1967. The scope of the study included seven themes: setting priorities, clarifying purposes, preserving and enhancing quality and diversity, advancing social justice, enhancing constructive change, achieving more effective governance, and assuring resources and their more effective use.

Education was a growth industry in the 1960s. It was one of America's biggest enterprises. Textbook publishing for all levels flourished. The production of the software and hardware of instructional materials became the business of some of the nation's largest corporations. In the publishing of books on education there was no period in the past to compare with it. The availability of grant money, the paperback volume, the popularity of the book of readings, the "publish or perish" syndrome among college faculty, the bulging student enrollments, and the fact that a great many authors had something they considered significant to say, in an epoch when education played a large part in the social concerns of Americans, all contributed to the surfeit of writings on education. A few of these may survive as the educational classics of these years; others, deservedly or not, will become ephemeral.

AMERICAN EDUCATION

ACADEMIC FREEDOM

Beale, Howard K. ARE AMERICAN TEACHERS FREE? New York: Charles Scribner's Sons, 1936. xxiv, 855 p.

An analysis of restraints upon the freedom of teaching in American schools. A report of the American Historical Association.

Hofstadter, Richard, and Metzger, Walter P. THE DEVELOPMENT OF ACADEMIC FREEDOM IN THE UNITED STATES. New York: Columbia University Press, 1952. xvi, 527 p.

Hofstadter has written part 1 covering the topic up to about 1860. Metzger, in part 2, deals with the issue through the early 1950s.

Hook, Sidney. ACADEMIC FREEDOM AND ACADEMIC ANARCHY. New York: Cowles Book Co., 1970. xviii, 269 p. Appendix.

Written from the campus events of the 1960s. Hook deplores as absurd many doctrines and practices that were urged and used as panaceas for campus peace. An appendix contains "Second Thoughts on Berkeley."

Jenkinson, Edward B. CENSORS IN THE CLASSROOM: THE MIND BENDERS. Carbondale: Southern Illinois University Press, 1979. xix, 184 p.

School textbook censorship by individuals and groups in the 1970s.

Kirk, Russell. ACADEMIC FREEDOM: AN ESSAY IN DEFINITION. Chicago: Henry Regnery Co., 1955. 210 p.

Study of academic freedom in the United States with specific cases used in illustration.

Manier, Edward, and Houck, John W. ACADEMIC FREEDOM AND THE CATHOLIC UNIVERSITY. Notre Dame: Fides Publishers, 1967. xi, 225 p.

Papers presented at a 1966 symposium held at Notre Dame with

short introduction for each. Some writers engage in the defense
of issues that would be taken for granted on secular campuses.

Nelson, Jack, and Roberts, Gene, Jr. THE CENSORS AND THE SCHOOLS.
Boston: Little, Brown, 1963. xii, 208 p.

Textbook censorship is the result of pressure groups seeking to
spread a particular pöint of view (or seeking to have one not
stated). Some are just misguided; others are bigots and extremists.

ACADEMY MOVEMENT

Marr, Harriet W. THE OLD NEW ENGLAND ACADEMIES. New York:
Comet Press, 1959. 311 p.

Academies in New England that were established before 1826.
The curriculum, finances, student life, and what became of these
institutions are some of the items covered.

Sizer, Theodore R. THE AGE OF ACADEMIES. New York: Teachers College, Columbia University, 1964. xii, 201 p.

The development and peak years of the academy, a major American
institution of secondary education during the first half of the nineteenth century.

ACCOUNTABILITY

Lessinger, Leon M., and Tyler, Ralph W., eds. ACCOUNTABILITY IN EDU-
CATION. Worthington, Ohio: Charles A. Jones Publishing Co., 1971.
viii, 85 p.

A monograph which is one of the earliest treatments of educational accountability, a concept which developed out of the late 1960s
and early 1970s. A contribution by United Federation of Teachers'
leader, Albert Shanker, expresses the fear that it may end up as
a "gimmick."

Martin, Don T.; Overholt, George E.; et al. ACCOUNTABILITY IN AMERI-
CAN EDUCATION: A CRITIQUE. Princeton, N.J.: Princeton Book Co.,
1976. ix, 83 p.

Accountability is a concept which emerged in the early 1970s.
Authors counter the claim that it should be the only approach to
educational practice.

Sicard, Frank J., and Jantz, Richard K., eds. ACCOUNTABILITY IN AMERI-
CAN EDUCATION. Boston: Allyn and Bacon, 1972. vi, 410 p.

Articles by educators who have been involved with educational accountability and related areas. Book has two parts: the call for accountability and the schools' response.

ADMINISTRATION OF SCHOOLS

General Works

Cubberley, Ellwood P. PUBLIC SCHOOL ADMINISTRATION. Boston: Houghton Mifflin, 1916. xviii, 479 p. Illus.

Statement of principles underlying organization and administration of public elementary and secondary schools presented by the then dean of the School of Education at Stanford University. A popular text that was published through the 1920s.

Miller, Van; Madden, George R.; et al. THE PUBLIC ADMINISTRATION OF AMERICAN SCHOOL SYSTEMS. 2d ed. New York: Macmillan, 1972. x, 428 p.

First appeared in 1965. There are three parts to the volume: background of school in American culture; tasks involved in educational organization; and the kinds of school administrators.

Sergiovanni, Thomas J., and Carver, Fred D. THE NEW SCHOOL EXECUTIVE: A THEORY OF ADMINISTRATION. New York: Dodd, Mead, 1973. 256 p.

Primarily for a course in educational administration, but also of help to those in the field. A behaviorally oriented book.

Elementary

Elsbree, Willard, et al. ELEMENTARY SCHOOL ADMINISTRATION AND SUPERVISION. 3d ed. New York: American Book Co., 1967. viii, 520 p.

A basic and popular text with a broad overview. First published in 1951.

Hencley, Stephen P., et al. THE ELEMENTARY SCHOOL PRINCIPALSHIP. New York: Dodd, Mead, 1970. 366 p.

A theory-based presentation of important aspects of the work of the elementary school principal. Practical help in many of the chapters.

Otto, Henry. ELEMENTARY SCHOOL ORGANIZATION AND ADMINISTRATION. 4th ed. New York: Appleton, Century, Crofts, 1964. xi, 409 p.

A basic treatment of the subject. Useful in university courses. The work has been a classic since 1934.

Stoops, Emery, and Johnson, Russelle. ELEMENTARY SCHOOL ADMINISTRA-TION. New York: McGraw-Hill, 1967. 352 p.

The several roles that the elementary school principal must play are discussed. Supervision of staff is also included.

Secondary

Douglass, Harl R. MODERN ADMINISTRATION OF SECONDARY SCHOOLS. Boston: Ginn and Co., 1963. ix, 601 p.

Somewhat dated but a well-known text in the field since its first appearance in 1932. Of use to both administrators in training and those in service.

Jones, James J., and Salisbury, C. Jackson. SECONDARY SCHOOL AD-MINISTRATION. New York: McGraw-Hill, 1969. 320 p.

An overview of the field of secondary school administration fill-ing the gap between the more traditional texts and those which present a theory approach.

Kraft, Leonard E., ed. THE SECONDARY SCHOOL PRINCIPAL IN ACTION. Dubuque: William C. Brown, 1971. xiii, 539 p.

The many functions of the principal's role are presented through reprints of articles by specialists in secondary education.

ADULT EDUCATION

Bibliography

Paulston, Rolland G., ed. NON-FORMAL EDUCATION: AN ANNOTATED BIBLIOGRAPHY. New York: Praeger Publishers, 1972. xxi, 332 p.

Adult education is a major area within nonformal schooling. Books, monographs, and articles are annotated.

General Works

Bryson, Lyman L. ADULT EDUCATION. New York: American Book Co., 1936. vi, 208 p.

By a prominent author and leader in adult education and com-munication of ideas from the 1930s through the 1950s.

Cass, Angelica, and Crabtree, Arthur P. ADULT ELEMENTARY EDUCATION. New York: Noble and Noble, 1956. 275 p.

Directed to adults who are learning elementary subjects. Book includes taaching methods along with administrative procedures.

Knowles, Malcolm S. THE ADULT EDUCATION MOVEMENT IN THE UNITED STATES. New York: Holt, Rinehart and Winston, 1962. 335 p.

A history of adult education from colonial times to the early 1960s.

AGRICULTURAL EDUCATION

Brown, Mary R., et al. AGRICULTURAL EDUCATION IN A TECHNICAL SOCIETY: AN ANNOTATED BIBLIOGRAPHY OF RESOURCES. Chicago: American Library Association, 1973. xii, 228 p.

Helpful to educators working in secondary or postsecondary agricultural education. Books, periodicals, monographs, and government documents are listed.

Jewell, James P. AGRICULTURAL EDUCATION INCLUDING NATURE STUDY AND SCHOOL GARDENS. U.S. Bureau of Education, Bulletin no. 2, 1907. Washington, D.C.: Government Printing Office, 1908. 148 p.

A history of elementary and secondary school agricultural education is included.

True, Alfred C. A HISTORY OF AGRICULTURAL EDUCATION IN THE UNITED STATES, 1785-1925. Rpt. of U.S. Department of Agriculture, Miscellaneous Publications, no. 36, 1929. New York: Arno Press, 1969. ix, 436 p. Illus.

AMERICAN INDIAN EDUCATION

Adams, Evelyn C. AMERICAN INDIAN EDUCATION: GOVERNMENT SCHOOLS AND ECONOMIC PROGRESS. New York: King's Crown Press, 1946. xiii, 122 p. Illus.

The federal government's efforts to "Americanize" Indians through schooling. The work covers the period from the Revolution to the first decades of the twentieth century.

Fuchs, Estelle, and Havighurst, Robert J. TO LIVE ON THIS EARTH: AMERICAN INDIAN EDUCATION. Garden City, N.Y.: Doubleday, 1972. xiii, 390 p. Illus.

A general but useful book. Havighurst, a distinguished educational sociologist, has done much research on education of the American Indian.

Golden, Gertrude. RED MOON CALLED ME. San Antonio: Naylor Co., 1954. 221 p. Illus.

> Memoirs of a teacher in the Government Indian Service.

Greenberg, Norman C., and Gilda, M. EDUCATION OF THE AMERICAN INDIAN IN TODAY'S WORLD. Dubuque: William C. Brown, 1964. vi, 76 p. Illus.

> An interdisciplinary work especially written for teachers and school administrators.

Powers, Joseph F. BROTHERHOOD THROUGH EDUCATION: A GUIDE FOR TEACHERS OF AMERICAN INDIANS. Fayette: Upper Iowa University, 1965. 171 p.

> Essentially for teachers having little experience with American Indians.

Szasz, Margaret. EDUCATION AND THE AMERICAN INDIAN: THE ROAD TO SELF-DETERMINATION, 1928-1973. Albuquerque: University of New Mexico Press, 1974. 272 p. Illus.

> A full-length treatment of federal American Indian education in the twentieth century. Its failures can be shared by the Bureau of Indian Affairs, Congress, and Bureau of the Budget.

ART EDUCATION

Bibliography

Bunch, Clarence, ed. ART EDUCATION: A GUIDE TO INFORMATION SOURCES. Art and Architecture Information Guide Series, vol. 6. Detroit: Gale Research Co., 1978. xv, 331 p.

> Many areas and levels of art education are included. From the sources it can be seen that art education began as utilitarian, it later changed to concern for aesthetics, and more recently emphasis has been on art as a part of living in an industrial society, and again has stressed "doing." Listings of books are annotated.

General Works

Bailey, Henry T. ART EDUCATION. Boston: Houghton Mifflin, 1914. xi, 101 p. Illus.

> Author was prominent late nineteenth- and early twentieth-century leader in art education. He was a teacher and editor of SCHOOL ARTS magazine. This work forms an early statement on the subject for this century.

Dow, Arthur W. THE THEORY AND PRACTICE OF TEACHING ART. New York: Teachers College, Columbia University, 1912. 73 p. Illus.

Dow, head of department of fine arts at Teachers College, did much to increase the importance of art in the public school curriculum.

Gaitskell, Charles D., and Hurwitz, Al. CHILDREN AND THEIR ART. 2d ed. New York: Harcourt Brace Jovanovich, 1970. 507 p. Illus.

Both theoretical and practical in approach. A chapter is devoted to teaching art to the gifted and slow learner.

Haskell, Lendall L. ART IN EARLY CHILDHOOD YEARS. Columbus: Charles E. Merrill, 1979. xi, 218 p. Illus.

Presents the theory of visual development in children. Drawing and craft experiences explained.

Lansing, Kenneth. ART, ARTISTS, AND ART EDUCATION. New York: McGraw-Hill, 1969. 350 p. Illus.

Heavily illustrated text, in color, for methods courses in art education. Aesthetic criteria, teaching processes, and recommended curriculum are features.

Linderman, Earl W., and Herberholz, Donald W. DEVELOPING ARTISTIC AND PERCEPTUAL AWARENESS: ART PRACTICE IN THE ELEMENTARY CLASSROOM. Dubuque: William C. Brown, 1969. xv, 146 p. Illus.

A guide to help teachers stimulate children to creative expression. Based on research findings from the fields of child psychology and art education.

Munro, Thomas, and Read, Herbert. THE CREATIVE ARTS IN AMERICAN EDUCATION. Cambridge, Mass.: Harvard University Press, 1960. 65 p.

The Inglis and Burton Lectures at Harvard with Munro on "The Interrelation of the Arts in Secondary Education," and Read on "The Third Realm of Education."

Paston, Herbert. LEARNING TO TEACH ART. Lincoln, Nebr.: Professional Educators Publications, 1973. 106 p.

A guide for the student teacher of art in elementary and secondary schools.

Smith, Walter. ART EDUCATION: SCHOLASTIC AND INDUSTRIAL. Boston: James R. Osgood, 1872. x, 398 p. Illus.

The best work on the teaching of art in the nineteenth century.

Both theory of art education and background information on color, design, and industrial drawing are presented. Smith taught at the Massachusetts School of Art and was state director of art education in that state.

ART OF TEACHING

Epstein, Joseph, ed. MASTERS: PORTRAITS OF GREAT TEACHERS. New York: Basic Books, 1981. 265 p.

Teaching is a performing art. The essays are descriptions of the performances of such great teachers as Morris Cohen, Alfred North Whitehead, Ruth Benedict, and thirteen others.

Fuess, Claude M., and Basford, Emory S., eds. UNSEEN HARVESTS, A TREASURY OF TEACHING. New York: Macmillan, 1947. xx, 678 p.

Selections about teaching from great teachers in literature.

Highet, Gilbert. THE ART OF TEACHING. New York: Alfred Knopf, 1950. xviii, 291 p., vii.

Not a methods book, but a most stimulating work on teaching in its largest sense written by a distinguished and popular Columbia University teacher of classics.

_____. THE IMMORTAL PROFESSION: THE JOYS OF TEACHING AND LEARNING. New York: Weybright and Tally, 1976. viii, 223 p.

Teaching and the classical tradition. Gilbert Murray, Albert Schweitzer, and Jesus of Nazareth are dealt with in some detail.

Kohl, Herbert R. ON TEACHING. New York: Schocken Books, 1976. 185 p.

Kohl, author and an advocate of open education, believes that teaching of basics is not incompatible with open classrooms. He includes other basics: cultural awareness and self-education, as examples.

Peterson, Houston, ed. GREAT TEACHERS PORTRAYED BY THOSE WHO STUDIED UNDER THEM. New Brunswick, N.J.: Rutgers University Press, 1946. xxi, 351 p.

Here are many of the great teachers (Anne Sullivan, Mark Hopkins, Woodrow Wilson, John Dewey, Ralph Waldo Emerson, and others) written about by distinguished pupils (Helen Keller, James Russell Lowell, Christopher Morley, and others).

AUDIOVISUAL INSTRUCTION

Dale, Edgar. AUDIOVISUAL METHODS IN TEACHING. 3d ed. New York: Holt, Dryden, 1969. xii, 716 p. Illus.

> One of the best texts in the field. The work first appeared in 1946 and has been greatly enlarged as years have passed to include the latest equipment and practices.

Freeman, Frank N. VISUAL EDUCATION: A COMPARATIVE STUDY OF MOTION PICTURES AND OTHER METHODS OF INSTRUCTION. Chicago: University of Chicago Press, 1924. viii, 391 p. Illus.

> An early work on the visual aids in education with emphasis on the new medium of motion pictures.

Limbacher, James L. A REFERENCE GUIDE TO AUDIOVISUAL INFORMATION. New York: R.R. Bowker Co., 1972. ix, 197 p.

> A listing of books and periodicals along with a selection on audiovisual terms and definitions.

Nelson, Leslie. INSTRUCTIONAL AIDS: HOW TO MAKE AND USE THEM. Dubuque: William C. Brown, 1970. xiv, 267 p. Illus.

> One of the most useful books of its kind. Plans are given for constructing all sorts of classroom instructional aids.

Saettler, Paul. A HISTORY OF INSTRUCTIONAL TECHNOLOGY. New York: McGraw-Hill, 1968. xv, 399 p. Illus.

> The definitive work on the history of audiovisual education from its roots up through programmed instruction.

Wittich, Walter A., and Schuller, Charles F. INSTRUCTIONAL TECHNOLOGY, ITS NATURE AND USE. 5th ed. New York: Harper and Row, 1973. xxvi, 737 p. Illus.

> Every type of audiovisual equipment listed with its proper use and instructional advantages.

BASIC EDUCATION

Hansen, Carl F. THE AMIDON ELEMENTARY SCHOOL: A SUCCESSFUL DEMONSTRATION IN BASIC EDUCATION. Englewood Cliffs, N.J.: Prentice Hall, 1962. 252 p.

> The development and results of a Washington, D.C., "no non-sense" school of the 1960s.

Koerner, James D., ed. THE CASE FOR BASIC EDUCATION. Boston: Little, Brown, 1959. 256 p.

A collection of essays by sixteen scholars (none of whom was involved in public education) on strengthening the curriculum in public schools. Editor is the executive secretary of the Council for Basic Education.

BIBLIOGRAPHIES OF EDUCATION: GENERAL

Besterman, Theodore, ed. EDUCATION: A BIBLIOGRAPHY OF BIBLIOGRA-PHIES. Totowa, N.J.: Towman and Littlefield, 1971. 306 p.

Bibliographies by countries and by topics (e.g., adult education, audiovisual education).

Bolton, Frederick E., ed. A SELECTED BIBLIOGRAPHY OF BOOKS AND MONOGRAPHS ON EDUCATION. Olympia, Wash.: n.p., 1921. 103 p.

This work listed two thousand volumes on education up to 1920.

Hall, G. Stanley, and Mansfield, John M., eds. HINTS TOWARD A SELECT AND DESCRIPTIVE BIBLIOGRAPHY OF EDUCATION. Boston: D.C. Heath, 1886. xv, 309 p.

Arranged by topics and indexed by authors. The earliest bibliography of American education.

Marks, Barbara S. NEW YORK UNIVERSITY LIST OF BOOKS IN EDUCA-TION. New York: Citation Press, 1968. 527 p.

Divided into chapters by special aspects of the subject. Each book is briefly annotated. Essentially it is a list of books that an education library should have. Prepared by the librarian of New York University's School of Education.

Monroe, Walter S., and Shores, Louis, eds. BIBLIOGRAPHIES AND SUMMA-RIES IN EDUCATION TO JULY 1935. New York: H.W. Wilson Co., 1936. xiv, 470 p.

Catalog of more than four thousand annotated works listed under authors and subjects.

Park, Joe, ed. THE RISE OF AMERICAN EDUCATION: AN ANNOTATED BIBLIOGRAPHY. Evanston: Northwestern University Press, 1965. xi, 216 p.

Most complete, annotated, general bibliography on American education to its time. Most major areas, especially in the historical and social foundations, are included with their definitive works. However, the work came out just before much of the turmoil of the 1960s with the resulting publication explosion.

BILINGUAL EDUCATION

Bibliography

Cordasco, Francesco, with Bernstein, George, comps. BILINGUAL EDUCATION IN AMERICAN SCHOOLS: A GUIDE TO INFORMATION SOURCES. Education Information Guide Series, vol. 3. Detroit: Gale Research Co., 1979. xv, 307 p.

> A very complete guide to its date of reference sources on history, programs, curriculum, administration, staffing, teacher training, and the legislation of bilingual education in the United States.

General Works

Anderson, Theodore, and Boyer, Mildred. BILINGUAL SCHOOLING IN THE UNITED STATES: HISTORY, RATIONALE, IMPLICATIONS, AND PLANNING. 2 vols. Detroit: Blaine Ethridge Books, 1976. Illus.

> Work was first published in 1970 at the Southwest Educational Development Laboratory at Austin, Texas, following the enactment of the Bilingual Education Act of 1967.

Cordasco, Francesco, ed. BILINGUALISM AND THE BILINGUAL CHILD. New York: Arno Press, 1978. 400 p.

> A collection of thirty-four previosly published articles on the topic. None earlier than 1965.

_____. BILINGUAL EDUCATION IN NEW YORK CITY: A COMPENDIUM OF REPORTS. New York: Arno Press, 1978. 248 p.

> Important because it presents three early reports (earliest in 1947) on the responses of public education authorities to Puerto Rican children in New York City schools.

_____. BILINGUAL SCHOOLING IN THE UNITED STATES: A SOURCEBOOK FOR EDUCATIONAL PERSONNEL. New York: McGraw-Hill, 1976. xxviii, 387 p.

> Historical backgrounds, definitions, linguistic perspectives programs, and practices in bilingual education.

Von Maltitz, Frances W. LIVING AND LEARNING IN TWO LANGUAGES: BILINGUAL-BICULTURAL EDUCATION IN THE UNITED STATES. New York: McGraw-Hill, 1975. xiii, 221 p.

> The origins and development of the movement with its rationale. The opposition to bilingual education is discussed.

BLACK AMERICANS, EDUCATION OF

Bibliographies

Chambers, Frederick, ed. BLACK HIGHER EDUCATION IN THE UNITED
STATES: A SELECTED BIBLIOGRAPHY ON NEGRO HIGHER EDUCATION.
Westport, Conn.: Greenwood Press, 1978. xxiv, 268 p. Index.

Includes doctoral and masters' dissertations, institutional histories,
periodicals and book references alphabetically arranged by author,
but not broken down into subtopics and not annotated. A subject
index is included.

Weinberg, Meyer, ed. EDUCATION OF THE MINORITY CHILD: A COMPRE-
HENSIVE BIBLIOGRAPHY OF 10,000 SELECTED ENTRIES. Chicago: Integrated
Education Association, 1970. xii, 530 p.

Much on black American children. Books, monographs, articles,
and theses are indexed under pertinent topics. Very comprehensive but not annotated.

General Works

Andrews, Charles C. THE HISTORY OF THE NEW YORK AFRICAN FREE
SCHOOLS. New York: Mahlon Day, 1830. 148 p.

An account of the schools founded by the New York Manumission
Society in 1787 for black children. In the appendix are examples
of the work accomplished by pupils.

Ballard, Allen B. THE EDUCATION OF BLACK FOLK: THE AFRO-AMER-
ICAN STRUGGLE FOR KNOWLEDGE IN WHITE AMERICA. New York:
Harper and Row, 1973. vi, 173 p.

First a historical presentation, then the problems as they exist.
Some recommendations: compensatory programs, intensive counseling, and strict class attendance.

Bond, Horace Mann. THE EDUCATION OF THE NEGRO IN THE AMERICAN
SOCIAL ORDER. New York: Prentice-Hall, 1934. xx, 501 p. Illus.

A landmark in educational sociology of black people by the emi-
nent black teacher, scholar, and college president. The coverage
is the post-Civil War period.

Bowles, Frank, and DeCosta, Frank A. BETWEEN TWO WORLDS: NEGRO
HIGHER EDUCATION. New York: McGraw-Hill, 1971. 326 p.

A broad look at the historically black college: the past, the
present, and future role.

Bullock, Henry A. A HISTORY OF NEGRO EDUCATION IN THE SOUTH, 1619 TO THE PRESENT. Cambridge, Mass.: Harvard University Press, 1967. xi, 339 p.

> Scant on the seventeenth and eighteenth centuries, but much on the post-Civil War period and the influence of philanthropy. The work includes the desegregation movements of the 1950s and 1960s.

Clift, Virgil A., et al., eds. NEGRO EDUCATION IN AMERICA: ITS ADEQUACY, PROBLEMS, AND NEEDS. 16th Yearbook, John Dewey Society. New York: Harper and Row, 1962. xxiii, 315 p.

> Contributions by several scholars on such topics as the history of the education of the Negro, contributions of Negro education, and the impact of recent Supreme Court decisions.

Cooley, Rossa B. SCHOOL ACRES. New Haven, Conn.: Yale University Press, 1930. 166 p.

> A study of rural schooling for blacks in the South.

Forten, Charlotte L. A FREE NEGRO IN THE SLAVE ERA: THE JOURNAL OF CHARLOTTE L. FORTEN. Introduction and notes by Ray Allen Billington. New York: Collier Books, 1961. 286 p.

> The diary of a northern Negro schoolteacher of the 1850s and 1860s. Especially valuable for her account of teaching liberated slaves on an island off the coast of South Carolina. Work was first published in 1953 as JOURNAL OF CHARLOTTE L. FORTEN (New York: Dryden Press, 1953).

Foster, Herbert L. RIBBIN', JIVIN', AND PLAYIN' THE DOZENS: THE UNRECOGNIZED DILEMMA OF INNER-CITY SCHOOLS. Cambridge, Mass.: Ballinger Publishing Co., 1974. 353 p.

> The verbal contacts between students and students and between students and teachers are vividly reported by an experienced teacher of inner-city black students.

Haskins, Jim. BLACK MANIFESTO FOR EDUCATION. New York: Morrow, 1973. xvi, 201 p.

> Ten black educators explore black studies for resources in teaching black students.

Holmes, D.O.W. THE EVOLUTION OF THE NEGRO COLLEGE. New York: Teachers College, Columbia University, 1934. xii, 221 p.

> A history of the origins and early years of the Negro colleges written before integration in higher education.

Kluger, Richard. SIMPLE JUSTICE: THE HISTORY OF BROWN v. BOARD OF EDUCATION AND BLACK AMERICA'S STRUGGLE FOR EQUALITY. New York: Alfred A. Knopf, 1976. 823 p.

> The development of the individual cases that led to the Brown decision. An epilogue relates what has happened from 1954 to 1974.

Labov, William. LANGUAGE IN THE INNER CITY: STUDIES IN THE BLACK VERNACULAR. Philadelphia: University of Pennsylvania Press, 1972. xxiv, 412 p. Illus.

> The range and complexity of black dialects are revealed. Of value to those working with many black inner-city children.

Mohraz, Judy J. THE SEPARATE PROBLEM: CASE STUDIES OF BLACK EDUCATION IN THE NORTH, 1900-1930. Westport, Conn.: Greenwood Press, 1979. xvi, 165 p.

> The educational practices of Chicago, Indianapolis, and Philadelphia, in the early twentieth century, so far as the schooling of black children was concerned.

Sowell, Thomas. BLACK EDUCATION: MYTHS AND TRAGEDIES. New York: David McKay, 1972. 396 p.

> A challenging report on college recruitment of black students and black studies' programs, among other controversial items. Proposals offered for remedying the situation.

Spivey, Donald. SCHOOLING FOR THE NEW SLAVERY: BLACK INDUS-TRIAL EDUCATION, 1868-1915. Westport, Conn.: Greenwood Press, 1978. xii, 162 p.

> The role of industrial education offered to black Americans after the Civil War. Booker T. Washington and Tuskegee Institute are discussed.

Woodson, Carter G. THE EDUCATION OF THE NEGRO PRIOR TO 1861. New York: G.P. Putman's Sons, 1915. vi, 545 p.

> The church and its clergy were generally the first to be involved with the schooling of black Americans. A valuable work of the pre-emancipation period by a distinguished black historian.

BLIND AND SIGHT-IMPAIRED, EDUCATION OF

Anagnos, Michael. THE EDUCATION OF THE BLIND IN THE UNITED STATES OF AMERICA. Boston: G.H. Ellis, 1904. 23 p.

Consists of two addresses given by the director of the Perkins Institution in Massachusetts.

Hanninen, Kenneth A. TEACHING THE VISUALLY HANDICAPPED. Columbus: Charles E. Merrill, 1975. vii, 232 p. Illus.

Written especially for those preparing to teach the visually handicapped in elementary or secondary schools. Topics include the integration of those with limited vision into regular classrooms.

Harley, Randall K., et al. THE TEACHING OF BRAILLE READING. Springfield, Ill.: Charles C Thomas, 1979. ix, 187 p. Illus.

The Braille system began in 1829 but has evolved through many changes to the present system of the six-dot cell and 189 characters for letters, words, punctuation, and special forms.

Lowenfeld, Berthold, ed. THE VISUALLY HANDICAPPED CHILD IN SCHOOL. New York: John Day Co., 1973. xvi, 384 p.

Eight chapters by specialists on teaching programs, psychological considerations, and other pertinent topics. Includes a history of the education of the visually handicapped.

CAREER EDUCATION

CAREER EDUCATION: A DISSERTATION INDEX. Ann Arbor, Mich.: University Microfilms International, 1976. vii, 333 p. Indexes.

A listing of university dissertations on the topic accepted between 1972 and 1975. A keyword index and author index are included.

Hoyt, Kenneth B., et al. CAREER EDUCATION: WHAT IT IS AND HOW TO DO IT. 2d ed. Salt Lake City: Olympus Publishing Co., 1974. 238 p.

A basic treatment of one of the newer departures of the early 1970s in educational practice. The book was first published in 1972.

_____. CAREER EDUCATION AND THE ELEMENTARY SCHOOL TEACHER. Salt Lake City: Olympus Publishing Co., 1973. 204 p.

Programs in career education begin in the elementary grades. The world of work is first explored.

_____. CAREER EDUCATION IN THE HIGH SCHOOL. Salt Lake City: Olympus Publishing Co., 1977. 461 p.

A continuance of graded work in a career education program. The vocational emphasis, usually with a work-study arrangement, is the common practice.

Lederer, Muriel. THE GUIDE TO CAREER EDUCATION. New York: Quadrangle, New York Times, 1974. xiv, 401 p. Illus.

> The definitive work to date on the subject. A major feature is a list of two thousand occupations that do not require a college degree.

CHAUTAUQUA

Gould, Joseph E. THE CHAUTAUQUA MOVEMENT. Albany: State University of New York, 1961. xiv, 108 p. Illus.

> Concentrates essentially on the beginnings of the Chautauqua movement, originating out of the need to train Sunday school teachers.

Harrison, Harry P. CULTURE UNDER CANVAS: THE STORY OF TENT CHAUTAUQUA. New York: Hastings House, 1958. 287 p. Illus.

> The story of the institution of Chautauqua, a potent democratic force in family education.

Morrison, Theodore. CHAUTAUQUA: A CENTER FOR EDUCATION, RELIGION, AND THE ARTS OF AMERICA. Chicago: University of Chicago Press, 1974. viii, 351 p. Illus.

> The origins, later development, and transformation of this nineteenth-century American adventure in adult and family education. A fine photographic record of the institution.

CHILDREN'S LITERATURE

Johnson, Edna, et al. ANTHOLOGY OF CHILDREN'S LITERATURE. 3d ed. Boston: Houghton Mifflin, 1970. xxxviii, 1,289 p. Illus.

> A popular and important work having undergone many revisions since its first appearance in 1935. Traditional literature (prose and poetry) plus modern contributions that are destined to last.

Kiefer, Monica. AMERICAN CHILDREN THROUGH THEIR BOOKS, 1700-1835. Philadelphia: University of Pennsylvania Press, 1948. xiv, 248 p. Illus.

> This work deals with a wide range of children's literature from colonial days through the early nineteenth century.

Kujoth, Jean S. BEST-SELLING CHILDREN'S BOOKS. Metuchen, N.J.: Scarecrow Press, 1973. viii, 305 p.

Best sellers for children (some from the nineteenth century and before) listed by author (annotated), by title, by year of publication, and by type, subject, and grade level.

Lukens, Rebecca J. A CRITICAL HANDBOOK OF CHILDREN'S LITERATURE. Glenview, Ill.: Scott, Foresman, 1976. 214 p. Illus.

The application of critical standards to children's literature. A basis is presented for discriminating among the good and inferior in books for children.

Meacham, Mary. INFORMATION SOURCES IN CHILDREN'S LITERATURE: A PRACTICAL REFERENCE GUIDE FOR CHILDREN'S LIBRARIANS, LITERATURE. Westport, Conn.: Greenwood Press, 1978. 280 p.

A valuable guide to the large quantity of literature for children. How-to build a basic collection and how-to find books in specific areas.

Meigs, Cornelia, et al. A CRITICAL HISTORY OF CHILDREN'S LITERATURE. New York: Macmillan, 1953. xxiv, 624 p.

The volume covers the history of children's books published in English from medieval tales to work of the early 1950s.

Rudman, Masha K. CHILDREN'S LITERATURE: AN ISSUES APPROACH. Lexington, Ky.: D.C. Heath, 1976. xix, 433 p.

Annotated bibliography arranged around such topics as divorce, death, war, sex, black people, Indians, and women; for the most part, issues of recent attention in writing for children.

COMMUNITY AND JUNIOR COLLEGES

Bibliography

Rarig, Emory, ed. THE COMMUNITY JUNIOR COLLEGE: AN ANNOTATED BIBLIOGRAPHY. New York: Teachers College, Columbia University, 1966. 114 p.

Books, monographs, and journal articles on the two-year colleges.

General Works

Blocker, Clyde E., et al. THE TWO-YEAR COLLEGE: A SOCIAL SYNTHESIS. Englewood Cliffs, N.J.: Prentice-Hall, 1965. xii, 298 p. Illus.

An analysis of the growing pains of the two-year college. Suggestions given for good community relations.

Eells, Walter C. THE JUNIOR COLLEGE. New York: Houghton Mifflin, 1931. xxviii, 933 p.

> Eells was a leader and writer in the junior college movement. This is an early textbook for courses in junior college administration.

Fields, Ralph R. THE COMMUNITY COLLEGE MOVEMENT. New York: McGraw-Hill, 1962. 360 p. Illus.

> Both a historical and a contemporary account of the community college. The programs of four such colleges are discussed in detail.

Koos, Leonard V. THE JUNIOR COLLEGE MOVEMENT. Boston: Ginn, 1925. xii, 436 p. Illus.

> One of the earliest works on the two-year college movement by one of its first proponents.

Monroe, Charles R. PROFILE OF THE COMMUNITY COLLEGE. San Francisco: Jossey-Bass, 1972. xiv, 435 p.

> A very complete treatment of the community college of the 1970s from research into the literature. The profiles make extensive use of the history of the movement.

O'Connell, Thomas E. COMMUNITY COLLEGES: A PRESIDENT'S VIEW. Urbana: University of Illinois Press, 1968. 172 p.

> The story of Berkshire Community College in Pittsfield, Massachusetts, established in 1960, written by its president. "How to Start a Community College" is one of the practical chapters.

Palinchak, Robert. THE EVOLUTION OF THE COMMUNITY COLLEGE. Metuchen, N.J.: Scarecrow Press, 1973. ix, 364 p. Bibliog.

> A history of the two-year college movement.

COMMUNITY-SCHOOL RELATIONS

Gordon, Ira J., ed. BUILDING EFFECTIVE HOME-SCHOOL RELATIONSHIPS. Boston: Allyn and Bacon, 1976. xi, 239 p.

> Discusses ways that parents and school people can work together for the enhancement of students' learning. The roles of administrators, teachers, and parents in this undertaking are presented. Home visitation is advocated and the role of the professional home visitor is set forth.

Grant, Carl A., ed. COMMUNITY PARTICIPATION IN EDUCATION. Boston: Allyn and Bacon, 1979. xiii, 262 p.

A collection of writings regarding the participation of various community groups in school governance.

Lightfoot, Sara L. WORLDS APART: RELATIONSHIP BETWEEN FAMILIES AND SCHOOLS. New York: Basic Books, 1978. xiii, 257 p.

The voices of both teachers and parents speak out on the complexities of relationship between the two.

COMPUTER-ASSISTED INSTRUCTION

Gerard, Ralph W., ed. COMPUTERS AND EDUCATION. New York: McGraw-Hill, 1967. 252 p.

Learning and technical aspects of computer-assisted learning are presented through papers by leaders in the field at a California conference.

Hicks, Bruce L., and Hunka, Stephen M. THE TEACHER AND THE COMPUTER. Philadelphia: W.B. Saunders, 1972. 219 p. Illus.

A text exploring the educational potential of the computer age. A wide range of CAI systems is included.

Levien, Roger E., ed. THE EMERGING TECHNOLOGY: INSTRUCTIONAL USES OF THE COMPUTER IN HIGHER EDUCATION. New York: McGraw-Hill, 1972. 585 p.

Since the 1960s computers have become a part of administration and instruction at universities. This work is based on a study by the Rand Corporation and shows the growth of technology as well as providing a terminology for computer users.

COOPERATIVE EDUCATION

Knowles, Asa, et al. HANDBOOK OF COOPERATIVE EDUCATION. San Francisco: Jossey-Bass, 1972. xxiii, 386 p.

Historical development and other articles on aspects of this rather recent practice in higher education.

Wilson, James W., ed. DEVELOPING AND EXPANDING COOPERATIVE EDUCATION. San Francisco: Jossey-Bass, 1978. ix, 95 p.

A look at cooperative education after about a decade of rapid growth.

COURTS AND EDUCATION

Edwards, Newton. THE COURTS AND THE PUBLIC SCHOOLS. Chicago: University of Chicago Press, 1933. xvi, 591 p.

> The legal basis for school organization and administration. Cited by the American Educational Research Association in 1939 as an outstanding contribution to education.

Elliott, Edward C., and Chambers, M.M. THE COLLEGES AND THE COURTS. Boston: D.B. Updike, 1936. x, 563 p.

> Court decisions regarding institutions of higher education into the 1930s.

Fellman, David, ed. THE SUPREME COURT AND EDUCATION. New York: Teachers College, Columbia University, 1962. 120 p.

> Contains some of the most significant cases (Brown, Cochran, Everson, McCollum, Zorach, and Engle).

Spurlock, Clark. EDUCATION AND THE SUPREME COURT. Urbana: University of Illinois Press, 1955. xv, 252 p.

> A collection of forty-five cases in which the Supreme Court has issued decisions affecting education.

Zirkel, Perry, ed. A DIGEST OF SUPREME COURT DECISIONS AFFECTING EDUCATION. Bloomington, Ind.: Phi Delta Kappa, 1978. xvi, 132 p.

> U.S. Supreme Court decisions on education from the nineteenth century to 1977, with brief synopses.

CRITICISM, ISSUES, AND REFORMS OF EDUCATION

Nineteenth Century

Carter, James G. ESSAYS UPON POPULAR EDUCATION. Boston: Bowles and Dearborn, 1826. iv, 60 p.

> Essays originally appeared in a Boston newspaper attacking private schooling for its effect on public schools. Carter was first to propose normal schools for better teacher training.

Eliot, Charles W. EDUCATIONAL REFORM: ESSAYS AND ADDRESSES. New York: Century Co., 1898, ix, 418 p.

> Writings for 1869 through the 1890s. The inaugural address as president of Harvard is included. Much on upper elementary (grammar) and secondary schools. Arno Press (New York, 1969) has reprinted this work.

Everett, Edward. IMPORTANCE OF PRACTICAL EDUCATION AND USEFUL KNOWLEDGE. Boston: Marsh, Capen, Lyon, and Webb, 1840. 419 p.

> Thoughts of the distinguished orator, clergyman, statesman, and president of Harvard College. The book was published under the sanction of the Massachusetts Board of Education.

Mann, Horace. LECTURES ON EDUCATION. Boston: William Fowle and N. Capen, 1845. x, 338 p.

> This early work incorporated materials from addresses, essays, lectures, and from his reports as secretary of the Massachusetts Board of Education. Much on the issues in public education of the mid-nineteenth century.

Rice, Joseph M. THE PUBLIC SCHOOL SYSTEM OF THE UNITED STATES. New York: Century Co., 1893. vi, 308 p.

> A critical report on the public schools by one of the first to use scientific methods in educational research. Rice was a physician and psychologist.

Taylor, J. Orville. THE DISTRICT SCHOOL, OR NATIONAL EDUCATION. Philadelphia: Carey, Lea, and Blanchard, 1835. 296 p.

> A treatise on the commitments of American public education by an early educationist. Taylor taught pedagogy at New York University as early as 1837. This work first appeared in 1834 as THE DISTRICT SCHOOL (Boston: Harper).

Twentieth Century to 1950

Bell, Bernard I. CRISIS IN EDUCATION: A CHALLENGE TO AMERICAN COMPLACENCY. New York: Whittlesey House, 1949. ix, 237 p.

> Canon Bell's criticism covers secondary and higher education in the light of his stance as a religionist and a perennialist in educational philosophy.

Butler, Nicholas M. CONTRIBUTIONS TO A PHILOSOPHY OF EDUCATION. New York: Charles Scribner's Sons, 1915. xiii, 385 p.

> This work is essentially the views of Butler on secondary and higher education. He was not sympathetic with the beginnings of pragmatic (progressive) thoughts on educational practice.

Conant, James B. EDUCATION IN A DIVIDED WORLD: THE FUNCTION OF THE PUBLIC SCHOOL IN OUR UNIQUE SOCIETY. Cambridge, Mass.: Harvard University Press, 1948. x, 249 p.

Conant believes that an understanding of the goals of American education will reduce the hostility that is often directed toward public schools.

Dewey, John. THE EDUCATIONAL SITUATION. Chicago: University of Chicago Press, 1902. 104 p.

An early statement concerning the need to articulate the work of elementary, secondary, and higher education.

Fine, Benjamin. OUR CHILDREN ARE CHEATED: THE CRISIS IN AMERICAN EDUCATION. New York: Henry Holt, 1947. xi, 244 p.

Author writes of the "school breakdown" he has found after a cross-country tour to visit many public schools. Recommendations for correction of ills are given.

Nock, Albert J. THEORY OF EDUCATION IN THE UNITED STATES. New York: Harcourt, Brace, 1932. 160 p.

Improvement of schooling must start with a revised educational theory, not just changing practices from time to time without regard to fundamental ideas.

The 1950s

Adler, Mortimer J., and Mayer, Milton S. THE REVOLUTION IN EDUCA-TION. Chicago: University of Chicago Press, 1958. 224 p.

A traditional position regarding the growing controversies of the 1950s as to the purposes of American education.

Bereday, George Z.F., and Volpicelli, Luigi, eds. PUBLIC EDUCATION IN AMERICA: A NEW INTERPRETATION OF PURPOSE AND PRACTICE. New York: Harper, 1958. 212 p.

Points of view by seventeen authors, mostly from leading schools of education, on issues that were controversial in the 1950s.

Bestor, Arthur E. EDUCATIONAL WASTELANDS: THE RETREAT FROM LEARN-ING IN OUR PUBLIC SCHOOLS. Urbana: University of Illinois Press, 1953. 266 p.

Bestor puts much of the blame for the apparent decline of educational standards upon the educational establishment itself.

_____. THE RESTORATION OF LEARNING: A PROGRAM FOR REDEEM-ING THE UNFULFILLED PROMISE OF AMERICAN EDUCATION. New York:

Alfred Knopf, 1955. xviii, 459 p.

> The call is for the reestablishment of standards in schooling at all levels.

Brameld, Theodore. ENDS AND MEANS IN EDUCATION: A MIDCENTURY APPRAISAL. New York: Harper, 1950. xii, 244 p.

> A plea for reconstructionism in education by a strong and articulate advocate. Such topics as indoctrination, communism, labor, intergroup relations, and atomic energy are discussed.

Hutchins, Robert M. THE CONFLICT IN EDUCATION IN A DEMOCRATIC SOCIETY. New York: Harper, 1953. x, 112 p.

> Some of the educational doctrines that had been widely accepted by the 1950s (social reform, adjustment, immediate needs) are examined and found wanting.

Lynd, Albert. QUACKERY IN THE PUBLIC SCHOOLS. Boston: Little, Brown, 1953. 282 p.

> A school board member in a Massachusetts town is an early 1950s critic of the teaching and learning achievement in public schools. The "educationists," essentially professors of education, are denounced for their lack of emphasis on basic subject knowledge.

Rickover, Hyman G. EDUCATION AND FREEDOM. New York: E.P. Dutton, 1959. 256 p.

> Based on speeches given by Admiral Rickover on education that "can meet the challenge of the atomic era." Levels of curriculum expectations must be raised. Opposition to life-adjustment education.

Smith, Mortimer B. THE DIMINISHED MIND: A STUDY OF PLANNED MEDIOCRITY IN OUR PUBLIC SCHOOLS. Chicago: Henry Regnery, 1954. 150 p.

> Smith deplores the decline of public school learning in disciplined knowledge. High schools, especially, are found guilty of coddling their students.

Woodring, Paul. LET'S TALK SENSE ABOUT OUR SCHOOLS. New York: McGraw-Hill, 1953. ix, 215 p.

> A reply to the 1940s and early 1950s critics of public education. Author does not find the situation bleak as portrayed by so many others.

1960s to Date

Bowles, Samuel, and Gintis, Herbert. SCHOOLING IN CAPITALIST AMERICA: EDUCATIONAL REFORM AND THE CONTRADICTIONS OF ECONOMIC LIFE. New York: Basic Books, 1976. 340 p.

A Socialist criticism of the public school as a place where children are disciplined to perform according to the demands of a capitalist society.

Brann, Eva T.H. PARADOXES OF EDUCATION IN A REPUBLIC. Chicago: University of Chicago Press, 1979. 184 p.

Brann advocates a base of the classical liberal arts as the most useful education for citizens of a modern republic.

Broudy, Harry S. THE REAL WORLD OF THE PUBLIC SCHOOLS. New York: Harcourt Brace Jovanovich, 1972. 271 p.

A sensible, down-to-earth (the real world) treatment of school problems. An analysis is made of some of the recent criticisms of public education.

Cremin, Lawrence A. PUBLIC EDUCATION. New York: Basic Books, 1976. 99 p.

The president of Teachers College, Columbia University, argues for a broader definition of public education, one that would include all institutions that educate the public, in and out of the formal school.

Featherston, Joseph. WHAT SCHOOLS CAN DO. New York: Liveright, 1976. x, 212 p.

A collection of essays reflecting upon the educational reform effort of the previous decade. Conclusion is drawn that too little significant change has taken place.

Goodlad, John I. THE DYNAMICS OF EDUCATIONAL CHANGE: TOWARD RESPONSIBLE SCHOOLS. New York: McGraw-Hill, 1975. xv, 267 p.

A major failure in attempting to bring about change is due to the fact that the school is a natural system rather than a mechanical one. The social system of the entire school must be considered when innovations are planned.

Goodman, Paul. COMPULSORY MISEDUCATION. New York: Horizon Press, 1964. 189 p.

The long period of schooling that is enforced is "inept and psychologically, politically, and professionally damaging" according to the author. He offers radical alternatives: farm as a school, city as a school, and no schooling for some children.

Gross, Ronald, and Gross, Beatrice, eds. RADICAL SCHOOL REFORM. New York: Simon and Schuster, 1969. 350 p.

A collection of writings by a number of critics (e.g., Herndon, Kozol, Goodman, Holt) who all say that children should have more freedom. Radical departures in educational practice are presented.

Holt, John. FREEDOM AND BEYOND. New York: E.P. Dutton, 1972. 273 p. Illus.

Holt envisions a deschooled society where free schools and open education are offered as alternatives to conventional schooling.

Illich, Ivan D. DESCHOOLING SOCIETY. New York: Harper and Row, 1971. xx, 116 p.

The call is for a cultural revolution wherein, among other things, there is an abandonment of the legal requirement of schooling. The author advocates skill centers where instruction can take place under a wide variety of teachers.

Katz, Michael B. CLASS BUREAUCRACY, AND SCHOOLS: THE ILLUSION OF EDUCATIONAL CHANGE IN AMERICA. New York: Praeger, 1971. 158 p.

The public schools are criticized for reinforcing existing patterns of the social structure.

Kimball, Solon T., and McClellan, James E., Jr. EDUCATION AND THE NEW AMERICA. New York: Random House, 1962. xiv, 402 p.

An examination of the reality of American life in the early 1960s and what education promised. Much on the nature of commitment in realizing educational objectives. Book contains an extensive bibliography on American educational thought from the 1920s up to 1960.

Lieberman, Myron. THE FUTURE OF PUBLIC EDUCATION. Chicago: University of Chicago Press, 1960. 294 p.

Power structure of public education is criticized. A suggestion is made that national professional groups might replace local boards of education. Much of the book deals with the teaching profession.

Mayer, Martin. THE SCHOOLS. New York: Harper and Row, 1961. xviii, 446 p.

The author, a professional writer, spent thirty months of visiting
and researching for this book. Chapters deal separately with
elementary, junior, and senior high schools. Other chapters dis-
cuss the subjects taught along with the educational technology.
He found the junior high school the most in need of improvement.

Melton, David. BURN THE SCHOOLS--SAVE THE CHILDREN. New York:
Thomas Y. Crowell, 1975. 281 p.

Author finds little or nothing worthwhile in our public schools.
Teachers don't teach and schools are not interested in their students. A severe berating with a broad sweep.

Postman, Neil. TEACHING AS A CONSERVING ACTIVITY. New York:
Delacorte Press, 1979. 244 p.

This author, once more or less an educational radical, now presents a more conservative treatise. Content, discipline, dress
codes, and respect for the school are stressed.

Postman, Neil, and Weingartner, Charles. TEACHING AS A SUBVERSIVE
ACTIVITY. New York: Delacorte Press, 1969. xv, 219 p.

The subversive activity is to teach students to ask questions.
Authors recommend the elimination of textbooks, tests, grades,
and course requirements.

Ravitch, Diane. THE REVISIONISTS REVISITED: A CRITIQUE ON THE RADI-
CAL ATTACK ON THE SCHOOLS. New York: Basic Books, 1978. 194 p.

The author takes on the radical revisionists of the 1960s and 1970s.
It is her contention that public education has been, and remains,
the institution which has helped the poor, the immigrants, and the
racial minorities to achieve economical and social ends.

Raywid, Mary Anne. THE AX-GRINDERS: CRITICS OF OUR PUBLIC SCHOOLS.
New York: Macmillan, 1962. 260 p.

The coverage of school critics goes back to the early 1950s.
Much is made of illegitimate critics. However, the author fails
to point out that all critics were not merely ax-grinders.

Silberman, Charles E. CRISIS IN THE CLASSROOM: THE REMAKING OF
AMERICAN EDUCATION. New York: Random House, 1970. xiv, 522 p.

A grim picture painted of American schools by a journalist and
education critic. This work led to wide experimentation with
the open classroom concept.

Vogle, Alfred T. THE OWL CRITICS. University: University of Alabama
Press, 1980. 189 p.

A book in defense of traditional education: a well-developed curriculum, taught by experienced teachers, followed by a testing program. The "owl critics" are cited as, for example, those who want to redesign the school to make the teacher a facilitator.

CURRICULUM DEVELOPMENT

Alpren, Morton, ed. THE SUBJECT CURRICULUM, GRADES K-12. Columbus: Charles E. Merrill, 1967. xiv, 561 p.

A comprehensive presentation of the scope of the public school curriculum. Most chapters begin with a historical perspective on the particular curriculum area. Especially suitable for a general course on public school curriculum.

Bobbitt, John F. HOW TO MAKE A CURRICULUM. Boston: Houghton Mifflin, 1924. 292 p.

A pioneer in the use of the survey as it related to public school curriculum planning. Author believed that an analysis of the society at a given time was the best basis for curriculum development.

Caswell, Hollis L., and Campbell, Doak S. CURRICULUM DEVELOPMENT. New York: American Book Co., 1935. xvii, 600 p.

This was a standard text in the field for a number of years. In spite of its general title, it is essentially a work on the elementary school curriculum.

Doll, Ronald. CURRICULUM IMPROVEMENT: DECISION MAKING AND PROCESS. 4th ed. Boston: Allyn and Bacon, 1978. xvii, 440 p.

A work on general curriculum (elementary and secondary) emphasizing the basis for decision making in planning, the process of curriculum improvement, and evaluation.

Lavatelli, Ceila, et al. ELEMENTARY SCHOOL CURRICULUM. New York: Holt, Rinehart and Winston, 1972. ix, 374 p. Illus.

A review of the learning process and then chapters on each curriculum area taught in the elementary school. The most recent research utilized. Suitable for a textbook on elementary curriculum.

National Society for the Study of Education. CURRICULUM MAKING: PAST AND PRESENT. Bloomington, Ill.: National Society for the Study of Education, 1927. 475 p.

Curriculum development during the 1920s presented by several reformers in the field. Professor Harold Rugg wrote an analysis of the innovations of the time.

Taba, Hilda. CURRICULUM DEVELOPMENT: THEORY AND PRACTICE. New York: Harcourt Brace Jovanovich, 1962. 529 p.

Data from the behavioral sciences used in building both elementary and secondary school curriculums.

Trump, J. Lloyd, and Miller, Delmas F. SECONDARY SCHOOL CURRICULUM IMPROVEMENT: MEETING CHALLENGES OF THE TIMES. 3d ed. Boston: Allyn and Bacon, 1979. xiv, 526 p.

All secondary school curriculum areas explored for basic changes. There are chapters devoted to several newer departures: career education, mini-courses, team teaching, and alternative programs. The most up-to-date work in the field.

DEAF AND HEARING-IMPAIRED, EDUCATION OF

Friedman, Lynn A. ON THE OTHER HAND: NEW PERSPECTIVE ON AMERICAN SIGN LANGUAGE. New York: Academic Press, 1977. xii, 245 p.

American Sign Language (ASL) is a manual and visual language used by over a half million deaf and hearing-impaired people. It is historically related to French Sign Language (FSL), introduced to America by Thomas Gallaudet in 1816.

Furth, Hans G. DEAFNESS AND LEARNING: A PSYCHOLOGICAL APPROACH. Belmont, Calif.: Wadsworth Publishing Co., 1973. 127 p.

The first part introduces the reader to the world of deafness in the United States. Subsequent chapters deal with teaching, testing, and research.

Nix, Gary W., ed. MAINSTREAM EDUCATION FOR HEARING IMPAIRED CHILDREN AND YOUTH. New York: Grune and Stratton, 1976. viii, 279 p.

Chapters prepared by specialists on the deaf and hearing-impaired as the result of an earlier national symposium. The practices and problems of mainstreaming are discussed.

Orlansky, Janice Z. MAINSTREAMING THE HEARING IMPAIRED CHILD: AN EDUCATION ALTERNATIVE. Austin, Tex.: Learning Concepts, 1977. 111 p. Illus.

A cartoon format used, making the book very easy and pleasant reading. A feature is a section "The Mainsteaming Story of One Child" where "Joel" is hearing-impaired and mainstreamed into a regular classroom.

DISCIPLINE

Bagley, William C. SCHOOL DISCIPLINE. New York: Macmillan, 1914. xiv, 259 p.

> Positive and noncoercive methods emphasized. This work, aimed at the young and beginning teacher, was a popular text in teaching and went through several printings up to 1926.

Cobb, Lyman. EVIL TENDENCY OF CORPORAL PUNISHMENT. New York: M.G. Newman, 1847. 270 p.

> Cobb, a self-educated schoolmaster and textbook author, was a Pestalozzian in his approach to teaching. He was an early opponent of corporal punishment.

Faust, Naomi F. DISCIPLINE AND THE CLASSROOM TEACHER. Port Washington, N.Y.: Kennikat Press, 1977. xi, 203 p.

> Practical tips on how to maintain an orderly and efficient classroom. Methods are offered for motivating students to control their own aggressive feelings.

Ginott, Haim G. TEACHER AND CHILD. New York: Macmillan, 1972. 323 p.

> How sane talk by the teacher can resolve many classroom conflicts.

Kujoth, Jean S. THE TEACHER AND SCHOOL DISCIPLINE. Metuchen, N.J.: Scarecrow Press, 1970. 314 p.

> A compilation of articles appearing in journals from 1963 to 1967. Valuable as a historic overview on what was being written on the topic of discipline in the 1960s.

Parody, Ovid F. THE HIGH SCHOOL PRINCIPAL AND STAFF DEAL WITH DISCIPLINE. New York: Teachers College Press, 1965. xiii, 104 p.

> The emphasis here is on the adolescent population of the high school with special attention given to disadvantaged youth in urban schools.

Rogers, Dorothy M. CLASSROOM DISCIPLINE: AN IDEA HANDBOOK FOR ELEMENTARY SCHOOL TEACHERS. New York: Center for Applied Research in Education, 1972. 213 p.

> Suggestions from the experience of a classroom teacher in the Chicago area and from other teachers in Evanston, Illinois. Very positive and practical ideas.

DRIVER EDUCATION

American Automobile Association. TEACHING DRIVER AND TRAFFIC SAFETY EDUCATION. New York: McGraw-Hill, 1965. 478 p.

An instructor's manual to supplement existing high school texts.

Anderson, William G. LEARNING TO DRIVE: SKILLS, CONCEPTS, AND STRATEGIES. Menlo Park, Calif.: Addison-Wesley, 1971. xii, 244 p. Illus.

A textbook manual for students.

DRUG ABUSE EDUCATION

Girdano, Daniel A., and Girdano, Dorothy D. DRUG EDUCATION: CONTENT AND METHODS. Reading, Mass.: Addison-Wesley, 1976. xviii, 270 p. Illus.

A manual for teachers or others who are involved in the planning of a drug abuse course or program.

EARLY CHILDHOOD EDUCATION

Almy, Millie. THE EARLY CHILDHOOD EDUCATOR AT WORK. New York: McGraw-Hill, 1975. ix, 276 p.

The functions of the professional in the field of early childhood education, an age range from infancy to age seven. The work is based upon research findings.

Goodlad, John I., et al. EARLY SCHOOLING IN THE UNITED STATES. New York: McGraw-Hill, 1973. xiv, 240 p.

A report of a three-year study of nursery schools in nine American cities (Atlanta, Chicago, Houston, Kansas City, Los Angeles, Nashville, Philadelphia, Seattle, and Rochester). It was found that too many such schools were "pedestrian and unimpressive."

Hipple, Marjorie L. EARLY CHILDHOOD EDUCATION. Pacific Palisades: Goodyear Publishing Co., 1975. 210 p.

Curriculum, facilities, equipment, materials, methods, and working with parents are featured.

Read, Katherine H. THE NURSERY SCHOOL: A HUMAN RELATIONSHIPS LABORATORY. 5th ed. Philadelphia: W.B. Saunders, 1971. 400 p. Illus.

A widely used book on the organization and administration of nursery schools. Equipment needed and activities for a program are listed.

ECONOMIC VALUE OF EDUCATION

Schultz, Theodore W. THE ECONOMIC VALUE OF EDUCATION. New York: Columbia University Press, 1963. xii, 92 p.

A look at the costs and returns from the investment in education.

EDUCATIONAL PSYCHOLOGY

Cronback, Lee J. EDUCATIONAL PSYCHOLOGY. New York: Harcourt Brace Jovanovich, 1963. 706 p.

A full presentation of psychological theory relating to educational practice. Lengthy case reports that illustrate psychological principles are a feature of this text.

Freeman, Frank N. THE PSYCHOLOGY OF THE COMMON BRANCHES. Boston: Houghton Mifflin, 1916. xii, 275 p. Illus.

Freeman was an important figure in the experimental psychology of school learning in the early twentieth century.

Gibson, Janice T. PSHCHOLOGY FOR THE CLASSROOM. Englewood Cliffs, N.J.: Prentice-Hall, 1976. 563 p.

Ties knowledge of psychological principles to the world of classroom teaching.

James, William. TALKS TO TEACHERS ON PSYCHOLOGY: AND TO STUDENTS ON SOME OF LIFE'S IDEALS. Introduction by Paul Woodring. New York: W.W. Norton, 1958. 192 p.

The book was first published in 1899 based upon lectures given by James to Cambridge, Massachusetts, teachers.

Thorndike, Edward L. EDUCATIONAL PSYCHOLOGY. 3 vols. New York: Teachers College, Columbia University, 1913-14. Illus.

A pioneer work in educational psychology from its first appearance in a lesser form in 1903. Thorndike's laws of learning were among the elements helping to form a science of education.

Trow, William C. EDUCATIONAL PSYCHOLOGY. 2d ed. Boston: Houghton Mifflin, 1950. ix, 761 p. Illus.

A popular college textbook. It was originally published in 1931.

EDUCATORS OF NOTE (AMERICAN)

General Works

Barnard, Henry. AMERICAN EDUCATIONAL BIOGRAPHY. Syracuse: C.W. Bardeen, 1874. 556 p. Illus.

Memoirs of educators and benefactors of education taken from articles in Barnard's AMERICAN JOURNAL OF EDUCATION.

Cattell, Jacques, ed. LEADERS IN EDUCATION. New York: R.R. Bowker, 1974. ix, 1,309 p.

Contemporary educators of prominence. James McKeen Cattell began this work (which has gone through many editions) in 1932.

Mattingly, Paul H. THE CLASSLESS PROFESSION: AMERICAN SCHOOL-MEN IN THE NINETEENTH CENTURY. New York University Press, 1975. 235 p.

An intellectual history of a number of nineteenth-century educational leaders and how their social backgrounds and schooling influenced their mission.

National Society for the Study of Education. LEADERS IN AMERICAN EDUCATION. Edited by Robert Havighurst for the Committee on Leaders in American Education of NSSE. Chicago: University of Chicago Press, 1971. xi, 504 p.

Ohles, John F. BIOGRAPHICAL DICTIONARY OF AMERICAN EDUCATORS. 3 vols. Westport, Conn.: Greenwood Press, 1978.

The biographies of sixteen hundred figures in American education from colonial times to 1976. The most complete and up-to-date work on the subject.

Winship, Albert E. GREAT AMERICAN EDUCATORS. New York: Werner School Book Co., 1900. 252 p. Illus.

The "great" include Mary Lyon, Page, H. Barnard, Philbrick, Bateman, Sheldon, Wickersham, J. Harvard, Hopkins, F.A.P. Barnard, and Finney. A brief historical sketch of American educational history, by chronology, concludes the book.

Felix Adler (1851-1933)

Adler, Felix. AN ETHICAL PHILOSOPHY OF LIFE PRESENTED IN ITS MAIN

OUTLINES. New York: D. Appleton, 1918. viii, 380 p.

> Autobiography of the founder of the Ethical Culture Society.
> His philosophical ideas are presented.

Elizabeth Cabot Cary Agassiz (1822-1901)

Paton, Lucy A. ELIZABETH CARY AGASSIZ. Boston: Houghton Mifflin, 1919. viii, 423 p.

> The story of a pioneer in the higher education of women, one
> of the founders of Radcliffe College, and the wife of Louis
> Agassiz, naturalist.

Amos Bronson Alcott (1799-1888)

McCuskey, Dorothy. BRONSON ALCOTT, TEACHER. New York: Macmillan, 1940. xii, 217 p.

> The life of the educator and transcendentalist whose radical edu-
> cational views for the times were reflected in the several private
> schools that he opened. This work is based upon Alcott's manuscripts.

James Burrill Angell (1829-1916)

Angell, James B. THE REMINISCENSES OF JAMES BURRILL ANGELL. New York: Longmans, Green, 1912. vii, 258 p.

> Angell was an early advocate of making higher education accessible
> to all. He was president of the University of Michigan from 1871 to
> 1909.

Smith, Shirley W. JAMES BURRILL ANGELL: AN AMERICAN INFLUENCE. Ann Arbor: University of Michigan Press, 1954. xiv, 380 p. Illus.

> The definitive work on Angell's contributions to higher education
> and his long service at the University of Michigan.

Samuel Chapman Armstrong (1839-93)

Talbot, Edith. SAMUEL CHAPMAN ARMSTRONG: A BIBLIOGRAPHICAL STUDY. New York: Doubleday, Page, 1904. vi, 301 p.

> An early leader in the education of American blacks as first
> head of Hampton Normal and Agricultural Institute, from 1868
> to 1893.

Frank Aydelotte (1880-1956)

Blanshard, Frances M. FRANK AYDELOTTE OF SWARTHMORE. Middleton, Conn.: Wesleyan University Press, 1970. xxii, 429 p. Illus.

> Aydelotte was influenced by the Oxford University system of higher education and introduced an honors program (the Swarthmore Plan) that was adopted by many American colleges. He was president of Swarthmore College from 1921 to 1930.

William Chandler Bagley (1874-1946)

Kandel, Isaac L. WILLIAM CHANDLER BAGLEY, STALWART EDUCATOR. New York: Teachers College, Columbia University, 1961. 131 p. Illus.

> Bagley was an exponent of the essentialist philosophy of education and was a critic of the extreme tendencies in progressive education.

Henry Barnard (1811-1900)

Brubacher, John S., ed. HENRY BARNARD ON EDUCATION. New York: McGraw-Hill, 1931. x, 298 p.

> A brief biographical treatment but considerable material in the form of excerpts on a host of educational topics. Barnard was the first U.S. commissioner of education and was editor of the AMERICAN JOURNAL OF EDUCATION, among many other undertakings in his long professional life.

Downs, Robert B. HENRY BARNARD. World Leaders Series, no. 59. Boston: Twayne Publishers, 1977. 138 p.

> A comprehensive treatment of Barnard's life and educational contributions.

Alexander Graham Bell (1847-1922)

Bruce, Robert V. BELL: ALEXANDER GRAHAM BELL AND THE CONQUEST OF SOLITUDE. Boston: Little, Brown, 1973. xi, 564 p. Illus.

> The inventor of the telephone worked with the education of the deaf most of his professional life.

Anthony Benezet (1713-84)

Brookes, George S. FRIEND ANTHONY BENEZET. Philadelphia: University of Pennsylvania Press, 1937. ix, 516 p. Illus.

Benezet was a Philadelphia teacher who worked for many early
social causes: rights for Indians and women, and female and
Negro education.

Martha Mc Chesney Berry (1866-1942)

Byers, Tracy. MARTHA BERRY, THE SUNDAY LADY OF POSSUM TROT.
New York: G.P. Putnam's Sons, 1932. 268 p. Illus.

Founder of Mount Berry School for Boys (1902), Martha Berry
School for Girls (1909), and Berry College (1926), in Georgia,
all dedicated to preparing poor rural students for vocations.

Mary Mc Leod Bethune (1875-1955)

Holt, Rackam. MARY MC LEOD BETHUNE. Garden City, N.Y.: Doubleday,
1964. 306 p. Illus.

The founder of Bethune-Cookman College (1904), a leading black
American educator, and one who was actively involved in many
national and international endeavors in the 1930s and 1940s.

James Blair (1656-1743)

Rouse, Parke. JAMES BLAIR OF VIRGINIA. Chapel Hill: University of
North Carolina Press, 1971. xiii, 336 p. Illus.

Blair was a religious, governmental, and educational figure in
colonial Virginia. He was the first and a long-time president
of the College of William and Mary (1693-1743).

Frank Learoyd Boyden (1879-1972)

McPhee, John. THE HEADMASTER: FRANK L. BOYDEN OF DEERFIELD.
New York: Farrar, Straus and Giroux, 1966. 149 p. Illus.

One of America's most famous secondary school heads. In 1902,
he came to Deerfield Academy, Massachusetts, a struggling institution founded in the late eighteenth century and, by his re-
tirement in 1968, made it into one of the nation's leading independent schools.

Nicholas Murray Butler (1862-1947)

Butler, Nicholas Murray. ACROSS THE BUSY YEARS. 2 vols. New York:
Charles Scribner's Sons, 1939-40. Illus.

An autobiography written during Butler's long Columbia University presidency (which continued until 1945). His association with the institution began with his student days in the early 1880s.

Whittemore, Richard F.W. NICHOLAS MURRAY BUTLER AND PUBLIC EDUCATION. New York: Teachers College Press, 1971. x, 164 p. Bibliog.

The most recent work on Butler, one of the most influential figures on the American education scene during the first half of the twentieth century.

Sister Marie Joseph Butler (1860-1940)

Burton, Katherine. MOTHER BUTLER OF MARYMOUNT. New York: Longmans, Green, 1944. xi, 290 p.

A member of the Sisters of Mercy, Sister Marie Joseph Butler founded the several Marymount schools and colleges (Tarrytown, New York; Los Angeles; Rome; and Paris). She was president of Marymount College, Tarrytown, New York, from 1918 to 1926.

Mary Ellen Chase (1887-1973)

Chase, Mary Ellen. A GOODLY FELLOWSHIP. New York: Macmillan, 1939. xiii, 305 p.

The story of a life spent in teaching, from a rural school in Maine to professor of English at Smith College in Massachusetts.

Thomas Clap (1703-67)

Tucker, Louis L. PURITAN PROTAGONIST: PRESIDENT THOMAS CLAP OF YALE COLLEGE. Chapel Hill: University of North Carolina Press, 1962. xv, 283 p. Illus.

Clap, a colonial Connecticut Puritan clergyman, was president of Yale from 1740 to 1766. He classified the books in the college, had a catalog published of the library, and issued new college regulations.

Ellwood Patterson Cubberley (1868-1941)

Cremin, Lawrence A. THE WONDERFUL WORLD OF ELLWOOD PATTERSON CUBBERLEY. New York: Teachers College, Columbia University, 1965. 81 p.

Cubberley was professor (1906-33) and dean (1917-33) of the School of Education, Stanford University. As an educational historian he viewed the history of American education as essentially the rise of the public school. This monograph is a valuable contribution to the historiography of American education.

Jesse Buttrick Davis (1871-1955)

Davis, Jesse B. THE SAGA OF A SCHOOLMASTER: AN AUTOBIOGRAPHY. Boston: Boston University Press, 1956. 311 p. Illus.

Posthumously published autobiography of a leader in the school guidance and counseling movement during the early part of the twentieth century.

John Dewey (1859-1952)

Boydston, Jo Ann. GUIDE TO THE WORKS OF JOHN DEWEY. Carbondale: Southern Illinois University Press, 1970. xv, 396 p.

Comments by scholars on the several areas of Dewey's written thought (psychology, ethics, education, art, etc.).

Boydston, Jo Ann, and Poulus, Kathleen. CHECKLIST OF WRITINGS ABOUT JOHN DEWEY. 2d ed. Carbondale: Southern Illinois University Press, 1978. ix, 476 p.

The writings about Dewey cover the years 1887 to 1977. This is an enlarged edition of the volume of 1974.

Dykhuizen, George. THE LIFE AND MIND OF JOHN DEWEY. Carbondale: Southern Illinois University Press, 1973. xxv, 429 p. Illus.

A very comprehensive and useful biography on this influential American philosopher and teacher. The chapter organization is based essentially on periods of his own education and the several university positions he held. The author knew Dewey since the 1940s.

Wirth, Arthur G. JOHN DEWEY AS EDUCATOR. New York: John Wiley, 1966. xvi, 322 p.

The book embraces Dewey's work from the University of Chicago, in 1894, to his appointment at Columbia, in 1904, years when he was most involved in the subject of pedagogy. The plan for his laboratory school at Chicago forms an appendix to the work.

Christopher Dock (c. 1698-1771)

Studer, Gerald C. CHRISTOPHER DOCK: COLONIAL SCHOOLMASTER. Scottsdale, Pa.: Herald Press, 1967. 445 p. Illus.

The biography and writings of the German-born Pennsylvania schoolmaster who wrote the first American book on school management (SCHOOLORDNUNG, 1770).

Stephen Pierce Duggan (1870-1950)

Duggan, Stephen P. A PROFESSOR AT LARGE. New York: Macmillan, 1943. xviii, 468 p.

> The autobiography of a professor of the history of education at the City College of New York and founder of the Institute of International Education.

Timothy Dwight (1752-1817)

Cuningham, Charles E. TIMOTHY DWIGHT, 1752-1817: A BIOGRAPHY. New York: Macmillan, 1942. viii, 403 p.

> A full-length biography of the clergyman, author, and college president. Dwight was president of Yale from 1795 to 1817, during a significant growth period in its intellectual development.

Charles William Eliot (1834-1926)

Hawkins, Hugh. BETWEEN HARVARD AND AMERICA: THE EDUCATIONAL LEADERSHIP OF CHARLES W. ELIOT. New York: Oxford University Press, 1972. xi, 404 p. Bibliog.

> The distinguished president of Harvard for forty-four years (1869-1909) during which the institution became a major university. The most recent work on Eliot.

James, Henry. CHARLES W. ELIOT, PRESIDENT OF HARVARD UNIVERSITY, 1869-1909. 2 vols. Boston: Houghton Mifflin, 1930. Appendix.

> An extensive work with a tabulation of Eliot's honors and a bibliography of his writings. An appendix gives the curriculum of Harvard at the outset to Eliot's administration.

Krug, Edward A., ed. CHARLES W. ELIOT AND POPULAR EDUCATION. New York: Teachers College, Columbia University, 1961. 166 p.

> Contains portions of the significant Committee of Ten Report on secondary schools (1892), as well as excerpts from addresses and articles by Eliot.

Neilson, William A., ed. CHARLES W. ELIOT, THE MAN AND HIS BE-LIEFS. 2 vols. New York: Harper, 1926.

> The most complete work on Eliot and approved by him for post-humous publication. Neilson was editor of the Harvard Classics, a distinguished English-language scholar, and president of Smith College.

George Emerson (1797-1881)

Emerson, George. REMINISCENCES OF AN OLD TEACHER. Boston: Alfred Mudge and Son, 1878. 153 p.

> Emerson relates his school and Harvard College days in New England and his experiences as headmaster of Boston English Classical School, the first public high school.

John Erskine (1879-1951)

Erskine, John. MY LIFE AS A TEACHER. Philadelphia: J.B. Lippincott, 1948. 249 p.

> As a teacher, poet, essayist, novelist, and musician, Erskine was a modern Renaissance man.

Edward Everett (1794-1865)

Frothingham, Paul R. EDWARD EVERETT, ORATOR AND STATESMAN. Boston: Houghton Mifflin, 1925. x, 495 p. Illus.

> Everett was a statesman, author, Harvard professor (1819–25), and president of Harvard (1845–48).

Abraham Flexner (1866-1959)

Flexner, Abraham. ABRAHAM FLEXNER: AN AUTOBIOGRAPHY. New York: Simon and Schuster, 1960. xvi, 302 p.

> Author of the significant Flexner Report on medical education (1910), secretary of the General Education Board, director of the Institute for Advanced Study at Princeton, and an associate of the Carnegie Foundation for the Advancement of Teaching.

Benjamin Franklin (1706-90)

Woody, Thomas. EDUCATIONAL VIEWS OF BENJAMIN FRANKLIN. New York: McGraw-Hill, 1931. xvi, 270 p.

> Franklin's efforts toward creating an academy for Philadelphia, leading to the University of Pennsylvania, and his establishment of the Library Company of Philadelphia and the American Philosophical Society, most certainly qualify him for listing among American educators of note.

Claude Moore Fuess (1885-1963)

Fuess, Claude M. INDEPENDENT SCHOOLMASTER. Boston: Little, Brown, 1952. xii, 371 p.

Long-time New England teacher and headmaster at Phillips
Academy, Andover, Massachusetts, from 1908 to 1948.

Thomas Hopkins Gallaudet (1787-1851)

Gallaudet, Edward Miner. THE LIFE OF THOMAS HOPKINS GALLAUDET.
New York: Henry Holt, 1888. viii, 339 p.

The life and work of the founder of the American School for the
Deaf, Hartford, Connecticut (1817), written by his son, also distinguished for his work with the deaf.

Virginia Gildersleeve (1877-1965)

Gildersleeve, Virginia. MANY A GOOD CRUSADE. New York: Macmillan,
1954. 434 p. Illus.

The memoirs of an educator whose leadership and vital person-
ality covered a span of thirty-six years as dean of Barnard College, from 1911 to 1947.

Daniel Coit Gilman (1831-1908)

Flexner, Abraham. DANIEL COIT GILMAN, CREATOR OF THE AMERICAN
TYPE OF UNIVERSITY. New York: Harcourt, Brace, 1946. ix, 173 p.

The first and long-time president of Johns Hopkins University
(1875-1901). One of the first to introduce to the United States
the idea of the university as a research institution rather than
just a place for instruction.

Gilman, Daniel C. THE LAUNCHING OF A UNIVERSITY AND OTHER
PAPERS: A SHEAF OF REMEMBRANCES. New York: Dodd, Mead, 1906.
386 p.

Public addresses and articles by Gilman. Important for a discussion of his days at the University of California and the beginnings of Johns Hopkins University.

Granville Stanley Hall (1844-1924)

Hall, G. Stanley. LIFE AND CONFESSIONS OF A PSYCHOLOGIST. New
York: Appleton-Century, 1923. ix, 623 p.

Hall's autobiography, which contains a great deal about his establishment of a psychological laboratory at Johns Hopkins and his
presidency of Clark University.

Ross, Dorothy. G. STANLEY HALL: THE PSYCHOLOGIST AS PROPHET. Chicago: University of Chicago Press, 1972. xiv, 482 p. illus.

> Hall's work, ADOLESCENCE, published in 1904, was a milestone in the child study movement. He founded the Child Study Association.

Paul Henry Hanus (1855-1941)

Hanus, Paul H. ADVENTURING IN EDUCATION. Cambridge, Mass.: Harvard University Press, 1937. viii, 259 p.

> The life of Hanus as a student and teacher, and an early history of pedagogy. He taught pedagogy at Harvard, beginning 1891, and was responsible for the establishment of the Graduate School of Education there in 1920.

William Torrey Harris (1835-1909)

Leidecker, Kurt F. YANKEE TEACHER: THE LIFE OF WILLIAM TORREY HARRIS. New York: Philosophical Library, 1946. xx, 648 p.

> As a philosopher, Harris was influenced by Hegel and was a friend of Emerson and Alcott at the Concord School of Philosophy. He was an influential superintendent of schools in St. Louis from 1868 to 1880.

Samuel Gridley Howe (1801-76)

Richards, Laura E. SAMUEL GRIDLEY HOWE. New York: D. Appleton-Century, 1935. 283 p. Illus.

> Howe was involved in the education of the blind and the mentally retarded along with many other social-reform concerns. This work was written by his daughter.

Schwartz, Harold. SAMUEL GRIDLEY HOWE: SOCIAL REFORMER, 1801-1876. Cambridge, Mass.: Harvard University Press, 1956. viii, 348 p.

> The most recent work on Howe. A scholarly biographical work with a detailed treatment of his involvement in the reform movement.

William James (1842-1910)

Allen, Gay W. WILLIAM JAMES: A BIOGRAPHY. New York: Viking Press, 1967. xx, 556 p. Illus.

> James, first professor of psychology at Harvard, was the author of TALKS TO TEACHERS ON PSYCHOLOGY (1899). He was an early proponent of the philosophy of pragmatism.

Thomas Jefferson (1743-1826)

Heslep, Robert D. THOMAS JEFFERSON AND EDUCATION. New York: Random House, 1969. 131 p.

> Jefferson's proposal to establish a comprehensive public education system for Virginia in 1779 was the first effort of its kind in the United States. He was responsible for the establishment of the University of Virginia in 1817.

Alvin Saunders Johnson (1874-1971)

Johnson, Alvin S. PIONEER'S PROGRESS. New York: Viking, 1952. x, 413 p.

> Autobiography of the founder of the New School for Social Research in New York City. He relates his varied student and teaching life leading to the New School experience.

Henry Johnson (1867-1953)

Johnson, Henry. THE OTHER SIDE OF MAIN STREET: A HISTORY TEACHER FROM SAUK CENTER. New York: Columbia University Press, 1943. viii, 263 p.

> Johnson was the author of a popular work, TEACHING OF HISTORY IN ELEMENTARY AND SECONDARY SCHOOLS, that went through many editions from 1908 to 1949. He taught at Teachers College, Columbia University, from 1906 to 1934.

Samuel Johnson (1696-1772)

Elias, Joseph J. THE NEW ENGLAND MIND IN TRANSITION: SAMUEL JOHNSON OF CONNECTICUT. New Haven, Conn.: Yale University Press, 1973. 292 p.

> American Anglican clergyman and first president of King's (Columbia) College.

David Starr Jordan (1851-1931)

Jordan, David S. THE DAYS OF MAN. 2 vols. Yonkers, N.Y.: World Book Co., 1922.

> The first president of Stanford University, 1891 to 1913, Jordan was a scientist by training and wrote a number of works on animals. His educational involvements, aside from Stanford, included

early leadership in the Association of American Universities, Carnegie Foundation for Advancement of Teaching, and the National Education Association.

William Heard Kilpatrick (1871-1965)

Tenenbaum, Samuel. WILLIAM HEARD KILPATRICK: TRAIL BLAZER IN EDUCATION. Introduction by John Dewey. New York: Harper, 1951. xiii, 318 p.

> The life of progressive education's greatest champion. He was a student of John Dewey and long a professor of education at Teachers College, Columbia University. He did much in applying Dewey's philosophy to classroom teaching.

Abbott Lawrence Lowell (1856-1943)

Yeomans, Henry A. ABBOTT LAWRENCE LOWELL, 1856-1943. Cambridge, Mass.: Harvard University Press, 1948. xiii, 564 p. Illus.

> The definitive work on Harvard's president from 1909 to 1933. The development of the House System and the establishment of the Society of Fellows are among his significant contributions.

Mary Lyon (1797-1849)

Gilchrist, Beth B. THE LIFE OF MARY LYON. Boston: Houghton Mifflin, 1910. x, 462 p. Illus.

> A work done at the request of President Mary Wooley of Mount Holyoke. All known letters and manuscript sources were persued. A valuable chapter is entitled, "As Her Students Knew Her," for at the time of this book's preparation there were still a few former students about.

Hitchcock, Edward. THE POWER OF CHRISTIAN BENEVOLENCE ILLUSTRATED IN THE LIFE AND LABORS OF MARY LYON. Northampton, Mass.: Hopkins, Bridgman, 1851. viii, 486 p. Illus.

> The first biography of the founder of Mount Holyoke College written soon after her death by the president of Amherst College. The work contains much primary source material from letters and documents.

Horace Mann (1796-1859)

Mann, Mary Peabody. LIFE OF HORACE MANN. Boston: Walker, Fuller, 1865. 602 p.

Written by his wife, this is the first biography of Mann to appear.
A considerable portion of the work makes use of his correspondence.

Messerli, Jonathan. HORACE MANN: A BIOGRAPHY. New York: Alfred
A. Knopf, 1972. xviii, 604 p., xxxvii. Illus.

The definitive biography of Mann. The work shows how deeply he
was involved with many aspects of the nineteenth-century reform
movement.

Tharp, Louise H. UNTIL VICTORY: HORACE MANN AND MARY PEABODY.
Boston: Little, Brown, 1953. xii, 367 p. Illus.

The life of Mary Peabody Mann, one of the Peabody sisters of
Salem, is woven into the well-written story of her husband,
Horace Mann.

Increase Mather (1639-1723)

Murdock, Kenneth B. INCREASE MATHER: THE FOREMOST AMERICAN
PURITAN. Cambridge, Mass.: Harvard University Press, 1925. xv, 442 p.
Illus.

Mather was a Puritan religious leader of colonial Massachusetts
and president of Harvard College from 1685 to 1701. He was
one of the most prolific writers of colonial America.

Benjamin Elijah Mays (1895--)

Mays, Benjamin E. BORN TO REBEL: AN AUTOBIOGRAPHY. New York:
Charles Scribner's Sons, 1971. xix, 380 p. Illus.

An autobiographical account of a prominent contemporary black
educator, clergyman, and author. He was president of Morehouse
College, Georgia, from 1940 to 1967.

William Holmes McGuffey (1800-1873)

Minnich, Harvey C. WILLIAM HOLMES McGUFFEY AND HIS READERS.
New York: American Book Co., 1936. xi, 203 p. Illus.

The life of McGuffey along with the impact of his influential
ECLECTIC READERS on generations of American children.

Eliphalet Nott (1773-1866)

Hislop, Codman. ELIPHALET NOTT. Middletown, Conn.: Wesleyan University
Press, 1971. xviii, 680 p. Illus.

A schoolmaster from age sixteen, Nott served as president of
Union College, Schenectady, New York, from 1804 to 1866.
He was also active in antislavery, temperance, religious and
civil liberty movements.

David Perkins Page (1810-48)

Phelps, William F. DAVID PAGE: HIS LIFE AND TEACHINGS. New York:
E. L. Kellogg, 1892. 30 p.

Page was first principal of Albany, New York, state normal school
and author of the influential, nineteenth-century work, THE
THEORY AND PRACTICE OF TEACHING (1847).

Francis Wayland Parker (1837-1902)

Campbell, Jack K. COLONEL FRANCIS W. PARKER: THE CHILDREN'S
CRUSADE. New York: Teachers College Press, 1967. vi, 283 p.

Parker's life from frontier settlement, through the Civil War, to
his association with John Dewey and others, leading to his educational work.

Elizabeth Palmer Peabody (1804-94)

Tharp, Louise H. THE PEABODY SISTERS OF SALEM. Boston: Little, Brown,
1950. x, 372 p.

Elizabeth Peabody, one of the three Peabody sisters, opened a
kindergarten in Boston in 1860, the first English-speaking one in
the United States.

Endicott Peabody (1857-1944)

Ashburn, Frank D. PEABODY OF GROTON. New York: Coward McCann,
1944. xii, 444 p. Illus.

Peabody was founder (1884) and first headmaster of the Groton
School, in Massachusetts, where he served until 1940. Many
prominent American figures received their secondary education
under his tutelage.

Bliss Perry (1860-1954)

Perry, Bliss. AND GLADLY TEACH: REMINISCENCES. Boston: Houghton
Mifflin, 1935. ix, 315 p.

The autobiography of the popular professor of English at Williams,

Princeton, and Harvard, and editor of the ATLANTIC MONTHLY, 1899-1909.

William Lyon Phelps (1865-1943)

Phelps, William Lyon. AUTOBIOGRAPHY WITH LETTERS. New York: Oxford University Press, 1939. xxiii, 986 p.

Phelps, a teacher of English literature, author, and literary critic, taught at Yale from 1892 to 1933. He advocated informality in the college classroom.

Elizabeth Ann Bayley Seaton (1774-1821)

Dirvin, Joseph I. MRS. SEATON, FOUNDRESS OF THE AMERICAN SISTERS OF CHARITY. New York: Farrar, Straus and Cudahy, 1962. 498 p. Illus.

The founder of the Sisters of Charity of St. Joseph is often called the founder of Roman Catholic parochial schools in the United States. St. Joseph's College, Emmitsburg, Maryland, began as a school in 1809 under her leadership.

Edward Austin Sheldon (1823-97)

Sheldon, Edward Austin. AUTOBIOGRAPHY OF EDWARD A. SHELDON. Edited by Mary Sheldon Barnes. New York: Ives-Butler, 1911. xii, 252 p.

Sheldon was an advocate of Pestalozzian methods, and, from 1862 to 1897, headed Oswego State Normal School in New York.

William Smith (1727-1803)

Smith, Horace W. LIFE AND CORRESPONDENCE OF THE REV. WILLIAM SMITH, D.D., FIRST PROVOST OF THE COLLEGE AND ACADEMY OF PHILADELPHIA. 2 vols. Philadelphia: Ferguson Brothers, 1880.

The best single source about the first head of that institution which became the University of Pennsylvania. The work was prepared by his great-grandson.

Ezra Stiles (1727-95)

Morgan, Edmund S. THE GENTLE PURITAN: A LIFE OF EZRA STILES, 1727-1795. New Haven, Conn.: Yale University Press, 1962. ix, 490 p. Illus.

Stiles, one of the most learned men in colonial America, was president of Yale from 1778 to 1795.

Henry Philip Tappan (1805-81)

Perry, Charles M. HENRY PHILIP TAPPAN: PHILOSOPHER AND UNIVERSITY PRESIDENT. Ann Arbor: University of Michigan Press, 1933. xi, 475 p. Illus.

> Tappan, a colorful nineteenth-century figure in higher education, tried unsuccessfully to remodel the University of Michigan into a German-type research institution.

Edward Lee Thorndike (1874-1949)

Joncich, Geraldine M. THE SANE POSITIVIST: A BIOGRAPHY OF EDWARD L. THORNDIKE. Middletown, Conn.: Wesleyan University Press, 1968. 634 p. Illus.

> The father of modern educational psychology and a prolific author of books, monographs, and articles on psychology and testing. He regarded measurement as the key to scientific progress in education and psychology.

Booker Taliaferro Washington (1856-1915)

Washington, Booker T. MY LARGER EDUCATION. Garden City, N.Y.: Doubleday, Page, 1911. viii, 313 p.

> Booker T. Washington's second autobiographical work, he deals with the Tuskegee experience in detail.

_____. UP FROM SLAVERY. New York: A.L. Burt, 1901. ix, 330 p.

> Autobiography of the eminent black educator and first head of Tuskegee Institute.

Noah Webster (1758-1843)

Ford, Emily Ellsworth. NOTES ON THE LIFE OF NOAH WEBSTER. 2 vols. New York: Privately published, 1912. Reprint. New York: Burt Franklin, 1971. Illus.

> A checklist of Webster's books included. Indispensable to a thorough study of Webster. The work was written by his granddaughter.

Morgan, John S. NOAH WEBSTER. New York: Mason, Charter, 1975. vii, 216 p.

> Three main emphases in this work are Webster as a patriot-pamphleteer, as an educator-textbook writer, and as a lexicographer. The most recent work on Webster.

Scudder, Horace E. NOAH WEBSTER. American Men of Letters Series. Boston: Houghton Mifflin, 1882. vi, 302 p.

There is much on the preparation of the dictionary. No bibliography.

Skeel, Emily. BIBLIOGRAPHY OF THE WRITINGS OF NOAH WEBSTER. New York: New York Public Library, 1958. xxxix, 655 p. Illus.

A limited, numbered edition. The work is embellished by many facsimile illustrations from Webster's works.

Warfel, Harry R. NOAH WEBSTER: SCHOOLMASTER TO AMERICA. New York: Macmillan, 1936. xiii, 460 p. Illus.

All aspects of Webster's long and varied life are covered. The work has been considered the definitive biography of this man of letters and educator.

Eleazar Wheelock (1711-79)

McCallum, James D. ELEAZAR WHEELOCK, FOUNDER OF DARTMOUTH COLLEGE. Hanover, N. H.: Dartmouth College Publications, 1939. ix, 236 p.

Wheelock, the founder of Moor's Indian Charity School, which lead to Dartmouth College, devoted his life to schooling American Indian boys.

Andrew Dickson White (1832-1918)

White, Andrew D. AUTOBIOGRAPHY OF ANDREW DICKSON WHITE. 2 vols. New York: Century, 1905. Illus.

White was instrumental in the founding of Cornell University, in 1865, and served as its first president until 1885. He was a member of the New York Senate, held many government posts, served on several commissions, and was an author.

Emma Hart Willard (1787-1870)

Lutz, Alma. EMMA WILLARD: DAUGHTER OF DEMOCRACY. Boston: Houghton Mifflin, 1929. xvi, 291 p.

The life of the founder, in 1821, of Troy Female Seminary. The major events in Emma Willard's life are presented chronologically.

Thomas Woodrow Wilson (1856-1924)

Bragdon, Henry W. WOODROW WILSON: THE ACADEMIC YEARS. Cambridge,

Mass.: Harvard University Press, 1967. xiii, 519 p.

> Wilson taught at Bryn Mawr, Wesleyan (Conn.), and Princeton. He served as president of Princeton from 1902 to 1910, resigning upon his election as governor of New Jersey.

John Witherspoon (1722-94)

Stohlman, Martha L. JOHN WITHERSPOON: PARSON, POLITICIAN, PATRIOT. Philadelphia: Westminster Press, 1976. 176 p. Illus.

> A Scottish-born Presbyterian clergyman, Witherspoon was president of Princeton from 1768 to 1794. He was the only educator and clergyman among the signers of the Declaration of Independence.

Henry Merritt Wriston (1889-1978)

Wriston, Henry W. ACADEMIC PROCESSION: REFLECTIONS OF A COLLEGE PRESIDENT. New York: Columbia University Press, 1959. 222 p.

> Wriston taught history at Wesleyan University in Connecticut and went on to become president of Lawrence College, in Wisconsin, and later Brown University. He served at the latter institution from 1937 to 1955 and was responsible for growth in endowment, students, and buildings.

ELEMENTARY EDUCATION

General Works

Caswell, Hollis L., and Foshay, Arthur W. EDUCATION IN THE ELEMENTARY SCHOOL. 3d ed. New York: American Book Co., 1957. 430 p. Illus.

> A general treatment of the elementary school of the 1950s, and a popular textbook that went through several revisions from its first appearance in 1942.

Dewey, John. THE CHILD AND THE CURRICULUM AND THE SCHOOL AND SOCIETY. Chicago: University of Chicago Press, 1956. 158 p. Illus.

> Two of Dewey's most important works on elementary education, written in 1902 and 1899 respectively, here included in one volume. The work of the University of Chicago laboratory school formed the basis of much of the educational thought contained therein.

Goodlad, John I., and Anderson, Robert H. THE NONGRADED ELEMEN-

TARY SCHOOL. Rev. ed. New York: Harcourt, Brace and World, 1963.
248 p. Illus.

> Research and practices concerning an elementary school organized
> without rigid grade levels.

Otto, Henry J., et al. PRINCIPLES OF ELEMENTARY EDUCATION. Rev.
ed. New York: Rinehart, 1955. xv, 455 p. Illus.

> A standard textbook in the field of elementary education that
> has enjoyed much use since its first printing in 1949.

Overly, Donald E., et al. THE MIDDLE SCHOOL: HUMANIZING EDUCA-
TION FOR YOUTH. Worthington, Ohio: Charles A. Jones Publishing Co.,
1972. v, 314 p. Illus.

> The history and rationale of the middle school movement with
> sections devoted to staff allocation, program objectives, and
> facilities needed.

Parkhurst, Helen. EDUCATION ON THE DALTON PLAN. New York: E.P.
Dutton, 1922. xviii, 278 p. Illus.

> Parkhurst established the Dalton School in New York in 1920.
> Her Dalton Plan divided the school subjects into contracts of
> work in which students proceeded at their own ability and speed.

Popper, Samuel H. THE AMERICAN MIDDLE SCHOOL. Waltham, Mass.:
Blaisdell Publishing Co., 1967. xxii, 378 p.

> Proposal of a 4-4-4 grade plan to replace the junior high school
> (the 6-3-3-3 grade plan).

Ragan, William B., et al. TEACHING IN THE NEW ELEMENTARY SCHOOL.
New York: Holt, Rinehart and Winston, 1972. xv, 368 p. Illus.

> By its title and contents, this volume is identified as one of the
> most modern texts in the field. Instructional technology, "cul-
> turally different children," and utilizing extra-teaching personnel
> are among the innovative features.

History of Elementary Education

Binder, Frederick M. THE AGE OF THE COMMON SCHOOL, 1830-1865.
New York: John Wiley, 1974. ix, 191 p.

> The nineteenth-century crusade for the public common school up
> to the end of the Civil War. A bibliographical essay is included
> among the sources given on the topic.

Cremin, Lawrence A. THE AMERICAN COMMON SCHOOL: AN HISTORIC CONCEPTION. New York: Teachers College, Columbia University, 1951. xvi, 248 p.

> The development of the public elementary school in the United States during the first half of the nineteenth century by a foremost scholar in the history of education.

Parker, Samuel C. THE HISTORY OF MODERN ELEMENTARY EDUCATION. Boston: Ginn and Co., 1912. xxiv, 504 p. Illus.

> Much on the European backgrounds of American common school education.

Reisner, Edward H. THE EVOLUTION OF THE COMMON SCHOOL. New York: Macmillan, 1930. xii, 590 p.

> American common school roots are traced to the vernacular schools of towns of the Middle Ages. The work brings the history of the elementary school down to the early twentieth century.

ENCYCLOPEDIAS OF EDUCATION

Deighton, Lee C., ed. THE ENCYCLOPEDIA OF EDUCATION. 10 vols. New York: Macmillan and the Free Press, 1971.

> A work with more than one thousand articles, most of which are followed by a bibliography. The most thorough encyclopedic treatment of American education.

Ebel, Robert L., ed. ENCYCLOPEDIA OF EDUCATIONAL RESEARCH. 4th ed. New York: Macmillan, 1969. xxviii, 1,522 p. Bibliog.

> First published in 1941 as a project of the American Education Research Association, under the editorship of Walter S. Monroe. Each entry is backed up with a copious bibliography of books, monographs, and journal articles. Entries by scholars are from "Academic Freedom" to "Vocational and Technical Education."

Famighetti, Bob, and Randall, Prudence B., eds. EDUCATION YEARBOOK, 1974-1975. New York: Macmillan, 1974. ix, 630 p.

> A comprehensive body of information from the current local, state, national, and international educational scene. The work first appeared for the years 1972-73.

Good, Carter V. DICTIONARY OF EDUCATION. 3d ed. New York: McGraw-Hill, 1973. xix, 736 p.

> Prepared under the auspices of Phi Delta Kappa. The terminology

in education increased greatly in the decades of the 1950s and 1960s. This work was first published in 1945.

Kiddle, Henry, and Schem, Alexander J., eds. THE CYCLOPAEDIA OF EDUCATION: A DICTIONARY OF INFORMATION. New York: E. Steiger, 1877. v, 868 p., xi.

The first encyclopedia of education in the English language. It was edited by the superintendent of schools in New York City and his assistant superintendent.

Monroe, Paul, ed. A CYCLOPEDIA OF EDUCATION. 5 vols. New York: Macmillan, 1911-13. Reprint. Detroit: Gale Research Co., 1968.

A massive and authoritative work with articles by such distinguished educators as James Angell, John Dewey, Ellwood Cubberley, Gabriel Compayre, Morris R. Cohen, William H. Kilpatrick, I.L. Kandel, Booker T. Washington, and John H. Finley.

Rivlin, Harry N., and Schueler, Herbert, eds. ENCYCLOPEDIA OF MODERN EDUCATION. New York: Philosophical Library, 1943. xvi, 902 p.

Educational topics, methods, concepts, and biographies in the twentieth century to 1943 by two hundred contributors, many prominent in the 1940s.

Smith, Edward W., et al. THE EDUCATOR'S ENCYCLOPEDIA. Englewood Cliff, N.J.: Prentice-Hall, 1961. xiii, 914 p. Appendix, bibliog.

The work is divided into fifteen divisions (e.g., curriculum areas, pupil personnel services, classroom management). There is a bibliography for each division and a glossary of educational terms in the appendix.

ENGLISH AND THE LANGUAGE ARTS, TEACHING OF

Applebee, Arthur N. TRADITIONS AND REFORM IN THE TEACHING OF ENGLISH: A HISTORY. Urbana, Ill.: National Council of Teachers of English, 1974. xi, 298 p. Bibliog.

Traces the history of the teaching of English in America, a subject that did not emerge as a major school requirement until the 1890s. Bibliography, chronology of teaching of English, curriculum offerings in English from the 1860s, and a list of required reading selections from the 1870s on.

Fadiman, Clifton, and Howard, James. EMPTY PAGES: A SEARCH FOR WRITING COMPETENCY IN SCHOOL AND SOCIETY. Belmont, Calif.: Fearon, Pitman Publishers, 1979. 232 p.

A work on teaching English composition. Authors are members of the Commission on Writing of the Council for Basic Education. Named by the AMERICAN SCHOOL BOARD JOURNAL as one of ten "must" books on education for 1979.

Fowler, Mary E. TEACHING LANGUAGE, COMPOSITION, AND LITERA-TURE. New York: McGraw-Hill, 1965. xii, 435 p. Illus.

A work for secondary school teachers of English, both beginners and experienced. Attention is paid to the study of English usage, the mass media of communication, and individual reading programs.

Hosic, James F. THE ELEMENTARY COURSE IN ENGLISH. Chicago: University of Chicago Press, 1911. ix, 150 p.

A language arts syllabus from kindergarten through grade eight with children's reading selections for each grade. An early work on the teaching of English.

Joyce, William W., and Banks, James A., eds. TEACHING THE LANGUAGE ARTS TO CULTURALLY DIFFERENT CHILDREN. Reading, Mass.: Addison-Wesley, 1971. x, 325 p. Illus.

A collection of articles on teaching English to children of other than the white race and/or of diverse ethnic groups.

Moffett, James. A STUDENT-CENTERED LANGUAGE ARTS CURRICULUM, GRADES K-13. New York: Houghton Mifflin, 1968. xxvii, 503 p.

The author proposes a program in teaching English throughout all the years of schooling that requires few textbooks or packaged materials except reading selections.

Morse, J. Mitchell. THE IRRELEVANT ENGLISH TEACHER. Philadelphia: Temple University Press, 1973. 152 p.

On teaching English to college students. Some controversial topics, such as "Black English," are discussed.

Squire, James R., and Applebee, Roger K. HIGH SCHOOL ENGLISH IN-STRUCTION TODAY. New York: Appleton-Century-Crofts, 1968. xvi, 311 p.

The "today" is the 1960s. This national study of high school English programs was sponsored in part by the National Council of Teachers of English. Over 150 high schools were examined.

Strickland, Ruth. THE LANGUAGE ARTS IN THE ELEMENTARY SCHOOL. 2d ed. Boston: D.C. Heath, 1957. 464 p. Illus.

All aspects of language, oral and written, are covered, and language as communication is stressed. For some years, a popular textbook in courses on the teaching of the language arts.

Tidyman, Willard F., et al. TEACHING THE LANGUAGE ARTS. 3d ed. New York: McGraw-Hill, 1969. viii, 466 p.

> For the elementary teacher. Material has been added on teaching language to the urban ghetto child.

Wiener, Harvey S. ANY CHILD CAN WRITE: HOW TO IMPROVE YOUR CHILD'S WRITING SKILLS FROM PRESCHOOL THROUGH HIGH SCHOOL. New York: McGraw-Hill, 1978. xiv, 255 p. Illus.

> A book suggesting how parents might help their children in writing skills, but also of use to any teacher working with students in need of such help.

Wolfe, Don M. CREATIVE WAYS TO TEACH ENGLISH: GRADES 7-12. 2d ed. New York: Odyssey Press, 1966. xxii, 554 p.

> Creative ways and means are suggested in improving the writing of high school students.

ETHICS IN THE TEACHING PROFESSION

Dorros, Sidney. TEACHING AS A PROFESSION. Columbus: Charles E. Merrill Publishing Co., 1968. vi, 122 p.

> There are chapters on professional ethics (giving the history and present status), certification, professional organizations, and teacher education.

Lieberman, Myron. EDUCATION AS A PROFESSION. Englewood Cliffs, N.J.: Prentice-Hall, 1956. 540 p.

> Sets forth criteria for professions in general and examines education in that light.

EVALUATION, TESTING, AND EDUCATIONAL MEASUREMENT

Buros, Oscar K. THE EIGHTH MENTAL MEASUREMENTS YEARBOOK. 2 vols. Highland Park, N.J.: Gryphon Press, 1978.

> This important work reviews and evaluates standard tests that are in use. The work has been continued since 1938.

Dearborn, Walter F. INTELLIGENCE TESTS: THEIR SIGNIFICANCE FOR SCHOOL AND SOCIETY. Boston: Houghton Mifflin, 1928. xxiv, 336 p. Illus.

Lectures on intelligence tests given at the Lowell Institute, Boston, in 1925. Dearborn was head of Harvard's Psycho-Educational Clinic.

Freeman, Frank N. MENTAL TESTS: THEIR HISTORY, PRINCIPLES AND APPLICATION. Boston: Houghton Mifflin, 1926. ix, 503 p. Illus.

A look at the mental testing movement in its second decade by an important educational psychologist of the early twentieth century.

Green, John A. INTRODUCTION TO MEASUREMENT AND EVALUATION. New York: Dodd, Mead, 1971. 391 p.

Good modern textbook to serve as an introduction to the field of educational measurement.

Hoffman, Banesh. THE TYRANNY OF TESTING. New York: Crowell-Collier, 1962. 223 p.

Criticism, especially of multiple-choice test questions, which sometimes present difficulties to students of acute intelligence.

Jensen, Arthur R. BIAS IN MENTAL TESTING. New York: Free Press, 1980. 786 p.

Jensen's latest work, organized around the issue of reliability of IQ tests: essentially he defends them. His claim is that selection on basis of objective tests is less biased than the use of other more subjective criteria.

Lewis, James, Jr. APPRAISING TEACHER PERFORMANCE. West Nyack, N.Y.: Parker Publishing Co., 1973. 227 p.

A book on teacher evaluation. Any evaluation procedures should be based upon objectives set up by teachers and administrators.

Lipsitz, Lawrence, ed. THE TEST SCORE DECLINE. Englewood Cliffs, N.J.: Englewood Technology Publications, 1977. x, 220 p.

A collection of papers, previously published, on the erosion of test scores which began in the 1960s.

Marshall, Jon C., and Hales, Loyde W. CLASSROOM TEST CONSTRUCTION. Reading, Mass.: Addison-Wesley Publishing Co., 1971. xiv, 335 p. Illus.

A concise and helpful work for teachers on the construction and analysis of classroom tests (not published standardized tests).

Terman, Lewis M., et al. THE STANFORD REVISION AND EXTENSION OF

THE BINET-SOMON SCALE FOR MEASURING INTELLIGENCE. Baltimore: Warwick and York, 1917. 179 p.

> An important historical work on testing. Terman devised the group intelligence tests used in the U.S. Army in World War I.

Thorndike, Edward L. AN INTRODUCTION TO THE THEORY OF MENTAL AND SOCIAL MEASUREMENTS. New York: Science Press, 1904. xii, 212 p.

> An early work of educational measurement. It was prepared for students as an aid in doing the statistical work required in experimental psychology.

Worthen, Blaine R., and Sanders, James R., eds. EDUCATIONAL EVALUATION: THEORY AND PRACTICE. Worthington, Ohio: Charles Jones, 1974. xi, 372 p.

> A book pulling together the best to that date in educational evaluation. A synthesizing from the literature problems in using standardized instruments in evaluation.

Wrightstone, Jacob W., et al. EVALUATION IN MODERN EDUCATION. New York: American Book Co., 1956. xi, 481 p. Appendix.

> A comprehensive textbook for undergraduate or graduate courses dealing with educational evaluation. The work is not over-technical. "Basic Statistical Concepts" are in the appendix.

FINANCIAL SUPPORT OF EDUCATION

Berke, Joel S. ANSWERS TO INEQUITY: AN ANALYSIS OF THE NEW SCHOOL FINANCE. Berkeley, Calif.: McCutchan, 1974. xv, 369 p.

> The "old" school finance dealt only with distribution of money received. The "new" finance is concerned more with the source of public money, state aid, and tax reform. Especial attention is paid to several court decisions (e.g., Serrano v. Priest) pertaining to public school funding.

Garms, Walter I., et al. SCHOOL FINANCE: THE ECONOMICS AND POLITICS OF PUBLIC EDUCATION. Englewood Cliffs, N.J.: Prentice-Hall, 1978. x, 466 p.

> An overview of the structure and finance of American public schools with a section devoted to reform of financial support.

Millett, John D. FINANCING HIGHER EDUCATION IN THE UNITED STATES. New York: Columbia University Press, 1952. xix, 503 p.

> A report of the Commission on Financing Higher Education in the United States.

Mort, Paul R., et al. PUBLIC SCHOOL FINANCE: ITS BACKGROUND, STRUCTURE, AND OPERATION. 3d ed. New York: McGraw-Hill, 1960. 512 p. Illus.

> With its several revisions, this work has been (since 1941) a popular textbook for courses in school finance.

Pincus, John, ed. SCHOOL FINANCE IN TRANSITION: THE COURTS AND EDUCATIONAL REFORM. Cambridge, Mass.: Ballinger Publisher Co., for the Rand Corp., 1974. viii, 324 p. Illus.

> The aftereffects of the California Supreme Court Serrano v. Priest case (1971) and reforms needed to uphold the principle established in this decision.

Reischauer, Robert D., et al. REFORMING SCHOOL FINANCE. Washington, D.C.: Brookings Institution, 1973. 185 p.

> Major fiscal problems facing public education in the United States. Tax reform, equalization of expenditures, vouchers, and assumption of costs by the states are considered.

FREE SCHOOL MOVEMENT

Graubard, Allen. FREE THE CHILDREN: RADICAL REFORM AND THE FREE SCHOOL MOVEMENT. New York: Pantheon Books, 1973. xiii, 306 p.

> The first comprehensive examination of the "free school" movement. The book covers how such schools came to be, what they are like, and the problems they face.

Kozol, Jonathan. FREE SCHOOLS. Boston: Houghton Mifflin, 1972. xii, 146 p.

> Kozol was involved in the "free school" movement from 1966. This is essentially a handbook on how to start and maintain a school of this sort.

GEOGRAPHY, TEACHING OF

Davis, William D. GEOGRAPHICAL ESSAYS. Boston: Ginn, 1909. vi, 777 p. Illus.

> Essays that had appeared from the 1880s in scholarly journals by a professor of geology at Harvard. There are sections on teaching geography in primary and grammar school grades, the high school, and the university, along with content material (e.g., "The Sculpture of Mountains by Glaciers").

Hanna, Paul R., et al. GEOGRAPHY IN THE TEACHING OF SOCIAL STUDIES: CONCEPTS AND SKILLS. Boston: Houghton Mifflin, 1966. x, 511 p. Illus.

> A guide to teaching geography as a central theme in a social studies program.

Manson, Gary A., and Ridd, Merrill K., eds. NEW PERSPECTIVES ON GEOGRAPHIC EDUCATION: PUTTING THEORY INTO PRACTICE. Dubuque: Kendall, Hart Publishing Co., under the National Council for Geographic Education, 1977. x, 214 p. Illus.

> The work is aimed at methods in geography for elementary and secondary schools. Chapters by a number of geographic educators on what to teach and how to teach it.

Morris, John W., ed. METHODS OF GEOGRAPHIC INSTRUCTION. Waltham: Ginn, 1968. 342 p. Illus.

> Book is arranged in six sections with chapters by scholars in geography and education. Some features: the history of the study of geography, instructional aids, and several approaches in geographic methodology.

GIFTED STUDENTS, EDUCATION OF

Bibliography

Laubenfels, Jean. THE GIFTED STUDENT: AN ANNOTATED BIBLIOGRAPHY. Westport, Conn.: Greenwood Press, 1977. xxi, 220 p.

> Books, articles in journals, monographs, and theses on the subject since the 1950s.

General Works

Axford, Lavonne B. A DICTIONARY OF EDUCATIONAL PROGRAMS FOR THE GIFTED. Metuchen, N.J.: Scarecrow Press, 1971. xxv, 282 p. Bibliog.

> Public school authorities and private schools that have programs for the educationally gifted are listed by state. A bibliography on the academically talented is included.

Gallagher, James J. TEACHING THE GIFTED CHILD. 2d ed. Boston: Allyn and Bacon, 1975. ix, 431 p. Illus.

> Characteristics of gifted students. Ideas and methodology in problem solving, language arts, science, mathematics, and social studies for these students.

Hildredth, Gertrude H. INTRODUCTION TO THE GIFTED. New York: McGraw-Hill, 1966. xvii, 572 p. Illus.

A study of characteristics of and programs for the gifted student from early childhood to college years.

Hollingworth, Leta S. GIFTED CHILDREN: THEIR NATURE AND NURTURE. New York: Macmillan, 1926. xxiv, 374 p. Illus.

The subject of bright children was a relatively recent one when this book was written. Intelligence testing was by then well established and the data was used to show the frequency of the gifted child in the school population. Reference is made to a number of the earliest studies (Cattell, Golton, and Terman, to name a few).

Rice, Joseph P. THE GIFTED: DEVELOPING TOTAL TALENT. Springfield, Ill.: Charles C Thomas, Publisher, 1970. xii, 339 p. Bibliog.

Among the features of the book are the classification of talents, building of model curriculums for gifted students, suggested administrative forms to be used in guidance, placement, and program planning.

Terman, Lewis M., et al. GENETIC STUDIES OF GENIUS. 5 vols. Stanford, Calif.: Stanford University Press, 1925-59.

The monumental study of the intellectually gifted child beginning with data collected on more than fourteen thousand children in the 1920s (volume 1, 1925). Volume 2 (1926) contains the stories of the early lives of three hundred geniuses from history. Volume 3 (1930) contains follow-up studies of one thousand gifted children from the original study. Volume 4 (1947) contains a follow-up of the gifted group after twenty-five years. Volume 5 (1959) deals with a thirty-five year follow-up of these gifted students.

GUIDANCE AND COUNSELING

Bloomfield, Meyer. THE VOCATIONAL GUIDANCE OF YOUTH. Boston: Houghton Mifflin, 1911. xii, 123 p.

A look ahead at vocational counseling by one of the early leaders in the guidance movement.

Brewer, John M., et al. HISTORY OF VOCATIONAL GUIDANCE: ORIGINS AND EARLY DEVELOPMENT. New York: Harper, 1942. viii, 344 p.

The first comprehensive account of the vocational guidance movement since its inception in the early twentieth century.

Davis, Jesse B. VOCATIONAL AND MORAL GUIDANCE. Boston: Ginn, 1914. xiii, 303 p.

The teacher was charged with the moral guidance, as well as the vocational guidance, of his students. The author was one of the early proponents of school guidance and counseling.

Lloyd-Jones, Esther, et al. GUIDANCE IN ELEMENTARY EDUCATION: A CASE BOOK. New York: Teachers College, Columbia University, 1958. 118 p.

A collection of sketches focusing on questions and issues among students, teachers, and administrators at the elementary school level.

Ohlsen, Merle M. GUIDANCE SERVICES IN THE MODERN SCHOOL. 2d ed. New York: Harcourt Brace Jovanovich, 1974. x, 500 p. Illus.

A basic introduction to fundamental school guidance services. The book stresses how guidance personnel can help students improve their social adjustment.

Peters, Herman J., and Shertzer, Bruce. GUIDANCE PROGRAM DEVELOPMENT AND MANAGEMENT. 3d ed. Columbus: Charles E. Merrill, 1974. xxii, 615 p.

A comprehensive presentation of the functions of all aspects of elementary and secondary school guidance. Much on management, facilities, and records.

Stafford, William B. SCHOOLS WITHOUT COUNSELORS: GUIDANCE PRACTICES FOR TEACHERS. Chicago: Nelson-Hall, 1974. xi, 215 p.

Addressed to the elementary school teacher who generally does not have access to a guidance office.

Walsh, William B., ed. COUNSELING CHILDREN AND ADOLESCENTS: AN ANTHOLOGY OF CONTEMPORARY TECHNIQUES. Berkeley, Calif.: McCutchan Publishing Corp., 1975. xiv, 406 p.

Behavioral counseling, existential counseling, play theory, eclectic counseling, and reality are among the sections. Work consists of previously published articles by professionals in each field.

Wrenn, C. Gilbert. THE WORLD OF THE CONTEMPORARY COUNSELOR. Boston: Houghton Mifflin, 1973. xi, 294 p.

The students' world of reality is not the same as that of the teacher or counselor. This book examines the changes in values, beliefs, and patterns of social living that have taken place in recent years.

HANDWRITING, TEACHING OF

Burns, Paul C. IMPROVING HANDWRITING INSTRUCTION IN ELEMENTARY SCHOOLS. Minneapolis: Burgess Publishing Co., 1962. 66 p. Illus.

A monograph by a specialist in elementary school language arts.

Freeman, Frank N. THE TEACHING OF HANDWRITING. Boston: Houghton Mifflin, 1914. xi, 155 p.

A work by an early twentieth-century educational psychologist.

Jenkins, John. THE ART OF WRITING REDUCED TO A PLAN AND EASY SYSTEM. Cambridge, Mass.: Flagg and Gould, 1813. 68 p.

An edition of the earliest (1791) American work on penmanship. This book was distributed to school children in Massachusetts.

Myers, Emma H. THE WHYS AND HOWS OF TEACHING HANDWRITING. Columbus: Zaner-Bloser Co., 1963. 160 p. Bibliog. Illus.

The work includes a bibliography on penmanship. Zaner-Bloser is a company devoted to methods and materials in handwriting instruction.

HEAD START

Zigler, Edward, and Valentine, Jeanette. PROJECT HEAD START: A LEGACY OF THE WAR ON POVERTY. New York: Free Press, 1979. 610 p.

A report on Head Start, preschool compensatory education, begun in 1965 as one of the educational aspects of President Lyndon Johnson's War on Poverty.

HEALTH EDUCATION

Anderson, Carl L. SCHOOL HEALTH PRACTICES. 3d ed. St. Louis: Mosby, 1964. 530 p.

The book covers all aspects of both elementary and secondary school health programs.

Byrd, Oliver E. SCHOOL HEALTH ADMINISTRATION. Philadelphia: W.B. Saunders, 1964. 491 p.

A total school health program set out along with other information on court cases and pupil and teacher health problems.

Willgoose, Carl E. HEALTH EDUCATION IN THE ELEMENTARY SCHOOL. 2d ed. Philadelphia: W.B. Saunders, 1964. 364 p.

A text on methods and materials in health education for elementary school teachers.

HIGHER EDUCATION

Administration

Brown, J. Douglas. THE LIBERAL UNIVERSITY: AN INSTITUTIONAL ANALYSIS. New York: McGraw-Hill, 1969. xx, 263 p.

The provost emeritus of Princeton writes of policy decisions that a college executive must make. Emphasis is on a university integrating its policies and procedures into an effective whole.

Cattell, James McKeen. UNIVERSITY CONTROL. New York: Science Press, 1913. viii, 484 p.

The author, a prominent psychologist at Columbia, was an early advocate of having faculty members participate in the governance of their respective institutions. Also included in this work are 299 letters by scholars in science holding academic positions.

Corson, John J. THE GOVERNANCE OF COLLEGES AND UNIVERSITIES. Rev. ed. New York: McGraw-Hill, 1975. xi, 297 p.

Deficiencies in the management of institutions of higher education and prescriptions for correcting them.

Dodds, Harold W. THE ACADEMIC PRESIDENT: EDUCATOR OR CARETAKER? New York: McGraw-Hill, 1962. 294 p.

An honest and provocative discussion on college administration by the president of Princeton from 1933 to 1957.

Eliot, Charles W. UNIVERSITY ADMINISTRATION. Boston: Houghton Mifflin, 1908. 266 p.

The views of Eliot, forty years as head of Harvard (1869-1909), on the governance of a university.

Epstein, Leon D. GOVERNING THE UNIVERSITY. San Francisco: Jossey-Bass, 1974. xi, 253 p.

A modern treatment of the governance of the large, state-supported universities.

Millett, John D. THE ACADEMIC COMMUNITY: AN ESSAY ON ORGANI-ZATION. New York: McGraw-Hill, 1962. 265 p.

An insightful account of higher education in the 1950s and early 1960s by the president of Miami University from 1953 to 1964.

Rauh, Morton A. THE TRUSTEESHIP OF COLLEGES AND UNIVERSITIES.
New York: McGraw-Hill, 1969. xv, 206 p.

> The function of university governing boards based upon interviews
> and surveys of over five thousand trustees.

Thwing, Charles F. COLLEGE ADMINISTRATION. New York: Century Co.,
1900. 321 p.

> The first guidebook prepared to help college presidents. Dedicated
> to Charles W. Eliot of Harvard.

_____. THE COLLEGE PRESIDENT. New York: Macmillan, 1926. x,
345 p.

> The author draws much of his material from his own experience
> as president of Western Reserve University.

Bibliographies

Beach, Mark, ed. A BIBLIOGRAPHIC GUIDE TO AMERICAN COLLEGES AND
UNIVERSITIES FROM COLONIAL TIMES TO THE PRESENT. Westport, Conn.:
Greenwood Press, 1975. vi, 314 p.

> A comprehensive bibliographical source on higher education in the
> states as well as in individual institutions.

Dressel, Paul L., and Pratt, Sally B., eds. THE WORLD OF HIGHER EDU-
CATION: AN ANNOTATED GUIDE TO MAJOR LITERATURE. San Francisco:
Jossey-Bass, 1971. xv, 238 p.

> Bibliography of higher education essentially from the 1960s on.

Eells, Walter C., ed. COLLEGE TEACHERS AND COLLEGE TEACHING: AN
ANNOTATED BIBLIOGRAPHY ON COLLEGE AND UNIVERSITY FACULTY
MEMBERS AND INSTRUCTIONAL METHODS. Atlanta: Southern Regional Ed-
ucation Board, 1957. xiii, 282 p.

> A comprehensive coverage into the 1950s, but before the explosion
> of publications during the 1960s.

Eells, Walter C., and Hollis, Ernest V., eds. ADMINISTRATION OF HIGH-
ER EDUCATION: AN ANNOTATED BIBLIOGRAPHY. Washington, D.C.:
U.S. Office of Education, 1960. vii, 410 p.

> Developed by the staff of the Division of Higher Education for
> its own use. An exhaustive list of journal articles, monographs,
> and books on college and university administration.

_____. THE COLLEGE PRESIDENCY, 1900-1960: AN ANNOTATED BIBLIOG-
RAPHY. Washington, D.C.: U.S. Office of Education, 1961. v, 143 p.

Journal articles, monographs, and books on the role of the college president in the twentieth century to 1960.

Willingham, Warren W., ed. THE SOURCE BOOK FOR HIGHER EDUCATION. New York: College Entrance Examination Board, 1973. xxii, 481 p.

A guide to literature and information on access to higher education.

College Teaching

Brown, David G. THE MOBILE PROFESSORS. Washington, D.C.: American Council on Education, 1967. xi, 212 p.

Material derived chiefly from questionnaires. Economic analysis is applied to job-changing professors. Changes are recommended regarding the supply and demand for college teachers.

Brown, James W., and Thornton, James W. COLLEGE TEACHING: A SYSTEMATIC APPROACH. 2d ed. New York: McGraw-Hill, 1971. 256 p.

The professors' instructional tasks are discussed, including the use of the newer media. Useful for graduate students who are assigned teaching duties.

Eble, Kenneth E. PROFESSORS AS TEACHERS. San Francisco: Josey-Bass, 1972. xiv, 202 p.

This work grew out of the Project to Improve College Teaching sponsored by the American Association of University Professors. It explores the optimum working conditions for effective teaching and studies the recognition and evaluation of teaching at the college level.

Livesey, Herbert. THE PROFESSORS: WHO THEY ARE, WHAT THEY DO, WHAT THEY REALLY WANT, AND WHAT THEY NEED. New York: Charterhouse, 1975. 343 p.

Prediction of hard days ahead for professors. There are interviews with prospective, present, and former college teachers. An indictment of professors in general coupled with proposals for reform.

Mandell, Richard D. THE PROFESSOR GAME. Garden City, N.Y.: Doubleday, 1977. x, 274 p.

A frank and sobering look at the profession of college teaching in the 1970s with a look back at "the glorious years of the 1960s."

Millett, Fred B. PROFESSOR: PROBLEMS AND REWARDS IN COLLEGE TEACHING. New York: Macmillan, 1961. 189 p.

A career book on college teaching by a professor of English at
Wesleyan University.

Milton, Ohmer, ed. ON COLLEGE TEACHING. San Francisco: Jossey-Bass,
1978. xvii, 404 p.

The editor, plus fourteen others, have contributed essays on the
improvement of college teaching. Essentially, the recommendations
are the introduction of new approaches and the improvement of
the traditional ones.

Smith, G. Terry, ed. NEW TEACHING, NEW LEARNING. San Francisco:
Jossey-Bass, 1971. xxi, 261 p.

Essays presented by professors and administrators at the twenty-sixth
National Conference of the American Association for Higher Education in 1971. The changes of the 1960s are reflected in the reports.

History

Brickman, William, and Lehrer, Stanley, eds. A CENTURY OF HIGHER ED-
UCATION: CLASSICAL CITADEL TO COLLEGIATE COLOSSUS. New York:
Society for the Advancement of Education, 1962. 293 p.

A one-hundred year overview of selected topics in higher education (e.g., graduate education, Negro education, women) written
by fourteen scholars.

Brubacher, John S., and Rudy, Willis. HIGHER EDUCATION IN TRANSITION:
AN AMERICAN HISTORY, 1636-1956. Rev. ed. New York: Harper, 1976.
vii, 536 p.

A revised edition of an earlier (1958) work bringing the chronicle
of higher education up to the student unrest of the 1960s. Many
aspects of the history of higher education are dealt with (e.g.,
student life, methods of instruction, curriculum, academic freedom).

Butts, R. Freeman. THE COLLEGE CHARTS ITS COURSE: HISTORICAL CON-
CEPTIONS AND CURRENT PROPOSALS. New York: McGraw-Hill, 1939.
xvi, 464 p.

History of the development of the college curriculum. The last
part of the book surveys the curriculum problems of the twentieth
century through the 1930s.

Canby, Henry S. ALMA MATER: THE GOTHIC AGE OF THE AMERICAN
COLLEGE. New York: Farrar, 1936. xiii, 259 p. Illus.

A critical memoir of a long college experience as a student and
later as a faculty member at Yale at the turn of the century.

Curti, Merle, and Nash, Roderick. PHILANTHROPY IN THE SHAPING OF AMERICAN HIGHER EDUCATION. New Brunswick, N.J.: Rutgers University Press, 1965. vi, 340 p.

> Philanthropy provided funds for much of the growth of higher education, especially in the private colleges. This book traces the growth from the colonial period to the 1960s.

Eddy, Edward D., Jr. COLLEGES FOR OUR LAND AND TIME: THE LAND GRANT IDEA IN AMERICAN EDUCATION. New York: Harper, 1957. xiv, 328 p.

> The story of the development of sixty-nine land grant colleges which were the result of the 1862 Morrill Act.

Hofstadter, Richard, and Smith, Wilson, eds. AMERICAN HIGHER EDUCA- TION: A DOCUMENTARY HISTORY. 2 vols. Chicago: University of Chicago Press, 1966.

> A chronology of the most significant documents in the history of American higher education, grouped also in periods of major themes. Each document is prefaced by the authors.

Lockmiller, David A. SCHOLARS ON PARADE: COLLEGES, UNIVERSITIES, COSTUMES AND DEGREES. New York: Macmillan, 1939. xiii, 290 p. Illus.

> A comprehensive history of the European inheritance in higher education, colonial American colleges, academic costumes, and degrees.

Nevins, Allan. THE STATE UNIVERSITIES AND DEMOCRACY. Urbana: University of Illinois Press, 1962. 171 p.

> The book presents the stages of development of state and land grant institutions of higher education. The final chapter describes contemporary issues facing all higher education.

Olson, Keith W. THE G.I. BILL, THE VETERANS, AND THE COLLEGES. Lexington: University of Kentucky Press, 1974. x, 139 p.

> The G.I. Bill of 1944 is described and the author reports upon the reception and performance of World War II veterans in the colleges.

Pierson, George W. THE EDUCATION OF AMERICAN LEADERS: COMPARA- TIVE CONTRIBUTIONS OF U.S. COLLEGES AND UNIVERSITIES. New York: Frederick A. Praeger, 1969. xxxii, 261 p.

> Where have outstanding Americans, from the outset, attended col- lege? Harvard takes the honors.

Rudolph, Frederick. THE AMERICAN COLLEGE AND UNIVERSITY: A HIS-
TORY. New York: Vintage Books, 1962. xxxvii, 516 p.

> The most up-to-date and concise history of American higher
> education up to 1960.

_____. CURRICULUM: A HISTORY OF THE AMERICAN UNDERGRADUATE
COURSE OF STUDY SINCE 1636. San Francisco: Jossey-Bass, 1977. xiii,
362 p.

> The curriculum of American colleges followed value changes and
> new demands placed upon those institutions.

Schmidt, George P. THE LIBERAL ARTS COLLEGE: A CHAPTER IN AMERI-
CAN CULTURAL HISTORY. New Brunswick, N.J.: Rutgers University Press,
1957. viii, 310 p. Illus.

> The author presents the history topical rather than chronological.
> Most of the significant aspects of the liberal arts colleges are
> covered. The story comes down to the complex institutions that
> were along in their development by the 1950s.

_____. THE OLD TIME COLLEGE PRESIDENT. New York: Columbia Uni-
versity Press, 1930. 251 p.

> The role of the college president between 1760 and 1860, when
> he was the major influence dominating an institution.

Storr, Richard J. THE BEGINNINGS OF GRADUATE EDUCATION IN AMERI-
CA. Chicago: University of Chicago Press, 1953. ix, 195 p.

> The roots of graduate education preceding the founding of Johns
> Hopkins University in 1876. The influence of German thought
> and practice on higher education.

Ten Brook, Andrew. AMERICAN STATE UNIVERSITIES: THEIR ORIGIN AND
PROGRESS. Cincinnati: R. Clarke and Co., 1875. viii, 410 p.

> The earliest history of the land grant colleges with especial treat-
> ment of the development of the University of Michigan.

Tewksbury, Donald G. THE FOUNDING OF AMERICAN COLLEGES AND
UNIVERSITIES BEFORE THE CIVIL WAR WITH PARTICULAR REFERENCE TO
THE RELIGIOUS INFLUENCES BEARING UPON THE COLLEGE MOVEMENT.
Hamden, Conn.: Archon Books, 1965. x, 254 p.

> Much emphasis on the church-related colleges of the early nine-
> teenth century. This work first appeared in 1932.

Thwing, Charles F. A HISTORY OF HIGHER EDUCATION IN AMERICA.
New York: D. Appleton, 1906. xiii, 501 p.

An early history of collegiate education in America from the colonial colleges through the nineteenth century, by the president of Western Reserve University and a writer on education.

True, Alfred C. A HISTORY OF AGRICULTURAL EDUCATION IN THE UNITED STATES, 1785-1925. Washington, D.C.: Government Printing Office, 1929. ix, 436 p. Illus.

A definitive history of the colleges and programs devoted to agricultural education. The Morrill Act of 1862, and the land grant colleges evolving from it, are major concerns.

Veysey, Laurence R. THE EMERGENCE OF THE AMERICAN UNIVERSITY. Chicago: University of Chicago Press, 1965. xiv, 505 p.

The academic structure and philosophy that developed in the decades after the 1860s.

Walsh, James J. EDUCATION OF THE FOUNDING FATHERS OF THE REPUBLIC: SCHOLASTICISM IN THE COLONIAL COLLEGES. New York: Fordham University Press, 1935. xii, 377 p.

The curriculum of seven colonial colleges is examined in terms of scholasticism, a remnant of the medieval universities.

Whitehead, John S. THE SEPARATION OF COLLEGE AND STATE: COLUMBIA, DARTMOUTH, HARVARD, AND YALE, 1776-1876. New Haven, Conn.: Yale University Press, 1973. x, 262 p.

Four colonial colleges are examined with relation to their early church affiliation and later emergence from ecclesiastical control.

Issues and Commentary: The Nineteenth Century

Angell, James B. THE HIGHER EDUCATION: A PLEA FOR MAKING IT ACCESSIBLE TO ALL. Ann Arbor, Mich.: Board of Regents, 1897. 19 p.

An 1879 commencement address by the president of the University of Michigan for thirty-eight years and a strong advocate of public education.

Burgess, John W. THE AMERICAN UNIVERSITY: WHEN SHALL IT BE? WHERE SHALL IT BE? WHAT SHALL IT BE? Boston: Ginn, Heath, 1884. 22 p.

An essay by a political science professor and later graduate dean at Columbia.

Fisk, Wilbur. SCIENCE OF EDUCATION. New York: McElrath and Bangs, 1832. 24 p.

Fisk's inaugural address at the 1831 opening of Wesleyan University in Connecticut. Probably the first time the expression "science of education" had been used.

Gilman, Daniel C. UNIVERSITY PROBLEMS IN THE UNITED STATES. New York: Century Co., 1898. 319 p.

A The first president of Johns Hopkins University reflects upon the nature and mission of the American university. His plans for Johns Hopkins are included.

Porter, Noah. AMERICAN COLLEGES AND THE AMERICAN PUBLIC. New York: Charles Scribner's Sons, 1878. viii, 408 p.

A conservative view of the nature and purpose of collegiate education in the nineteenth century by a professor and later president of Yale. A revision of an earlier work of 1870.

Tappan, Henry P. UNIVERSITY EDUCATION. New York: G.P. Putnam, 1851. 120 p.

A desire is expressed to have American universities built on the German model, dedicated to scientific inquiry. The author was president of the University of Michigan from 1852 to 1863, and one of the founders of the American Association for the Advancement of Education.

Wayland, Francis. THOUGHTS ON THE PRESENT COLLEGE SYSTEM IN THE UNITED STATES. Boston: Kendall and Lincoln, 1842. vi, 160 p.

The president of Brown University urged an expansion of the college curriculum and the addition of the B.S. and B. Litt. degrees.

Issues and Commentary: The Twentieth Century to 1940

Angell, James R. AMERICAN EDUCATION. New Haven, Conn.: Yale University Press, 1937. iv, 282 p.

A collection of articles and speeches on higher education by Yale's president from 1921 to 1937.

Flexner, Abraham. THE AMERICAN COLLEGE: A CRITICISM. New York: Century Co., 1908. x, 237 p.

A review of the procedure from the admission of a student to his graduation. The first book by a distinguished education leader and author. Contemporary reviewers called this book dogmatic in tone.

Harper, William R. THE TRENDS IN HIGHER EDUCATION. Chicago: University of Chicago Press, 1905. xii, 390 p.

> A series of observations made by the president of the University
> of Chicago showing the increased democratization of higher
> education.

Hutchins, Robert M. THE HIGHER LEARNING IN AMERICA. New Haven,
Conn.: Yale University Press, 1936. 120 p.

> An early statement by President Hutchins of the University of
> Chicago presenting causes of the alleged confusion that beset
> higher education; with recommendations for solutions.

Jordan, David S. THE VOICE OF THE SCHOLAR, WITH OTHER ADDRESSES
ON THE PROBLEMS OF HIGHER EDUCATION. San Francisco: Francis P.
Elder, 1903. 278 p.

> Jordan, a naturalist and first president of Stanford University
> (1891 to 1913), writes on such topics as women and the university,
> higher education of the business man, and a national university
> ("University of the United States").

Slosson, Edwin C. GREAT AMERICAN UNIVERSITIES. New York: Macmillan,
1910. xvi, 528 p. Illus.

> An early twentieth-century discussion of Harvard, Yale, Princeton,
> Stanford, California, Michigan, Wisconsin, Minnesota, Illinois,
> Cornell, Pennsylvania, Johns Hopkins, Chicago, and Columbia,
> the "greats" of the time.

Veblen, Thorstein. THE HIGHER LEARNING IN AMERICA. New York:
Huebsch, 1918. vii, 286 p.

> The author's contention is that the pursuit of learning suffers from
> bureaucracy and from business principles applied to higher education.

Issues and Commentary: The 1940s and 1950s

Barzun, Jacques. TEACHER IN AMERICA. Garden City, N.Y.: Doubleday,
1945. vi, 321 p.

> The work is essentially about college and university teaching and
> administration, written from the position of a distinguised Columbia
> University professor (and later dean).

Frankel, Charles, ed. ISSUES IN UNIVERSITY EDUCATION: ESSAYS BY
TEN AMERICAN SCHOLARS. New York: Harper, 1959. 175 p.

> A cooperative project by ten scholars in various fields (including
> J. Robert Oppenheimer) which constitutes a 1950s view of what
> were important issues in the university. The cheapening of the
> academic degree was one of the concerns.

GENERAL EDUCATION IN A FREE SOCIETY: THE REPORT OF THE HARVARD COMMITTEE. Cambridge, Mass.: Harvard University Press, 1945. xix, 267 p.

> The Harvard Report of 1945 which set forth a rationale and program of general education for higher education. The work had much influence on college curriculums throughout the nation.

HIGHER EDUCATION FOR AMERICAN DEMOCRACY: A REPORT OF THE PRESIDENT'S COMMISSION ON HIGHER EDUCATION. 6 vols. Washington, D.C.: Government Printing Office, 1947.

> A commission appointed by President Truman at the close of World War II. It dealt with goals, staffing, financing, and expansion of opportunities.

PRESIDENT'S COMMITTEE ON EDUCATION BEYOND THE HIGH SCHOOL: NEEDS AND RESOURCES. Washington, D.C.: Government Printing Office, 1957. Unpaged.

> The report with recommendations of a committee on higher education appointed by President Eisenhower.

Van Doren, Mark. LIBERAL EDUCATION. New York: Henry Holt, 1943. xi, 185 p.

> A traditional view of the liberal arts is defended, and the author laments the decreased emphasis in this area during World War II.

Issues and Commentary: The 1960s to Date

Barzun, Jacques. THE AMERICAN UNIVERSITY: HOW IT RUNS, WHERE IT IS GOING. New York: Harper and Row, 1968. xii, 319 p.

> Part of the book reads like a handbook in university administration. Other parts give a philosophical critique of the university. The author concludes that the university has forsaken its true role and has wandered far afield.

Bell, Daniel. THE REFORMING OF GENERAL EDUCATION: THE COLUMBIA COLLEGE EXPERIENCE IN ITS NATIONAL SETTING. New York: Columbia University Press, 1966. xvi, 320 p.

> The most important reexamination of collegiate general education since the 1945 Harvard Report. A program is outlined for Columbia College.

Berube, Maurice R. THE URBAN UNIVERSITY IN AMERICA. Westport, Conn.: Greenwood Press, 1978. 149 p.

> Such issues as open enrollment, racial problems, urban studies, and expansion are focused upon.

Boroff, David. CAMPUS USA: PORTRAITS OF AMERICAN COLLEGES IN ACTION. New York: Harper and Row, 1961. xiv, 210 p.

> Although published in 1961, the work really portrays the selected colleges (national, local, and women's) in the late 1950s and 1960. It was a straightforward look at these institutions and enjoyed great popularity upon its publication.

Carmichael, Oliver C. GRADUATE EDUCATION: A CRITIQUE AND A PROGRAM. New York: Harper and Row, 1961. 213 p.

> A criticism of graduate education as inefficient because of attrition rate, poor articulation between undergraduate and graduate education, among other items. A recommendation is made for a three-year master's degree program for college teaching (there was a great need in the early 1960s).

Carnegie Commission on Higher Education. PRIORITIES FOR ACTION: FINAL REPORT OF THE CARNEGIE COMMISSION ON HIGHER EDUCATION. New York: McGraw-Hill, 1973. 240 p.

> The commission report has several themes: setting priorities, clarifying purposes, preserving and enhancing quality and diversity, advocacy, social justice, enhancing constructive change, achieving more effective governance, and assuring resources and their effective use.

Dugger, Ronnie. OUR INVADED UNIVERSITIES: FORM, REFORM, AND NEW STARTS. New York: W.W. Norton, 1974. 457 p. Illus.

> The work focuses upon the University of Texas in its examination of political involvement and collegiate education. The author advocates mass public higher education free of over-competitiveness, over-specialization, and political invasion.

Eurich, Alvin C., ed. CAMPUS 1980: THE SHAPE OF THE FUTURE IN AMERICAN HIGHER EDUCATION. New York: Delacorte Press, 1968. xvi, 327 p.

> Seventeen educators look into the future. Such topics as the community college, educational technology, and undergraduate curriculum are discussed.

Frankena, William K., ed. THE PHILOSOPHY AND FUTURE OF GRADUATE EDUCATION. Ann Arbor: University of Michigan Press, 1980. x, 259 p.

> A look ahead at the graduate school situation in the face of declining enrollments and job shortages in many scholarly professions. Papers delivered at a conference on graduate education at the University of Michigan in 1978.

Gallagher, Buell G. CAMPUS IN CRISIS. New York: Harper and Row, 1974. ix, 288 p.

>A former president of the City College of New York looks at higher education and its values, and he turns there to solve many social crises.

Grant, Gerald, and Riesman, David. THE PERPETUAL DREAM: REFORM AND EXPERIMENT IN THE AMERICAN COLLEGE. Chicago: University of Chicago Press, 1978. vi, 474 p.

>The reforms of the 1960s are presented as a part of the old American dream toward perfectability. Many of the newer reforms are not rejections of the 1960s, but continuing necessary experimentation.

Gross, Theodore L. ACADEMIC TURMOIL: THE REALITY AND PROMISE OF OPEN EDUCATION. New York: Anchor Press, Doubleday, 1980. 250 p.

>The troubled story of open admission at the City College of New York as written by the former dean of humanities. The book also contains suggestions for the teaching of reading and writing to ill-prepared students.

Hall, Laurence, et al. NEW COLLEGES FOR NEW STUDENTS. San Francisco: Jossey-Bass, 1974. xxi, 210 p.

>An account of several collegiate institutions and their methods of teaching aimed at a changed student body (women, older people, recent immigrants, and poor people).

Jencks, Christopher, and Riesman, David. THE ACADEMIC REVOLUTION. Garden City, N.Y.: Doubleday, 1968. xvii, 580 p.

>The development of American colleges, along with American society, with an evaluation of the past, present, and future of this relationship. The book presents an observation of the campus during the early Vietnam years. .

Kerr, Clark. THE USES OF THE UNIVERSITY. Cambridge, Mass.: Harvard University Press, 1963. vii, 140 p.

>The president of the University of California at Berkeley warns of the dangers of creating "knowledge factories," where neglect of students could turn them into an alienated group. A precursor of the troubles of the later 1960s.

Lamont, Lansing. CAMPUS SHOCK: A FRISTHAND REPORT OF COLLEGE LIFE TODAY. New York: E.P. Dutton, 1979. 144 p.

>The book is based on interviews with hundreds of students and

faculty members on a dozen campuses. Essentially, it portrays the "darker side" of college life (e.g., cheating, the race for grades) in the early 1970s.

McConnell, Thomas R. A GENERAL PATTERN FOR AMERICAN PUBLIC HIGHER EDUCATION. New York: McGraw-Hill, 1962. 198 p.

With the 1960s influx of students into colleges,several questions are faced: who will go to college, where, and for what?

MacDonald, Gary B., ed. FIVE EXPERIMENTAL COLLEGES. New York: Harper and Row, 1974. xiv, 257 p.

The story of Bensalem, Antioch-Putney, Franconia, Old Westbury, and Fairhaven. All are experimental, innovative colleges coming out of the 1960s.

McGrath, Earl J. SHOULD STUDENTS SHARE THE POWER? Philadelphia: Temple University Press, 1970. 124 p.

A study of the role of college students in the governance of institutions of higher education.

Mahew, Lewis B. LEGACY OF THE SEVENTIES. San Francisco: Jossey-Bass, 1977. xvi, 366 p.

The origins, themes, and consequences of the revolution of the 1960s and 1970s in higher education are examined. A good summary of the changes taking place during those years.

_____. THE CARNEGIE COMMISSION ON HIGHER EDUCATION. San Francisco: Jossey-Bass, 1974. xii, 441 p.

A report and critical analysis of the commission established in 1967 to plan guidelines for higher education in the remainder of the twentieth century.

Pusey, Nathan M. AMERICAN HIGHER EDUCATION, 1945-1970: A PERSONAL REPORT. Cambridge, Mass.: Harvard University Press, 1978. 204 p.

This book covers what happened at Harvard from the close of World War II through the 1960s academic revolution. Pusey was president of Harvard from 1953 to 1971, and before that of Appleton College in Wisconsin.

Ridgeway, James. THE CLOSED CORPORATION: AMERICAN UNIVERSITIES IN CRISIS. New York: Random House, 1968. 273 p.

The author, an editor of the NEW REPUBLIC, reports on an inquiry into the relationship among universities, industry, government, and foundations. The American university is the nation's largest

corporation. Disestablishment of higher education from its power-
ful relations is discussed.

Taylor, Harold A. STUDENTS WITHOUT TEACHERS: THE CRISIS OF THE
UNIVERSITY. New York: McGraw-Hill, 1969. xiv, 333 p.

   The subject is the nature of the student movement in the colleges,
   with causes for unrest. The work is by a former president of
   Sarah Lawrence College, and an activist and innovator in his
   thinking on higher education.

Von Hoffman, Nicholas. THE MULTIVERSITY: A PERSONAL REPORT ON
WHAT HAPPENED TO TODAY'S STUDENTS AT AMERICAN UNIVERSITIES.
New York: Holt, Rinehart and Winston, 1966. xxi, 201 p.

   A book about the malaise on the campuses during the early 1960s.
   There is a discussion of the fragmentation of faculty purpose, the
   confusion of goals among students, and the way depersonalization
   of college education affects those who are there.

Woodring, Paul. THE HIGHER LEARNING IN AMERICA: A REASSESSMENT.
New York: McGraw-Hill, 1968. xv, 236 p.

   Essays by a professor of psychology and a former education editor of the
   SATURDAY REVIEW. The student unrest of the early 1960s is discussed.
   A plea is made for more attention to undergraduate teaching.

General Bibliography by State

Beach, Mark. A BIBLIOGRAPHICAL GUIDE TO AMERICAN COLLEGES
AND UNIVERSITIES. Westport, Conn.: Greenwood Press, 1975. vi, 314 p.

   All institutions of higher education for which published histories
   are available are included in this valuable reference source.
   Books, monographs, and journal articles are listed.

General Historical Works by State

COLORADO

Le Rossignol, James E. HISTORY OF HIGHER EDUCATION IN COLORADO.
U.S. Bureau of Education, Circulars of Information, no. 1. Washington, D.C.:
Government Printing Office, 1903. 67 p.

   University of Colorado, the State Agricultural College, the State
   Normal School, Colorado College, and the University of Denver
   are treated.

McGiffert, Michael. THE HIGHER LEARNING IN COLORADO: AN HIS-
TORICAL STUDY, 1860-1940. Denver: Sage Books, 1964. xiii, 307 p.

A survey of all institutions of public and private higher education in
Colorado from their beginnings to the end of the Depression decade.

INDIANA

Woodburn, James A. HIGHER EDUCATION IN INDIANA. U.S. Bureau of Education, Circulars of Information, no. 1. Washington, D.C.: Government Printing Office, 1891. 200 p. Illus.

Historic background of the territory, the common school system,
and eleven collegiate institutions are dealt with.

IOWA

Parker, Leonard F. HIGHER EDUCATION IN IOWA. U.S. Bureau of Education, Circulars of Information, no. 6. Washington, D.C.: Government Printing
Office, 1893. 190 p.

History of common, secondary, and normal schools is included
in addition to the State University, State Agricultural College,
and the denominational colleges.

KANSAS

Blackmar, Frank W. HIGHER EDUCATION IN KANSAS. U.S. Bureau of Education, Circulars of Information, no. 2. Washington, D.C.: Government Printing Office, 1900. 166 p.

KENTUCKY

Lewis, Alvan F. HISTORY OF HIGHER EDUCATION IN KENTUCKY. U.S.
Bureau of Education, Circulars of Information, no. 3. Washington, D.C.:
Government Printing Office, 1899. 350 p.

Originally a Johns Hopkins University doctoral thesis.

MAINE

Hall, Edward W. HISTORY OF HIGHER EDUCATION IN MAINE. U.S.
Bureau of Education, Circulars of Information, no. 3. Washington, D.C.:
Governement Printing Office, 1903. 241 p.

There are chapters on the major institutions (Bates, Bowdoin,
Colby, and University of Maine), with lesser coverage given to
Bangor Theological Seminary, the normal schools, and some private
schools (secondary academies and seminaries).

MARYLAND

Steiner, Bernard C. THE HISTORY OF UNIVERSITY EDUCATION IN MARY-

LAND. Baltimore: Johns Hopkins University Press, 1891. 73 p.

Included in volume 9, Johns Hopkins University Studies in Historical and Political Science, Herbert B. Adams, editor. The selection also includes a piece on Johns Hopkins University (1876-91)
by Daniel C. Gilman.

MASSACHUSETTS

Bush, George G. HISTORY OF HIGHER EDUCATION IN MASSACHUSETTS.
U.S. Bureau of Education, Circulars of Information, no. 6. Washington, D.C.:
Government Printing Office, 1891. 445 p.

Includes a bibliography of Harvard University to the 1890s.

MICHIGAN

Dunbar, Willis F. THE MICHIGAN RECORD IN HIGHER EDUCATION. A
History of Education in Michigan Series, vol. 4. Edited by Wynand Wichers.
Detroit: Wayne State University Press, 1963. 463 p. Illus.

McLaughlin, Andrew C. HISTORY OF HIGHER EDUCATION IN MICHIGAN.
U.S. Bureau of Education, Circulars of Information, no. 4. Washington, D.C.:
Government Printing Office, 1891. 179 p.

By a prominent American historian of the late nineteenth and
early twentieth centuries.

MISSOURI

Snow, Marshall S. HIGHER EDUCATION IN MISSOURI. U.S. Bureau of
Education, Circulars of Information, no. 2. Washington, D.C.: Government
Printing Office, 1898. 164 p.

The State University, Washington University, and four smaller
private institutions are covered.

NEW JERSEY

Sammartino, Peter. A HISTORY OF HIGHER EDUCATION IN NEW JERSEY.
South Brunswick, N.J.: A.S. Barnes, 1978. 196 p.

A relatively brief work for a state with sixty colleges, several of
them with considerable history. Essentially this is an overview.
The author was the first and longtime president of Fairleigh
Dickinson University.

NEW YORK

Sherwood, Sidney. THE UNIVERSITY OF THE STATE OF NEW YORK: HISTORY OF HIGHER EDUCATION IN THE STATE OF NEW YORK. Washington, D.C.: Government Printing Office, 1900. 539 p. Illus.

> The establishment of the Board of Regents with a review of all public and private institutions of higher learning in the state at the end of the nineteenth century.

NORTH CAROLINA

Drake, William E. HIGHER EDUCATION IN NORTH CAROLINA BEFORE 1860. New York: Carlton Press, 1967. vi, 283 p.

> Chapters are organized by general topics (denominationalism, manners and morals, etc.), not by institutions.

OHIO

Knight, George W., and Commons, John R. THE HISTORIES OF HIGHER EDUCATION IN OHIO. U.S. Bureau of Education, Circulars of Information, no. 5. Washington, D.C.: Government Printing Office, 1891. 258 p.

> Ohio had thirty-two colleges before the close of the nineteenth century and all of them are covered in this work.

PENNSYLVANIA

Haskins, Charles H., and Hull, William I. A HISTORY OF HIGHER EDUCATION IN PENNSYLVANIA. U.S. Bureau of Education, Circulars of Information, no. 4. Washington, D.C.: Government Printing Office, 1902. 272 p.

> Author compiled information provided from faculty members of the many colleges and universities in Pennsylvania.

Sack, Saul. HISTORY OF HIGHER EDUCATION IN PENNSYLVANIA. 2 vols. Harrisburg: Pennsylvania Historical and Museum Commission, 1963.

> The most scholarly and complete of the several state histories of higher education. The arrangement is by institution as well as chapters on pertinent topics (women, curriculum, graduate studies, etc.).

RHODE ISLAND

Tolman, William H. HISTORY OF HIGHER EDUCATION IN RHODE ISLAND. U.S. Bureau of Education, Circulars of Information, no. 1. Washington, D.C.: Government Printing Office, 1894. 210 p.

Was originally the author's doctoral thesis at Johns Hopkins University. Essentially, the volume is about Brown University.

SOUTH CAROLINA

Meriwether, Colyer. HISTORY OF HIGHER EDUCATION IN SOUTH CAROLINA WITH A SKETCH OF THE FREE SCHOOL SYSTEM. U.S. Bureau of Education, Circulars of Information, no. 3. Washington, D.C.: Government Printing Office, 1889. 247 p.

> In addition to the treatment of collegiate education, there is a sketch of the free common school system in the state.

TENNESSEE

Merriam, Lucius S. HIGHER EDUCATION IN TENNESSEE. U.S. Bureau of Education, Circulars of Information, no. 5. Washington, D.C.: Government Printing Office, 1893. 287 p.

> A thorough and scholarly work by a Cornell professor.

WISCONSIN

Allen, W.F., and Spencer, David F. HIGHER EDUCATION IN WISCONSIN. U.S. Bureau of Education, Circulars of Information, no. 1. Washington, D.C.: Government Printing Office, 1891. 68 p.

> Extensive treatment of early years at the University of Wisconsin. Brief historical sketches of several private institutions of higher learning.

Major Institutions by State

ALABAMA

ALABAMA, UNIVERSITY OF (1831).

Sellers, James B. HISTORY OF THE UNIVERSITY OF ALABAMA. University: University of Alabama Press, 1953. v, 580 p. Illus.

> This volume (printed as volume 1) covers the period from 1818, when Congress passed an act on sale of public lands in Alabama Territory stipulating that a township be set aside for a "seminary of learning," to 1902, the presidency of William S. Wyman. Apparently only one volume was published.

TUSKEGEE INSTITUTE (1881, as Tuskegee Normal and Industrial Institute; 1937, present name).

Thrasher, Max B. TUSKEGEE: ITS STORY AND ITS WORK. Introduction by Booker T. Washington. Boston: Small, Maynard, 1900. Reprint. New York: Negro Universities Press, 1969. xvi, 215 p. Illus.

Washington was the school's first principal and distinguished black American educator. The history of the institution is brought up to 1900.

ALASKA

ALASKA, UNIVERSITY OF (1917, as Alaska Agricultural College and School of Mines; 1935, present name).

Cashen, William R. FARTHEST NORTH COLLEGE PRESIDENT: CHARLES E. BUNNELL AND THE EARLY HISTORY OF THE UNIVERSITY OF ALASKA. Fairbanks: University of Alaska Press, 1972. xvii, 387 p. Illus.

As the subtitle reads, this is essentially the story of President Bunnell (1878-1956) and his long years (1921-49) at the institution.

ARIZONA

ARIZONA, UNIVERSITY OF (1885).

Martin, Douglas D. THE LAMP IN THE DESERT: THE STORY OF THE UNIVERSITY OF ARIZONA. Tucson: University of Arizona Press, 1960. xiii, 304 p. Illus.

Established by territorial legislative act of 1885, but it was not until 1891 that classes began in Tucson, and then only in agriculture and mining. A preparatory course was necessary as Arizona had no high schools. Great growth came in the twentieth century. The history is brought to 1960.

ARKANSAS

ARKANSAS, UNIVERSITY OF (1871).

Leflar, Robert A. FIRST 100 YEARS: CENTENNIAL HISTORY OF THE UNIVERSITY OF ARKANSAS. Fayetteville: University of Arkansas Foundation, 1972. xii, 403 p. Illus.

The centennial history of this state university founded as "Arkansas Industrial University" under provisions of the Morrill (Land Grant) Act of 1862.

CALIFORNIA

CALIFORNIA, UNIVERSITY OF (1855, as College of California, a private institution; 1868, as University of California, a state institution).

Ferrier, William W. ORIGIN AND DEVELOPMENT OF THE UNIVERSITY OF CALIFORNIA. Berkeley, Calif.: Sather Gate Book Shop, 1930. xi, 710 p.

A good source for information on the College of California, the private predecessor institution to the University of California. The history of the latter is presented through the 1920s.

Stadtman, Verne A. THE UNIVERSITY OF CALIFORNIA, 1868-1968. New York: McGraw-Hill, 1970. x, 594 p.

A centennial history of the Berkeley institution which is the mother of the many University of California campuses. This work include the "Berkeley Rebellion" which had its beginnings in 1964.

CLAREMONT COLLEGE (1887)

Clary, William W. THE CLAREMONT COLLEGES: A HISTORY OF THE DEVELOPMENT OF THE CLAREMONT GROUP PLAN. Claremont, Calif.: Claremont University Center, 1970. xxii, 314 p.

The Claremont Colleges comprise Pomona (1887), Claremont University Center (1925), Scripps (1926), Claremont (1946), Harvey Mudd (1955), and Pitzer (1963). The work was written by a long-time trustee and a founder of three of the colleges.

MILLS COLLEGE (1852, as the Young Ladies Seminary; 1885 as Mills College).

Keep, Rosalind A. FOURSCORE AND TEN YEARS: A HISTORY OF MILLS COLLEGE. Oakland, Calif.: Mills College, 1946. xiii, 203 p. Illus.

The pioneer institution of higher education for women in western United States. It opened in 1852 as the Young Ladies Seminary at Benicia, and developed into Mills Seminary College in 1877 and Mills College in 1885. Cyrus Mills purchased the early seminary and became its head in 1866, hence the present name of the institution.

OCCIDENTAL COLLEGE (1887).

Cleland, Robert G. THE HISTORY OF OCCIDENTAL COLLEGE, 1887-1937. Los Angeles: Ward Ritchie Press, 1937. xiii, 115 p. xvi. Illus.

Written by the dean of the college on the occasion of its fiftieth anniversary. It was founded under Presbyterian auspices and was called Occidental University at the outset. An academy for college preparation was attached to it in its early days, there being only one high school in Los Angeles.

SOUTHERN CALIFORNIA, UNIVERSITY OF (1880)

Servis, Manuel P., and Wilson, Iris H. SOUTHERN CALIFORNIA AND ITS UNIVERSITY. Los Angeles: Ward Ritchie Press, 1969. xix, 319 p. Illus.

Originally founded under the auspices of the Methodist Episcopal Church in Southern California, the institution is now the second most important private university in that state. Two chapters are devoted to the sports at the university, and one to the part played by the institution in the development of southern California.

STANFORD UNIVERSITY (1885).

Elliott, Orrin L. STANFORD UNIVERSITY: THE FIRST TWENTY-FIVE YEARS. Stanford, Calif.: Stanford University Press, 1937. xiii, 624 p. Illus.

The grant of endowment dates from 1885, but the institution opened in 1891 as Leland Stanford Junior University, one of the nineteenth-century universities built from private wealth. The vicissitudes during the early years (up to 1925) are related in this work.

Mirrieless, Edith R. STANFORD: THE STORY OF A UNIVERSITY. New York: G.P. Putnam's Sons, 1959. 255 p. Illus.

The history of this institution is brought up to 1958, the beginning of a period of enlargement of student body, staff, and faculty. Interesting prediction is made that by 1959 college tuition and living would be $2,000 a year.

WHITTIER COLLEGE (1887, first meeting of Friends for a college; 1896, present name).

Cooper, Charles W. WHITTIER: INDEPENDENT COLLEGE IN CALIFORNIA. Los Angeles: Ward Ritchie Press, 1967. xvii, 405 p. Illus.

Institution was founded by the Society of Friends at a meeting held in 1887 in the town of Whittier, named for the Quaker poet. Three academies established from 1888 to 1891 all failed to prosper. Whittier College was named in 1896, and the first graduating class was in 1904. Several references are made to Richard Nixon, member of the class of 1934.

COLORADO

COLORADO, UNIVERSITY (1861).

Allen, Frederick S., et al. THE UNIVERSITY OF COLORADO, 1876-1976. New York: Harcourt Brace Jovanovich, 1976. xii, 319 p. Illus.

A centennial publication written by five faculty authors. A territorial act of 1861 established the university, but it did not open until 1877.

CONNECTICUT

CONNECTICUT, UNIVERSITY OF (1881, as Storrs Agricultural School; 1893, as a college; 1939, present name).

Stemmons, Walter. CONNECTICUT AGRICULTURAL COLLEGE: A HISTORY. Storrs: n.p., 1931. 258 p.

Efforts to get the Connecticut legislature to change the name of the agricultural college to that of a state college went on for many years. This work covers its years as an institution for agricultural education.

TRINITY COLLEGE (1823, as Washington College; 1845, persent name).

Weaver, Glenn. THE HISTORY OF TRINITY COLLEGE. Hartford, Conn.: Trinity College Press, 1967. xii, 363 p. Illus.

A scholarly and beautifully presented work of this early nineteenth-century institution founded under the auspices of the Episcopal Church. This book is listed as volume 1 and brings the history into the twentieth century. Volume 2 was planned for 1973, but has not yet appeared.

WESLEYAN UNIVERSITY (1831).

Price, Carl F. WESLEYAN'S FIRST CENTURY, WITH AN ACCOUNT OF THE CENTENNIAL CELEBRATION. Middletown, Conn.: Wesleyan University, 1932. 384 p.

Established by the Methodist Church, but now a nondenominational liberal arts college. This work deals with the earlier years and the one hundredth anniversary.

YALE UNIVERSITY (1701, as the Collegiate School; 1718, present name).

Dexter, Franklin B., ed. DOCUMENTARY HISTORY OF YALE UNIVERSITY. New Haven, Conn.: Yale University Press, 1916. xviii, 382 p.

A basic resource for the early colonial history of Yale. Significant documents are included from the proposals and charter of 1701 to a letter of President Thomas Clap in 1745.

Kelly, Brooks M. YALE: A HISTORY. New Haven, Conn.: Yale University Press, 1974. xi, 588 p. Illus.

The most recent treatment of this third oldest colonial college founded in 1701 at Branford, Connecticut, as the Collegiate School.

Pierson, George W. YALE: COLLEGE AND UNIVERSITY, 1871-1937. 2 vols. New Haven, Conn.: Yale University Press, 1952-55. Illus.

In two volumes (volume 1, 1871-1921; volume 2, 1921-1937) Yale's Professor Pierson presents the story of Yale from the administration of Noah Porter, beginning in 1871, through the years of James Rowland Angell, ending in 1937. The Harkness residential plan, which began in 1930, is described.

Warch, Richard. SCHOOL OF THE PROPHETS: YALE COLLEGE, 1701-1740. New Haven, Conn.: Yale University Press, 1973. xii, 339 p. Illus.

The first forty years of Yale are chronicled with their religious, social, and intellectual dimensions.

DELAWARE

DELAWARE, UNIVERSITY OF (1743, as an academy; 1833 as Newark College; 1921, present name).

A BRIEF HISTORY OF THE UNIVERSITY OF DELAWARE. Newark, Del.: n.p., 1940. 32 p.

A pamphlet outlining the development of this state university from Francis Allison's academy of 1743 (in Chester County, Pa.) through successor institutions, Newark Academy (1765), Newark College (1833), Delaware College (1843), the agricultural college (1867), to the University of Delaware.

DISTRICT OF COLUMBIA

CATHOLIC UNIVERSITY OF AMERICA (1889).

Ellis, John T. THE FORMATIVE YEARS OF THE CATHOLIC UNIVERSITY OF AMERICA. Washington, D.C.: American Catholic Historical Association, 1946, xiv, 415 p. Illus.

Founded in 1889 from deliberations of the Third Roman Catholic Plenary Council held in 1884. This work covers the years leading up to establishment of the university. The last chapter deals with its opening.

GALLAUDET COLLEGE (1864)

Atwood, Albert W. GALLAUDET COLLEGE: ITS FIRST ONE-HUNDRED YEARS. Lancaster, Pa.: Intelligence Printing Co., 1964. 183 p. Illus.

The college developed from the Columbia Institution for Instruction of Deaf, Dumb, and Blind, established in 1855. In 1864, it became the Columbia Institution for the Deaf, and its collegiate department was organized. The present name is for Thomas Hopkins Gallaudet, a pioneer educator of the deaf.

GEORGE WASHINGTON UNIVERSITY (1821, incorporated as Columbian College; 1904, present name).

Kayser, Elmer L. BRICKS WITHOUT STRAW: THE EVOLUTION OF GEORGE WASHINGTON UNIVERSITY. New York: Appleton-Century-Crofts, 1970. xiv, 352 p. Illus.

The story of the institution in the nation's capital which began under Baptist influences, and has evolved through three names and on three sites in the city. The years from 1950 to 1970 are briefly covered.

GEORGETOWN UNIVERSITY (1789, as an academy; 1801, collegiate curriculum; 1815, right to grant degrees).

Daley, John M. GEORGETOWN UNIVERSITY: ORIGIN AND EARLY YEARS. Washington, D.C.: Georgetown University Press, 1957. xxi, 324 p. Illus.

This work traces the history of Georgetown University back to early Roman Catholic education endeavors in Maryland, beginning in 1634 with the arrival of some Jesuits. The establishment of Georgetown Academy in 1789, with its opening in 1791, soon led directly to a college curriculum and degree granting. This work brings the story down through 1833, when the institution was Georgetown College.

Durkin, Joseph T. GEORGETOWN UNIVERSITY: THE MIDDLE YEARS (1840-1900). Washington, D.C.: Georgetown University Press, 1963. vii, 333 p. Illus.

The work was written for the one hundred and twenty-fifth anniversary of the university's founding. The coverage follows chronologically the earlier Daley work (1957) and brings the history up to the early twentieth century.

HOWARD UNIVERSITY (1867).

Dyson, Walter. HOWARD UNIVERSITY, THE CAPSTONE OF NEGRO EDUCATION: A HISTORY, 1867-1949. Washington, D.C.: Graduate School of Howard University, 1941. xiv, 553 p. Illus.

The charter was granted by Congress in 1867 and the college was named for General Oliver Otis Howard, head of the Freedmen's Bureau. There is much on the development of the graduate and several professional schools. The history is brought up to just before World War II.

Logan, Rayford W. HOWARD UNIVERSITY: THE FIRST HUNDRED YEARS, 1867-1967. New York: New York University Press, 1969. 658 p. Illus.

A detailed and well-documented history of one of the most influential, predominantly black institutions of higher learning.

FLORIDA

FLORIDA STATE UNIVERSITY (1857, as West Florida Seminary; 1947, present name).

Campbell, Doak S. A UNIVERSITY IN TRANSITION: FLORIDA STATE COL-

LEGE FOR WOMEN AND FLORIDA STATE UNIVERSITY. Tallahassee:
Florida State University, 1964. ix, 132 p.

> At the outset, this institution was a private school for women,
> becoming a state college in 1905. Since 1947, it has been
> coeducational. This history deals essentially with the transforma-
> tion of the institution.

FLORIDA, UNIVERSITY OF (1853, as East Florida Seminary; 1905, present
name).

Proctor, Samuel. "The University of Florida: Its Early Years, 1853-1906."
Doctoral dissertation, University of Florida, Gainesville, 1956. xii, 561 p.

> An unpublished dissertation chronicling the early years of the in-
> stitution when it was located on Ocala and Lake City. The move
> to Gainesville was made in 1906.

ROLLINS COLLEGE (1885).

Hanna, Alfred J. THE FOUNDING OF ROLLINS COLLEGE. Winter Park:
Rollins Press, 1936. vii, 69 p. Illus.

> A monograph-size work on the early years of Rollins. College
> was founded under the auspices of the Congregational Church and
> was named for Alonzo Rollins, Chicago merchant and benefactor.

GEORGIA

GEORGIA INSTITUTE OF TECHNOLOGY (1885).

Brittain, Marion L. THE STORY OF GEORGIA TECH. Chapel Hill: University of North Carolina Press, 1948. xiv, 385 p. Appendix, Illus.

> Classes began in 1885 when it was called Georgia School of
> Technology. This volume was written by a president emeritus
> and the history is brought down to World War II. A detailed
> chronology is included.

EMORY UNIVERSITY (1836).

English, Thomas H. EMORY UNIVERSITY, 1915-1965: A SEMICENTENNIAL
HISTORY. Atlanta: Emory University, 1966. xi, 269 p. Illus.

> This institution history concentrates on the twentieth century
> years as Emory University. The earlier years as Emory College
> are chronicled in an introductory chapter.

GEORGIA, UNIVERSITY OF (1785, chartered; 1801, opened).

Brooks, Robert P. THE UNIVERSITY OF GEORGIA UNDER SIXTEEN ADMIN-
ISTRATIONS, 1785-1955. Athens: University of Georgia Press, 1956. ix,
260 p.

Important developments are recorded under the respective presi-
dencies up to 1955. University of Georgia is known as the first
state university due to its early chartering, although classes did
not begin until the early nineteenth century.

MOREHOUSE COLLEGE (1867, as Augusta Institute; 1913, present name).

Jones, Edward A. A CANDLE IN THE DARK: A HISTORY OF MOREHOUSE
COLLEGE. Valley Forge, Pa.: Judson Press, 1967. 320 p. Appendix, Illus.

Founded as Augusta Institute in Augusta, Georgia. A predominantly black college now affiliated with Atlanta University. It was
named for Henry Morehouse, an early trustee and prominent Baptist.
An extensive appendix includes several documents relating to its
history and a bibliography of the writings of Benjamin E. Mays.

HAWAII

HAWAII, UNIVERSITY OF (1907, as College of Agriculture and Mechanic
Arts; 1920, present name).

Nickerson, Thomas. THE UNIVERSITY OF HAWAII, 1907-1957: HIGHER
EDUCATION IN THE PACIFIC. Honolulu: University of Hawaii, 1957.
56 p. Illus.

The story of one of the more recent state universities, originating
under the territorial government. The Center for Cultural and
Technical Interchange Between East and West is affiliated with
this university.

IDAHO

IDAHO, UNIVERSITY OF (1889).

Gibbs, Rafe. BEACON FOR MOUNTAIN AND PLAIN: STORY OF THE
UNIVERSITY OF IDAHO. Moscow: University of Idaho, 1962. x, 420 p.
Illus.

This university was designated as Idaho's land-grant college.
First instruction was given in 1892. Professional and graduate
schools opened in the early twentieth century.

ILLINOIS

CHICAGO, UNIVERSITY OF (1857).

Goodspeed, Thomas W. A HISTORY OF THE UNIVERSITY OF CHICAGO:
THE FIRST QUARTER-CENTURY. Chicago: University of Chicago Press,
1957. xvii, 522 p. Illus.

A new edition of an important institutional history first published in 1916. The work presents the history from incorporation in 1857 through the middle years (1916) of the administration of Harry P. Judson, second president.

Murphy, William M., and Bruckner, D.J.R., eds. THE IDEA OF THE UNI-VERSITY OF CHICAGO. Chicago: University of Chicago Press, 1976. xiv, 533 p.

Selections from the papers of the first eight presidents of the university, William R. Harper through Edward H. Levy.

ILLINOIS, UNIVERSITY OF (1867, as Illinois Industrial University; 1885, present name).

Johnson, Henry C., Jr., and Johanningmeier, Erwin V. TEACHERS FOR THE PRAIRIE: THE UNIVERSITY OF ILLINOIS AND THE SCHOOLS, 1868-1945. Urbana: University of Illinois Press, 1972. xx, 508 p.

The history of teacher education at the University of Illinois.

Nevins, Allan. ILLINOIS. New York: Oxford University Press, 1917. vi, 378 p. Illus.

The first history of this university. Written by a distinguished American historian and one of its graduates.

Solberg, Winton U. THE UNIVERSITY OF ILLINOIS, 1867-1894: AN IN-TELLECTUAL AND CULTURAL HISTORY. Urbana: University of Illinois Press, 1968. x, 494 p. Illus.

The institution was founded on the proceeds of the Morrill (Land Grant) Act. The account gives a great deal of the background and the early frustration in getting the college chartered. The history is brought to 1894, the administration of Andrew Draper and the beginnings of the modern University of Illinois.

KNOX COLLEGE (1837, as Knox Manual Labor College; 1857, present name).

Calkins, Ernest E. THEY BROKE THE PRAIRIE. New York: Charles Scribner's Sons, 1937. xi, 451 p.

An account of the settlement of the upper Mississippi valley by educational and religious pioneers and the history of Knox College in particular. The college was the site of a Lincoln-Douglas debate in 1858.

NORTHWESTERN UNIVERSITY (1851).

Scott, Franklin D., ed. A PICTORIAL HISTORY OF NORTHWESTERN UNI-VERSITY, 1851-1951. Evanston, Ill.: Northwestern University Press, 1951. 198 p. Illus.

This work is a profusely illustrated treatment, with adequate text, of the one-hundred years of Northwestern's history. The institution was founded under the patronage of the Methodist Church.

INDIANA

INDIANA UNIVERSITY (1820, as Indiana Seminary; 1828, as Indiana College; 1838, present name).

Clark, Thomas D. INDIANA UNIVERSITY: MIDWESTERN PIONEER. 4 vols. Bloomington: Indiana University Press, 1970-77. Illus.

> One of the most ambitious and complete institutional histories of the many American state universities. Volume 4 consists of the historical documents pertaining to the university.

NOTRE DAME, UNIVERSITY OF (1842, Fr. Sorin's school; 1844, charter and present name).

Schlereth, Thomas J. THE UNIVERSITY OF NOTRE DAME: A PORTRAIT OF ITS HISTORY AND CAMPUS. Notre Dame: University of Notre Dame Press, 1976. xix, 252 p. Illus.

> A profusely illustrated, very readable and attractive volume. Notre Dame was established by the Congregation of the Holy Cross (CSC), a Roman Catholic order.

PURDUE UNIVERSITY (1869).

Hepburn, William W., and Sears, Louis M. PURDUE UNIVERSITY: FIFTY YEARS OF PROGRESS. Indianapolis: Hollenbeck Press, 1925. vi, 208 p.

> The Morrill (Land Grant) Act College in Indiana. Named for John Purdue, a benefactor. Classes began in 1874.

IOWA

IOWA STATE UNIVERSITY OF SCIENCE AND TECHNOLOGY (1858, chartered as Iowa Agricultural College; 1959, present name).

Ross, Earle D. THE LAND GRANT IDEA AT IOWA STATE COLLEGE. Ames: Iowa State College Press, 1958. x, 310 p. Illus.

> School was chartered before the Morrill (Land Grant) Act, but was soon a recipient of its aid. Classes began at Ames in 1869.

IOWA, UNIVERSITY OF (1847).

Carstensen, Vernon R. THE HISTORY OF THE STATE UNIVERSITY OF IOWA. Iowa City: n.p., 1938. 115 p.

> This work is an abstract of a thesis and deals essentially with the collegiate department from its beginning to 1878.

KANSAS

KANSAS STATE UNIVERSITY (1858, as Bluemont Central College; 1863, as Kansas State Agricultural College; 1959, present name).

Carey, James C. KANSAS STATE UNIVERSITY, A QUEST FOR IDENTITY. Lawrence: Regents Press of Kansas, 1977. xii, 333 p. Illus.

> Kansas was the first state to designate a specific college under the provisions of the Morrill (Land Grant) Act, and this institution at Manhattan, Kansas, was the first state-supported college in that state. A chapter in this history is devoted to the administration of Milton Eisenhower (1943-1950), brother to the president.

KANSAS, UNIVERSITY OF (1864).

Griffin, Clifford S. THE UNIVERSITY OF KANSAS: A HISTORY. Lawrence: University Press of Kansas, 1974. xiv, 808 p. Illus.

> An 1859 predecessor institution known as Lawrence University came before the state chartered and supported one. The university got established in Lawrence due to a $15,000 gift from supporters. This well-documented institutional history carries the story into the 1960s, the period of greatest growth.

KENTUCKY

KENTUCKY, UNIVERSITY OF (1865).

Hopkins, James F. THE UNIVERSITY OF KENTUCKY: ORIGINS AND EARLY YEARS. Lexington: University of Kentucky Press, 1951. ix, 305 p. Illus.

> A good source in tracing the rather involved early history of this university. The Agricultural and Mechanical College of Kentucky was joined to Kentucky University, a private college (later known as Transylvania University), in 1865. In 1878, the A & M College separated and in 1908 became the State University of Kentucky.

TRANSYLVANIA UNIVERSITY (1780, act of Virginia Assembly; 1783, Transylvania Seminary; 1798, Transylvania University).

Wright, John D., Jr. TRANSYLVANIA: TUTOR TO THE WEST. Lexington, Ky.: Transylvania University, 1975. xii, 444 p. Illus.

> This institution was an educational pioneer in the trans-Allegheny West of the late eighteenth century. Medical and law departments were established by 1799. In 1865 Transylvania joined with Kentucky University (another private institution founded in 1858) to form Kentucky University. In that same year, the state established the Agricultural and Mechanical College and attached it to Kentucky University. After the separation of the state institution in 1878, the private institution continued, and in 1907 the early name, Transylvania University, was resumed.

LOUISIANA

LOUISIANA STATE UNIVERSITY (1853, as Louisiana State Seminary; 1870, present name).

Fleming, Walter L. LOUISIANA STATE UNIVERSITY, 1860-1896. Baton Rouge: Louisiana State University Press, 1936. x, 499 p.

> This institution developed from a state seminary under a military system of governance. It moved from Rapidas to Baton Rouge in 1869. The Agricultural and Mechanical College of Louisiana was united to the university in 1877. There are several references in this history concerning the race question during Reconstruction, especially the relations of the university with black people in Baton Rouge. This work covers only the nineteenth-century period, ending with the administration of James Nicholson in 1896.

TULANE UNIVERSITY OF LOUISIANA (1835, as Medical College of Louisiana; 1847, as University of Louisiana; 1883, present name).

Dyer, John P. TULANE: THE BIOGRAPHY OF A UNIVERSITY, 1834-1965. New York: Harper and Row, 1966. x, 370 p. Illus.

> From a feeble University of Louisiana, the name was changed and the institution flourished after an 1882 gift from Paul Tulane of $288,700.

MAINE

BATES COLLEGE (1855, as Maine State Seminary; 1864, present name).

Anthony, Alfred W. BATES COLLEGE AND ITS BACKGROUND. Philadelphia: Judson Press, 1936. 284 p.

> Written by a one-time professor and later trustee of Bates. The story of a small Baptist seminary's development into nondenominational college of arts and sciences.

BOWDOIN COLLEGE (1794).

Hatch, Louis C. THE HISTORY OF BOWDOIN COLLEGE. Portland, Maine: Loring, Short and Harmon, 1927. xii, 500 p. Illus.

> The history of Maine's oldest college (at the time Maine was a district under the Commonwealth of Massachusetts) to the early 1920s written by a historian and a graduate of the class of 1895.

COLBY COLLEGE (1813, as Maine Literary and Theological Institution; 1867, present name).

Marriner, Ernest C. THE HISTORY OF COLBY COLLEGE. Waterville, Maine: Colby College Press, 1963. 659 p.

The story of this Baptist institution's transformation and subsequent history, first as Waterville College, and after 1867 as Colby College, a coeducational arts and science college.

MAINE, UNIVERSITY OF (1865).

Smith, David C. THE FIRST CENTURY: A HISTORY OF THE UNIVERSITY OF MAINE, 1865-1965. Orono: University of Maine at Orono Press, 1979. xviii, 295 p. Illus.

This attractive volume marks the centennial of Maine's Morrill (Land Grant) Act College, beginning as Maine State College and later as the University of Maine.

MARYLAND

JOHNS HOPKINS UNIVERSITY (1876).

French, John C. A HISTORY OF THE UNIVERSITY FOUNDED BY JOHNS HOPKINS. Baltimore: Johns Hopkins Press, 1946. xii, 492 p. Illus.

The history of the first truly American university (with a distinguished graduate school) through the period of World War II; written by a former librarian of the institution.

Hawkins, Hugh. PIONEER: A HISTORY OF THE JOHNS HOPKINS UNIVERSITY, 1874-1889. Ithaca, N.Y.: Cornell University Press, 1960. xiv, 368 p.

The benefactions of the Baltimore merchant, Johns Hopkins, and the work of Daniel Gilman, first president of the university.

MARYLAND, UNIVERSITY OF (1807, chartered as College of Medicine of Maryland; 1920, present institution).

Callcott, George H. A HISTORY OF THE UNIVERSITY OF MARYLAND. Baltimore: Maryland Historical Society, 1966. viii, 422 p. Illus.

The predecessor medical school developed into a University of Maryland, a private institution. Maryland Agricultural College (chartered in 1856, before the Morrill Act) became Maryland State College in 1916. In 1920, the state college joined with the private university to form the present state-supported University of Maryland.

ST. JOHN'S COLLEGE (1696, as King William's School; 1784, present name).

COMMEMORATION OF THE ONE HUNDREDTH ANNIVERSARY OF ST. JOHN'S COLLEGE. Baltimore: William K. Boyle and Son, 1890. 175 p.

The sermons and addresses in this work, given in June of 1889, include information on the early history of this seventeenth- and eighteenth-century institution.

UNITED STATES NAVAL ACADEMY (1845)

Riesenberg, Felix. THE STORY OF THE NAVAL ACADEMY. New York: Random House, 1958. 176 p. Illus.

An overview of the highlights in the history of this service academy established by George Bancroft, secretary of the navy during the presidency of John Quincy Adams.

MASSACHUSETTS

AMHERST COLLEGE (1821).

Fuess, Claude M. AMHERST: THE STORY OF A NEW ENGLAND COLLEGE. Boston: Little, Brown, 1935. xiii, 372 p. Illus.

One of the classics of American college histories by a distinguished graduate and long-time headmaster of Phillips Academy, Andover, Massachusetts. The college was an outgrowth of Amherst Academy, opened in 1814.

BOSTON COLLEGE (1863).

Dunigan, David R. A HISTORY OF BOSTON COLLEGE. Milwaukee: Bruce Publishing Co., 1947. xviii, 362 p. Illus.

An institution conducted under the authority of the Roman Catholic order of the Society of Jesus. Although a college by name, it is really a university with several distinguished graduate schools. It moved to its present campus in Chestnut Hill in 1913.

BOSTON UNIVERSITY (1869).

Ault, Warren O. BOSTON UNIVERSITY: THE COLLEGE OF LIBERAL ARTS, 1873-1973. Boston: Trustees of Boston University, 1973. xii, 283 p. Illus.

This history, written by an emeritus professor of history at the institution, covers only the liberal arts faculty of this large urban university. The college early admitted women "on the same conditions as gentlemen."

BRANDEIS UNIVERSITY (1948).

Sachar, Abram L. A HOST AT LAST. Boston: Little, Brown, 1976. 308 p. Illus.

A nondenominational but Jewish-sponsored university opened in Waltham, Massachusetts, on grounds of the defunct Middlesex University. The institution's rapid rise is presented by the first president and chancellor.

HARVARD UNIVERSITY (1636).

Copeland, Melvin T. AND MARK AN ERA: THE STORY OF THE HARVARD

BUSINESS SCHOOL. Boston: Little, Brown, 1958. xvi, 368 p. Appendix, illus.

> The Graduate School of Business Administration was established in 1908 during the administration of President Charles Eliot. A chapter is devoted to the influential case method of instruction. The history is written by the George Baker professor of administration who was at the school from 1909 to 1953. The work is not indexed. Appendix lists faculty and officers from the opening to 1958.

Morison, Samuel E. THE FOUNDING OF HARVARD COLLEGE. Cambridge, Mass.: Harvard University Press, 1935. xxvi, 472 p. Illus.

> Harvard's distinguished professor of history wrote this work for the three hundredth anniversary of the university's founding. The volume covers the institution during the seventeenth century.

_____. THREE CENTURIES OF HARVARD. Cambridge, Mass.: Harvard University Press, 1936. viii, 512 p.

> A comprehensive volume on the history of the oldest college in the United States. Prepared for the tercentenary in 1936.

Powell, Arthur G. THE UNCERTAIN PROFESSION: HARVARD AND THE SEARCH FOR EDUCATIONAL AUTHORITY. Cambridge, Mass.: Harvard University Press, 1980. viii, 341 p. Illus.

> An analytic history of Harvard's Graduate School of Education established in 1920. The book presents the several emphases, with rationales, in the education of teachers and administrators over the years of the school's existence.

Sutherland, Arthur E. THE LAW AT HARVARD: A HISTORY OF IDEAS AND MEN. Cambridge, Mass.: Belknap Press, 1967. xv, 408 p. Illus.

> The history begins with the story of Isaac Royal, an eighteenth-century benefactor who made first endowment for law (not realized until 1815). School opened in 1817 under administration of John Thornton Kirkland. Written by the Bussey professor of law on the school's 150th anniversary.

MASSACHUSETTS INSTITUTE OF TECHNOLOGY (1861).

Prescott, Samuel C. WHEN M.I.T. WAS "BOSTON TECH," 1861-1916. Cambridge, Mass.: Technology Press, 1954. xviii, 350 p. Illus.

> The work of the four Rogers brothers in science and education is discussed. Instruction began in 1865 on Boylston Street in Boston, hence "Boston Tech." William B. Rogers was the first president. The book closes with the opening of the new Cambridge campus in 1916.

MASSACHUSETTS, UNIVERSITY OF (1863, as Massachusetts Agricultural College; 1947, present name).

Cary, Harold W. THE UNIVERSITY OF MASSACHUSETTS: A HISTORY OF
ONE HUNDRED YEARS. Amherst: University of Massachusetts, 1962. 247 p.
Illus.

> Classes began in 1867 as a Morrill (Land Grant) Act College.
> Developed relatively late into an arts and sciences college and
> state university.

MOUNT HOLYOKE COLLEGE (1837, as Mount Holyoke Female Seminary;
1888, present name).

Cole, Arthur C. A HUNDRED YEARS OF MOUNT HOLYOKE COLLEGE:
THE EVOLUTION OF AN EDUCATIONAL IDEAL. New Haven, Conn.: Yale
University Press, 1940. ix, 426 p. Illus.

> The ideas and work of Mary Lyon in the opening of the Mount
> Holyoke Female Seminary and its subsequent history as a promi-
> nent women's college, the first of the "Seven Sisters." The
> story is brought to the one hundredth anniversary in the mid-1930s.

NORTHEASTERN UNIVERSITY (1892, as Evening Institute of Boston YMCA;
1916, as Northeastern College).

Marston, Everett C. ORIGIN AND DEVELOPMENT OF NORTHEASTERN
UNIVERSITY, 1898-1960. Boston: Northeastern University, 1961. v, 234 p.
Appendix, illus.

> The story of one of the largest urban universities which grew out
> of the desire of the Boston YMCA to establish an "evening In-
> stitute for Young Men," beginning in 1896, to teach practical
> subjects. Law, the first collegiate offering, was offered in 1898.
> The institution was incorporated as a university in 1936. An
> appendix includes a detailed chronology.

RADCLIFFE COLLEGE (1879, as Society for Collegiate Instruction of Women;
1894, present name).

Howells, Dorothy E. A CENTURY TO CELEBRATE: RADCLIFFE COLLEGE,
1879-1979. Cambridge, Mass.: Radcliffe College, 1978. viii, 152 p. Illus.

> Book has an attractive format, profusely illustrated with text pre-
> senting the highlights in the history of what was called at the
> outset, "The Harvard Annex." The institution was named for
> Lady Ann (Radcliffe) Mowlson, Harvard's seventeenth-century
> woman donor.

SMITH COLLEGE (1875).

Seelye, L. Clark. THE EARLY HISTORY OF SMITH COLLEGE, 1871-1910.
Boston: Houghton Mifflin, 1923. ix, 242 p. Appendix, illus.

Forty years of the history of the college founded through benevolence of Sophia Smith, who died in 1870. Classes began in
1875. The appendix includes the will of Miss Smith and the
charter of the college.

TUFTS UNIVERSITY (1852).

Miller, Russell E. LIGHT ON THE HILL: A HISTORY OF TUFTS COLLEGE,
1852-1952. Boston: Beacon Press, 1966. 734 p. Illus.

College was sponsored by the Universalist Church at the outset.
Now a nonsectarian institution with professional schools and
Jackson College, a women's liberal arts college. University status
came in 1955 after the publication of this centennial volume.

WELLESLEY COLLEGE (1870, as Wellesley Female Seminary; 1873, present
name).

Glascock, Jean, ed. WELLESLEY COLLEGE 1875-1975: A CENTURY OF
WOMEN. Wellesley: Wellesley College, 1975. xv, 496 p. Illus.

This work, prepared by fourteen authors, is the most recent and
best history of this college. Issued for the institution's centennial.

WILLIAMS COLLEGE (1793).

Durfee, Calvin. A HISTORY OF WILLIAMS COLLEGE. Boston: A. Williams
and Co., 1860. x, 432 p. Appendix, illus.

The college evolved from the Free School at Williamstown, chartered in 1785, an academy in western Massachusetts, which came
into being from the will of Col. Ephraim Williams (which is included in the appendix). The administration of the renowned
Mark Hopkins receives contemporary treatment (he was president
at the time of the publication of this work).

MICHIGAN

MICHIGAN STATE UNIVERSITY (1855, as Michigan Agricultural College;
1964, present name).

Kuhn, Madison. MICHIGAN STATE: THE FIRST HUNDRED YEARS, 1855-
1955. East Lansing: Michigan State University Press, 1955. xi, 501 p.
Illus.

This institution is credited with being the first state agricultural
college in America, and served as a model for other Morrill
(Land Grant) Act schools. The college changed its name several
times before the adoption of the current one.

MICHIGAN, UNIVERSITY OF (1817).

Hinsdale, Burke A. HISTORY OF THE UNIVERSITY OF MICHIGAN. Ann Arbor: University of Michigan, 1906. 376 p. Illus.

> An early history of this distinguished state university. It includes biographical sketches of the regents and members of the university senate from the beginnings to the start of the twentieth century.

Peckam, Howard E. THE MAKING OF THE UNIVERSITY OF MICHIGAN, 1817-1967. Ann Arbor: University of Michigan Press, 1967. vi, 276 p.

> The most recent work on this major state university. It is a comprehensive history. Author notes that it was written for "Michigan residents, students, alumni, and parents . . . not for my faculty colleagues." Although the institution was chartered early in the nineteenth century, as the "Catholepisemiad of Michigan" (in the language of the legislative act), it was a long time in getting off the ground. Classes did not begin on the collegiate level until 1841.

MINNESOTA

MINNESOTA, UNIVERSITY OF (1851).

Gray, James. THE UNIVERSITY OF MINNESOTA, 1851-1951. Minneapolis: University of Minnesota Press, 1951. xviii, 609 p.

> Classes began at this state university in 1869. This history is divided into ten sections which are arranged around the administrations of the several presidents.

MISSISSIPPI

MISSISSIPPI STATE UNIVERSITY (1878, as Agricultural and Mechanical College of Mississippi; 1932, as Mississippi State College).

Bettersworth, John K. PEOPLE'S UNIVERSITY: THE CENTENNIAL HISTORY OF MISSISSIPPI STATE. Jackson: University Press of Mississippi, 1980. vii, 504 p.

> An update, marking the institution's centennial, of a 1953 history by the same author.

MISSISSIPPI, UNIVERSITY OF (1844).

Cabaniss, Allen. THE UNIVERSITY OF MISSISSIPPI: ITS FIRST HUNDRED YEARS. 2d ed. Hattiesburg: University and College Press of Mississippi, 1971. xiii, 207 p. Illus.

> This work first appeared in 1948 for the one-hundredth anniversary of "Ole Miss." It brought the university's history up through World War II.

MISSOURI

MISSOURI, UNIVERSITY (1839).

Stephens, Frank F. A HISTORY OF THE UNIVERSITY OF MISSOURI. Columbia: University of Missouri Press, 1962. xvi, 661 p.

> A "Columbia College" was already in operation in the town where the state university was to open. This predecessor institution served for preparatory classes for the new university at the outset, but the former was phased out when the state university's classes began in 1843.

WESTMINSTER COLLEGE (1851, as Fulton College; 1853, present name).

Parrish, William E. WESTMINSTER COLLEGE: AN INFORMAL HISTORY, 1851-1969. Fulton, Mo.: Westminster College, 1971. xv, 280 p. Illus.

> A small liberal arts college with ties to the Presbyterian Church. It became internationally known by the 1946 visit and "Iron Curtain" address of Winston Churchill. A chapter is devoted to this event.

MONTANA

MONTANA, UNIVERSITY OF (1893).

Merriam, Harold G. THE UNIVERSITY OF MONTANA: A HISTORY. Missoula: University of Montana Press, 1970. xiii, 194 p. Illus.

> During many years of its history the institution was called "Montana State University" when the state system of higher education was designated as "University of Montana." The name was changed back to the original one in 1965.

NEBRASKA

NEBRASKA, UNIVERSITY OF (1869).

Manley, Robert N., and Sawyer, R. McLaren. CENTENNIAL HISTORY OF THE UNIVERSITY OF NEBRASKA. 2 vols. Lincoln: University of Nebraska, Centennial Press, 1969-73. Illus.

> Volume 1 covers the history of the university from 1869 to 1919, and volume 2 from 1920 to 1969. The University of Omaha merged with this institution in 1968.

NEVADA

NEVADA, UNIVERSITY OF (1874, as a secondary school; 1887, first college classes).

Hulse, James W. THE UNIVERSITY OF NEVADA: A CENTENNIAL HIS-
TORY. Reno: University of Nevada Press, 1974. xii, 258 p. Illus.

> A centennial history with an attractive format of this state univer-
> sity which had its beginnings as a preparatory school in Elko. It
> moved to Reno in 1885, and college-level work was offered in
> 1887.

NEW HAMPSHIRE

DARTMOUTH COLLEGE (1769).

Hill, Ralph N., ed. THE COLLEGE ON THE HILL: A DARTMOUTH CHRON-
ICLE. Hanover, N.H.: Dartmouth Publications, 1964. 357 p. Illus.

> The long history is summed up in six chapters, each by a different
> author. A beautifully illustrated volume with period prints.

Richardson, Leon B. HISTORY OF DARTMOUTH COLLEGE. 2 vols. Hanover,
N.H.: Dartmouth College Publications, 1932.

> Dartmouth had its origins in Moor's Indian Charity School opened
> in 1755 in Lebanon, Connecticut, by Eleazar Wheelock. Volume
> 1 covers the early period to the administration of Nathan Lord.
> Volume 2 begins with Lord's thirty-five year tenure, from 1828
> to 1863, and continues through the 1920s.

NEW HAMPSHIRE, UNIVERSITY OF (1866, as New Hampshire State College
of Agriculture and Mechanic Arts; 1923, present name).

Sackett, Everett B. NEW HAMPSHIRE'S UNIVERSITY: THE STORY OF A
NEW ENGLAND LAND GRANT COLLEGE. Somersworth: New Hampshire
Publishing Co., 1974. x, 210 p. Illus.

> An attractive and well-illustrated volume of this land-grant college.
> Classes began in 1868 as a division of Dartmouth College, special-
> izing in agriculture and mechanics. College moved to a new
> campus in Durham in 1893.

NEW JERSEY

PRINCETON UNIVERSITY (1746, as College of New Jersey; 1896, present
·name).

Leitch, Alexander. A PRINCETON COMPANION. Princeton, N.J.: Princeton University Press, 1978. 559 p.

> A collection of four hundred articles by faculty members and alumni
> covering many aspects of Princeton life, past and present. Biog-
> raphies of the university's seventeen presidents are included.

Maclean, John. HISTORY OF THE COLLEGE OF NEW JERSEY. 2 vols. Philadelphia: J.B. Lippincott, 1877.

An early history of Princeton by its tenth president. A valuable work on the eighteenth-century origins and subsequent history to 1854.

Wertenbaker, Thomas J. PRINCETON, 1746-1896. Princeton, N.J.: Princeton University Press, 1946. v, 424 p. Illus.

The College of New Jersey through its first 150 years, with much on the important years of President James McCosh leading to Princeton's status as a university, by one of its distinguished professors of American history.

RUTGERS UNIVERSITY (1766, as Queens College; 1825, as Rutgers College; 1945, designated a state university).

Demarest, William H.S. A HISTORY OF RUTGERS COLLEGE, 1766-1924. New Brunswick, N.J.: Rutgers College, 1924. 570 p. Illus.

Written by a Rutgers president, from 1906 to 1925. An excellent source of information on the troubled early years of this institution. Classes began in 1771, but the interruption of the Revolution caused them to be peripatetic and intermittent for some years.

McCormick, Richard P. RUTGERS: A BICENTENNIAL HISTORY. New Brunswick, N.J.: Rutgers University Press, 1966. xvi, 336 p. Illus.

Prepared for the occasion of the two hundredth anniversary of the chartering of Queens College, the colonial predecessor of Rutgers University. This volume covers the significant growth of the college into the State University of New Jersey.

NEW MEXICO

NEW MEXICO STATE UNIVERSITY (1888, as Las Cruces College; 1960, present name).

Kropp, Simon F. THAT ALL MAY LEARN: NEW MEXICO STATE UNIVERSITY, 1888-1964. Las Cruces: New Mexico State University, 1972. 401 p. Illus.

In 1889 the territorial legislature transformed the independent Las Cruces College into a land-grant institution as New Mexico College of Agriculture and Mechanic Arts. The growth of additional programs in other arts and sciences came during the twentieth century.

NEW MEXICO, UNIVERSITY OF (1889).

Hughes, Dorothy. PUEBLO ON THE MESA: THE FIRST FIFTY YEARS AT THE UNIVERSITY OF NEW MEXICO. Albuquerque: University of New Mexico

Press, 1939. xi, 151 p. Illus.

> This work deals with the early history of the institution. This well-illustrated volume has much on the beginnings of the territorial university which opened in Albuquerque in 1892 before there was even a secondary school in the territory. A preparatory school was opened with the college.

NEW YORK

ELMIRA COLLEGE (1853, as Elmira Collegiate Seminary; 1890, present name).

Barber, W. Charles. ELMIRA COLLEGE: THE FIRST HUNDRED YEARS. New York: McGraw-Hill, 1955. xiv, 290 p. Illus.

> An early American women's institution of higher education, the first in New York, offering work of collegiate grade.

CITY COLLEGE OF NEW YORK (1847, as the Free Academy of New York; 1866, present name).

Rudy, S. Willis. THE COLLEGE OF THE CITY OF NEW YORK: A HISTORY, 1847-1947. New York: City College Press, 1949. x, 492 p. Illus.

> The history of the oldest municipal college in the United States. The work ends at the period of World War II and the college presidency of Harry Noble Wright.

COLUMBIA UNIVERSITY (1754 as King's College; 1784, present name).

Coon, Horace. COLUMBIA: COLOSSUS ON THE HUDSON. New York: E.P. Dutton, 1947. 388 p. Illus.

> The eighteenth and early nineteenth centuries are treated briefly. There is much on the long and important administration of Nicholas Murray Butler, 1901 to 1945, when the graduate and professional schools developed.

Cremin, Lawrence A.; Shannon, David; et al. A HISTORY OF TEACHERS COLLEGE, COLUMBIA UNIVERSITY. New York: Columbia University Press, 1954. vi, 289 p. Illus.

> The roots of this professional school date from the Industrial Education Association founded by Grace Dodge in 1884. In 1887 it became New York College for the Training of Teachers, and in 1889 it was chartered as Teachers College. The relationship with Columbia began in 1893, and in 1898 it became part of the university.

Humphrey, David C. FROM KING'S COLLEGE TO COLUMBIA, 1746-1800. New York: Columbia University Press, 1976. x, 413 p. Illus.

> A great deal of material is presented on the developments leading

up to the chartering of King's College in 1754. This detailed
history carries the institution's life to the early years as Columbia
College (established 1784) under William Samuel Johnson as president.

White, Marian C. A HISTORY OF BARNARD COLLEGE. New York: Columbia University Press, 1954. viii, 222 p. Illus.

The history of the women's college affiliated with Columbia University and named for Frederick A.P. Barnard, the Columbia president influential in the founding of the school. The story is
brought to the administration of Millicent McIntosh. This is one
of the 1954 bicentennial histories of Columbia.

CORNELL UNIVERSITY (1865).

Becker, Carl L. CORNELL UNIVERSITY: FOUNDERS AND THE FOUNDING.
Ithaca, N.Y.: Cornell University Press, 1943. viii, 240 p.

The contributions of Ezra Cornell and Andrew White, and a review of the Morrill Act (1862) and the New York state land
grant as they affected the founding of Cornell.

Bishop, Morris, A HISTORY OF CORNELL. Ithaca, N.Y.: Cornell University
Press, 1962. xii, 651 p. Illus.

The work of Ezra Cornell, a prosperous benefactor, and Andrew
White, first president. The volume presents the university's growth
through the presidency of Deane Mallott to the early 1960s.

HAMILTON COLLEGE (1793, as Hamilton-Oneida Academy; 1812, as Hamilton
College).

Pilkington, Walter. HAMILTON COLLEGE, 1812-1962. Clinton, N.Y.:
Hamilton College, 1962. 311 p. Illus.

Rev. Samuel Kirkland's plans for educating Indians led to the
founding of an academy, and out of this school developed Hamilton
College.

HUNTER COLLEGE (1870, as the Normal College of the City of New York;
1914, present name).

Patterson, Samuel W. HUNTER COLLEGE: EIGHTY-FIVE YEARS OF SERVICE.
New York: Lantern Press, 1955. xiii, 263 p.

The story of the transformation of a normal school for women into
an important coeducational municipal college within the City University of New York. The institution was named for Thomas Hunter,
the first head. This volume does not contain an index.

NEW YORK UNIVERSITY (1831, as the University of the City of New York;
1896, present name).

Chamberlain, Joshua L., ed. NEW YORK UNIVERSITY: ITS HISTORY, INFLUENCE, EQUIPMENT AND CHARACTERISTICS. Universities and Their Sons Series. 2 vols. Boston: R. Herndon Co., 1901. Illus.

> Volume 1 has two parts, the first dealing with the history from the 1830 promotional efforts to 1901 and was written by Chancellor Henry McCracken and Professor Ernest Sihler. The second part, with biographies of the early officers, was written by Willis F. Johnson. Volume 2 contains biographies of alumni to 1901 and was written by Sihler.

Hug, Elsie A. SEVENTY-FIVE YEARS IN EDUCATION: THE ROLE OF THE SCHOOL OF EDUCATION, NEW YORK UNIVERSITY, 1890-1965. New York: New York University Press, 1965. xii, 276 p.

> An account of "School of Pedagogy," describing its origins and its subsequent development. NYU offered courses in pedagogy as early as 1932, probably the first institution of higher learning to do so.

Jones, Theodore F., ed. NEW YORK UNIVERSITY, 1832-1932. New York: New York University Press, 1933. xiv, 459 p. Illus.

> This is the most recent comprehensive history of this major urban university. The beginnings of the several graduate faculties are included.

RENSSELAER POLYTECHNIC INSTITUTE (1824, as Rensselaer School; 1861, present name).

Rezneck, Samuel. EDUCATION FOR A TECHNICAL SOCIETY: A SESQUI-CENTENNIAL HISTORY OF RENSSELAER POLYTECHNIC INSTITUTE. Troy, N.Y.: Rensselaer Polytechnic Institute, 1968. xvii, 520 p. Illus.

> America's first technical college founded by Stephen Van Rensselaer for the "application of science to the common purposes of life." It became Rensselaer Institute in 1832, and in 1950 reorganization brought about a three-year program. The book's appendixes include a chronology, list of officers, trustees, and faculty, and some courses of study.

ROCHESTER, UNIVERSITY OF (1850).

Rosenberger, Jesse L. ROCHESTER: THE MAKING OF A UNIVERSITY. Rochester, N.Y.: University of Rochester, 1927. xiii, 333 p. Illus.

> University was brought into being by a group of Baptists in upper-state New York. It was opened for classes the same year it was chartered. The Eastman School of Music, a gift of George Eastman, was opened in 1921. The history continues to the mid 1920s.

SYRACUSE UNIVERSITY (1870).

Galpin, W. Freeman. SYRACUSE UNIVERSITY: THE PIONEER DAYS. 2 vols. Syracuse: Syracuse University Press, 1952-60. Illus.

> Genessee College (1849) was a predecessor, but was not directly related to the founding of Syracuse University. Volume 1 covers the history of the predecessor institution and brings the university's history up through the nineteenth century. Volume 2, "The Growing Years," deals with the twentieth century.

UNION COLLEGE (1785, as Schenectady Academy; 1795, present name).

Fox, Dixon R. UNION COLLEGE: AN UNFINISHED HISTORY. Schenectady, N.Y.: Union College, Graduate Council, 1945. 84 p.

> A short volume written by the college's twelfth president on the institution's sesquicentennial. It is essentially an essay and has no chapter subdivisions.

UNITED STATES MILITARY ACADEMY (1802).

Ambrose, Stephen E. DUTY, HONOR, COUNTRY: A HISTORY OF WEST POINT. Baltimore: Johns Hopkins Press, 1966. xv, 357 p. Illus.

> The academy grew out of the U.S. Army Corps of Engineers, but soon the curriculum was expanded to increase the offerings to other branches of the army. This work stresses the many aspects of cadet life and the leadership of the academy over the years.

VASSAR COLLEGE (1861, as Vassar Female College; 1867, present name).

Plum, Dorothy A., and Dowell, George B. THE MAGNIFICENT ENTERPRISE: A CHRONICLE OF VASSAR. Poughkeepsie, N.Y.: Vassar College, 1961. viii, 138 p. Illus.

> The history of a leading institution of higher education for women. It pioneered in music and physical education. Named for Matthew Vassar, a prominent brewer and philanthropist who made the initial gift for the college. The book is in the form of a chronology, beginning in 1792, with the birth of Vassar, and continuing through events of the 1961 centennial year.

YESHIVA UNIVERSITY (1866, as Yeshivat Etz Chaim; 1928, present name).

Klapperman, Gilbert. THE STORY OF YESHIVA UNIVERSITY: THE FIRST JEWISH UNIVERSITY IN AMERICA. New York: Macmillan, 1969. xv, 301 p. Illus.

> This urban university came about from the merging in 1915 of two institutions, Yeshivat Etz Chaim (1866) and Rabbi Isaac Eichanan Theological Seminary (1897). University status was acquired in 1945.

NORTH CAROLINA

BLACK MOUNTAIN COLLEGE (1933).

Duberman, Martin. BLACK MOUNTAIN: AN EXPLORATION IN COMMU-
NITY. New York: E.P. Dutton, 1972. 527 p. Illus.

> The story of an experimental college that existed from 1933 to
> 1956; written by a distinguished professor history at Lehman Col-
> lege, City University of New York. The major sources are numer-
> ous interviews with the major figures in the life of the institution.
> Why did it fail? The growth of informal power rather than rules
> and structure is put forth as the reason.

DUKE UNIVERSITY (1939, as Union Institute; 1859, as Trinity College; 1924,
present name).

Porter, Earl W. TRINITY AND DUKE, 1892-1924: FOUNDATIONS OF
DUKE UNIVERSITY. Durham, N.C.: Duke University Press, 1964. xii,
274 p. Illus.

> The university has roots to Union Institute, later a normal school,
> and then Trinity College, a Methodist institution. This work deals
> with the Trinity period with emphasis on the men (presidents, pro-
> fessors, and philanthropists) who were responsible for its growth.
> The Duke endowment was responsible for the change of name in
> 1924.

NORTH CAROLINA, UNIVERSITY OF (1789).

Powell, William S. THE FIRST STATE UNIVERSITY: A PICTORIAL HISTORY
OF THE UNIVERSITY OF NORTH CAROLINA. Chapel Hill: University of
North Carolina Press, 1972. x, 309 p. Illus.

> The first of the state colleges to open (1795) as a state university.
> The history is presented in a handsome volume, profusely illustrated.
> The life of the university is well presented--students, faculty, ad-
> ministrators, classes, and athletics.

Wilson, Louis R. THE UNIVERSITY OF NORTH CAROLINA, 1900-1930:
THE MAKING OF A MODERN UNIVERSITY. Chapel Hill: University of
North Carolina Press, 1957. xxi, 633 p. Illus.

> The years treated are those when the university made the change
> from a liberal arts college to a full-fledged university.

NORTH DAKOTA

NORTH DAKOTA, UNIVERSITY OF (1883).

Geiger, Louis G. UNIVERSITY OF THE NORTHERN PLAINS: A HISTORY
OF THE UNIVERSITY OF NORTH DAKOTA, 1883-1958. Grand Forks: Uni-

versity of North Dakota Press, 1958. xiv, 491 p. Illus.

> Classes began in 1884, the year after the incorporation by Dakota
> Territory. In addition to the work of the college, there were a
> preparatory school and a normal department. This history relates
> the university's life during the Great Depression and World War
> II, and in a chapter, "A New Day," presents the growth since
> the end of the war into the 1950s.

OHIO

ANTIOCH COLLEGE (1853).

Henderson, Algo D., and Hall, Dorothy. ANTIOCH COLLEGE: ITS DE-
SIGN FOR LIBERAL EDUCATION. New York: Harper, 1946. xiv, 280 p.

> Henderson was president of the college in the 1940s and this work
> is essentially his program. It was one of the first colleges to have
> a work-study plan. There is no reference made to the nineteenth-
> century history of Antioch under Horace Mann and others.

CASE WESTERN RESERVE UNIVERSITY (1826, as Western Reserve College;
1967, present name).

Cramer, C.H. CASE WESTERN RESERVE: A HISTORY OF THE UNIVERSITY,
1826-1976. Boston: Little, Brown, 1976. viii, 401 p. Illus.

> The story of two Ohio institutions, Western Reserve College and
> Case Institute of Technology and their federation into Case West-
> ern Reserve College.

UNIVERSITY OF CINCINNATI (1819, as Cincinnati College; 1870, present
name).

McGrane, Reginald C. THE UNIVERSITY OF CINCINNATI: A SUCCESS
STORY IN URBAN HIGHER EDUCATION. New York: Harper and Row, 1963.
xiii, 364 p. Illus.

> The complications and viscissitudes of the predecessor institutions
> of this municipal university are delineated. McGuffey's first
> ECLECTIC READER came out in 1836 while he was president here.

DENISON UNIVERSITY (1831, as Granville Literary and Theological Institution;
1856, present name).

Chessman, G. Wallace. DENISON: THE STORY OF AN OHIO COLLEGE.
Granville, Ohio: Denison University, 1957. xiv, 451 p. Illus.

> The institution was founded by the Baptists of northeastern Ohio.
> Shepardson College for Women merged with Denison in 1886.

HIRAM COLLEGE (1850, as Western Reserve Eclectic Institute; 1867, present
name).

Treudley, M.B. PRELUDE TO THE FUTURE: FIRST HUNDRED YEARS OF HIRAM COLLEGE. New York: Association Press, 1950. 288 p. Illus.

The years of James Garfield, as a student, teacher, and principal, are well covered. The college attained full collegiate rank in 1867.

KENYON COLLEGE (1824).

Greenslade, Thomas B. KENYON COLLEGE: ITS THIRD HALF CENTURY. Gambia, Ohio: Kenyon College, 1975. viii, 301 p. Illus.

The history of this liberal arts college offers a brief review of the early years but concentrates on the more recent years from the 1920s to 1975. The institution was founded as an Episcopal Church college but became nondenominational in recent years.

MARIETTA COLLEGE (1797, as Muskingum Academy; 1835, college charter).

Beach, Arthur G. A PIONEER COLLEGE: THE STORY OF MARIETTA. Chicago: John F. Cuneo, 1935. xiv, 325 p. Illus.

Published on the one-hundredth anniversary of the college charter of 1835. A gradual evolution took place in the transformation of the early academy into the college. The work is in five parts covering groupings of years to 1935. It is not indexed.

MIAMI UNIVERSITY (1809).

Havighurst, Walter. THE MIAMI YEARS, 1809-1959. New York: G.P. Putnam's Sons, 1958. 254 p. Illus.

This state-supported college opened for classes in 1824. William H. McGuffey taught here from 1826 to 1836.

OBERLIN COLLEGE (1838, as Oberlin Collegiate Institute; 1850, present name).

Fletcher, Robert S. A HISTORY OF OBERLIN COLLEGE FROM ITS FOUNDA-TIONS THROUGH THE CIVIL WAR. New York: Arno Press, 1971. xvii, 1,004 p. Illus.

One of the first colleges to have coeducational classes. Oberlin was a center of abolitionism in the pre-Civil War period. This work was first published in two volumes at Oberlin College in 1943.

OHIO STATE UNIVERSITY (1870, as Ohio Agricultural and Mechanical College; 1878, present name).

Pollard, James E. HISTORY OF THE OHIO STATE UNIVERSITY. Columbus: Ohio State University Press, 1952. vii, 434 p. Appendix. Illus.

This is the story of the university's first seventy-five years, bringing it up to World War II. A brief chronology of the high points in its history is in the appendix.

OHIO UNIVERSITY (1804).

Hoover, Thomas N. THE HISTORY OF OHIO UNIVERSITY. Athens: Ohio University Press, 1954. iv, 274 p. Illus.

> Opened in 1809 as the first college in the old Northwest Territory. The college museum houses a collection of items from this territory. The chapters in the book are arranged by the several presidents' administrations. William H. McGuffey was president from 1839 to 1843.

OHIO WESLEYAN UNIVERSITY (1842).

Hubbart, Henry C. OHIO WESLEYAN'S FIRST HUNDRED YEARS. Delaware: Ohio Wesleyan University, 1943. vii, 358 p. Illus.

> The college opened in 1844, the preparatory school opened a year or so before. Methodist leaders in Ohio were responsible for its establishment. In 1877 it absorbed Ohio Wesleyan Female College. Despite its name, Ohio Wesleyan has remained a college, not a true university.

WOOSTER, COLLEGE OF (1866).

Notestein, Lucy L. WOOSTER OF THE MIDDLE WEST. 2 vols. Kent: Kent State University Press, 1937-71. Illus.

> Volume 1 covers the years 1866 to 1910. Volume 2, added over thirty years later, encompasses 1911 to 1944. The college was founded by the Presbyterian Church. The author used the notes of her father, Jonas Notestein, classics professor, in preparing the first volume.

OKLAHOMA

OKLAHOMA STATE UNIVERSITY (1890, as Oklahoma Agricultural and Mechanical College; 1957, present name).

Rulon, Philip R. OKLAHOMA STATE UNIVERSITY, SINCE 1890. Stillwater: Oklahoma State University Press, 1975. xvi, 386 p. Illus.

> The story of the land-grant college of Oklahoma in the setting of the early post-territorial history of the state. The volume brings the history to 1957 when the present name was adopted.

OKLAHOMA, UNIVERSITY OF (1890).

Gittinger, Roy. THE UNIVERSITY OF OKLAHOMA, 1892-1942. Norman: University of Oklahoma Press, 1942. xii, 282 p. Illus.

The institution was established the year that the territory of
Oklahoma was formed and the year after the Indian territory was
to take students as they found them: first students were mostly
preparatory. This is a history of fifty years.

OREGON

OREGON STATE UNIVERSITY (1858, as Corvallis College; 1868, as Agricultural College of State of Oregon; 1961, present name).

Groshong, James W. THE MAKING OF A UNIVERSITY, 1868-1968. Corvallis: Oregon State University, 1968. 32 p. Illus.

This monograph presents the steps in the college's development as
a true university. The institution began as a private one, became
the state land-grant college in 1868, and came entirely under
state control in 1885.

OREGON, UNIVERSITY OF (1872).

Sheldon, Henry D. HISTORY OF THE UNIVERSITY OF OREGON. Portland:
Binfords and Mort, 1940. 288 p. Illus.

The state incorporation in 1872 was for the Union University
Association. After much discussion over location, classes began
in Eugene in 1876. This history brings the institution up through
the 1930s when a new structure for higher education in Oregon,
a state board of governance, came into being.

PENNSYLVANIA

BUCKNELL UNIVERSITY (1846, as University at Lewisburg; 1866, present
name).

Oliphant, J. Orin. THE RISE OF BUCKNELL UNIVERSITY. New York:
Appleton-Century-Crofts, 1965. xii, 448 p. Illus.

Founded by a group of Baptists and renamed in 1886 for William
Bucknell, a benefactor from Philadelphia. This is the story of
a liberal arts college miscalled a university for most of its history.
The development of its three colleges (arts and sciences, business
administration, and engineering) is set forth.

DICKINSON COLLEGE (1783).

Sellers, Charles C. DICKINSON COLLEGE: A HISTORY. Middletown, Pa.:
Wesleyan University Press, 1973. xvii, 626 p. Illus.

The college had its beginnings as a Latin grammar school as early
as 1769. Its seal uses 1773, the date of a grant of land for a
schoolhouse, as its founding date. The college charter was granted in 1783. It was a Presbyterian Church-affiliated institution in

its early years. The problems of college–church–state relationships are discussed.

FRANKLIN AND MARSHALL COLLEGE (1787, as Franklin College; 1853, present name).

Klein, Frederic S. SINCE 1787: THE FRANKLIN AND MARSHALL COLLEGE STORY. Lancaster, Pa.: Franklin and Marshall College, 1968. 45 p. Illus.

A short monograph arranged chronologically by significant dates, 1787 to 1954. A very scant historical treatment.

HAVERFORD COLLEGE (1833, as Haverford School; 1856, present name).

Jones, Rufus M. HAVERFORD COLLEGE: A HISTORY AND AN INTERPRE-TATION. New York: Macmillan, 1933. xi, 244 p.

The first institution of higher education established under auspices of the Society of Friends. The history is written by a distinguished Quaker scholar.

LAFAYETTE COLLEGE (1826).

Skillman, David B. THE BIOGRAPHY OF A COLLEGE: BEING THE HISTORY OF THE FIRST CENTURY OF LAFAYETTE COLLEGE. 2 vols. Easton, Pa.: Lafayette College, 1932. Appendixes, illus.

The college was founded by townspeople of Easton, Pennsylvania, in tribute to the Marquis de Lafayette. It had early affiliation with the Presbyterian Church. Appendixes include the charter, laws, and college officers.

LEHIGH UNIVERSITY (1865).

Bowen, Catherine D. A HISTORY OF LEHIGH UNIVERSITY. South Bethlehem, Pa.: Lehigh Alumni Bulletin, 1924. 105 p. Illus.

The university was established by Asa Packer, one of the founders of the Lehigh Valley Railroad. The orientation of the institution has always been essentially toward the sciences. This work is by a distinguished biographer, the daughter of a past president of Lehigh.

PENNSYLVANIA STATE UNIVERSITY (1854, as Farmer's High School of Pensylvania; 1862, as Agricultural College of Pennsylvania; 1874, as Pennsylvania State College; 1953, present name).

Dunaway, Wayland F. HISTORY OF THE PENNSYLVANIA STATE COLLEGE. State College: Pennsylvania State College, 1946. xiv, 540 p. Illus.

Classes began in 1855 with courses on the secondary level for farmers. The book traces the development of the institution as a state college up to the beginning of World War II.

PENNSYLVANIA, UNIVERSITY OF (1755, as College, Academy, and Charitable School of Philadelphia; 1791, present name).

Cheyney, Edward P. HISTORY OF THE UNIVERSITY OF PENNSYLVANIA, 1740-1940. Philadelphia: University of Pennsylvania Press, 1940. x, 461 p.

> Written to commemorate the two hundredth anniversary. The university traces its roots to the establishment of a building in 1740 intended for a charity school and for the occasional preaching by the Rev. George Whitefield.

Thorpe, Francis N. BENJAMIN FRANKLIN AND THE UNIVERSITY OF PENN-SYLVANIA. Washington, D.C.: Government Printing Office, 1893. 450 p. Illus.

> About half of this work deals with Franklin's ideas on education and his part in the establishment of the Academy of Philadelphia, the predecessor of the college and university. Important documents in the early history of the institution are included.

WASHINGTON AND JEFFERSON COLLEGE (1787, charter for Washington Academy; 1806, Washington College; 1791, Canonsburg Academy; 1802, Jefferson College; united with present name in 1865).

Coleman, Helen T.W. BANNERS IN THE WILDERNESS: EARLY YEARS OF WASHINGTON AND JEFFERSON COLLEGE. Pittsburgh, Pa.: University of Pittsburgh Press, 1956. xvii, 285 p. Illus.

> A western Pennsylvania institution originating as two eighteenth-century academies with subsequent development into two colleges, named for Jefferson and Washington. The evolution into the united college is well developed in this work.

RHODE ISLAND

BROWN UNIVERSITY (1764, as Rhode Island College; 1804, present name).

Bronson, Walter C. THE HISTORY OF BROWN UNIVERSITY, 1764-1914. Providence, R.I.: Brown University, 1914. x, 548 p. Appendix.

> A history written by a professor of English for the one hundreds and-fiftieth anniversary of the founding by a group of Baptists and by the colony of Rhode Island and Providence Plantations. The appendix includes charters, early laws, and college seals.

Guild, Reuben G. HISTORY OF BROWN UNIVERSITY WITH ILLUSTRATIVE DOCUMENTS. Providence, R.I.: Providence Press, xv, 443 p. Illus.

> A limited, subscription volume that is replete with information on the early periods of the college's history. Written by the university's librarian.

RHODE ISLAND, UNIVERSITY OF (1888, as Rhode Island State Agricultural School; 1909, as Rhode Island State College; 1951, present name).

Eschenbacher, Herman F. THE UNIVERSITY OF RHODE ISLAND: A HISTORY OF LAND GRANT EDUCATION IN RHODE ISLAND. New York: Appleton-Century-Crofts, 1967. x, 584 p. Illus.

> The first delegation of the Morrill (Land Grant) Act in Rhode Island was for a department at Brown University. Finally, the state established this agricultural school, which achieved collegiate status in 1892 and full university rank in 1951. The liberal arts curriculum was introduced in 1944. The work is very carefully documented.

SOUTH CAROLINA

CHARLESTON, COLLEGE OF (1785)

Easterby, James H. A HISTORY OF THE COLLEGE OF CHARLESTON, FOUNDED 1770. Charleston: Trustees of the College of Charleston, 1935. 379 p. Illus.

> Published for the sesquicentennial of the college charter. The institution was of secondary school level until 1806. This study presents the many vicissitudes in its long history. In 1837 it became the first municipal college in the United States.

SOUTH CAROLINA, UNIVERSITY OF (1801)

Hollis, Daniel W. UNIVERSITY OF SOUTH CAROLINA. 2 vols. Columbia: University of South Carolina Press, 1951-56. Illus.

> Volume 1 marked the sesquicentennial of the charter as "South Carolina College" and deals with the early history. Volume 2 was published for the sesquicentennial of the 1805 opening and presents the transformation of the college into a university.

SOUTH DAKOTA

SOUTH DAKOTA, UNIVERSITY OF (1862)

Cummins, Cedric. THE UNIVERSITY OF SOUTH DAKOTA, 1862-1966. Vermillion: University of South Dakota, 1975. v, 334 p. Illus.

> This is the first full-treatment history of this first university in Dakota territory. It opened in 1882, twenty years after its incorporation. Interestingly, its first head was an immigrant Russian Jew, Ephraim Epstein.

TENNESSEE

FISK UNIVERSITY (1865, as Fisk School; 1867, present name).

Jones, Thomas E., and Richardson, Joe E. A HISTORY OF FISK UNIVERSITY,

1865-1946. University: University of Alabama Press, 1980. 227 p. Illus.

> Founded under the influence of the American Missionary Association, and named for General Clinton Fisk, an official of the Freedmen's Bureau and a benefactor. The college department began in 1871. A chapter is devoted to distinguished alumni, W.E.B. DuBois (class of 18888) being one of them.

TENNESSEE, UNIVERSITY OF (1794, as Blount College; 1879, present name).

Folmsbee, Stanley J. TENNESSEE ESTABLISHED A STATE UNIVERSITY: FIRST YEARS OF THE UNIVERSITY OF TENNESSEE, 1879-1887. Vol. 64, no. 3. Knoxville: University of Tennessee Record, 1961. 214 p.

> The early years of the institution in its evolution from Blount College through East Tennessee College to the University of Tennessee.

Montgomery, James R. THE VOLUNTEERS STATE FORGES ITS UNIVERSITY: THE UNIVERSITY OF TENNESSEE, 1887-1919. Vol. 69, no. 6. Knoxville: University of Tennessee Record, 1966. vii, 231 p.

> The history of the university in its middle years.

_____. THRESHOLD OF A NEW DAY: THE UNIVERSITY OF TENNESSEE, 1919-1946. Vol. 74, no. 6. Knoxville: University of Tennessee Record, 1971. vii, 432 p. Illus.

> Events and developments at the university in the twentieth century to the return of veterans from World War II.

VANDERBILT UNIVERSITY (1872, as Central University of Methodist Episcopal Church South; 1873, present name).

Mims, Edwin. HISTORY OF VANDERBILT UNIVERSITY. Nashville: Vanderbilt University Press, 1946. 497 p. Illus.

> The 1873 gift of Cornelius Vanderbilt converted a small Methodist seminary (chartered but not opened) into a prominent university. The work ends with the World War II period.

TEXAS

SOUTHERN METHODIST UNIVERSITY (1911).

Thomas, Mary M. H. SOUTHERN METHODIST UNIVERSITY: FOUNDING AND EARLY. Dallas: Southern Methodist University Press, 1974. xiii, 224 p. Appendix, illus.

> A Methodist-supported institution established early in the twentieth century. First classes were held in 1915. The history is brought up to 1940, the Depression years, a period of mounting debt and other institutional difficulties. The appendix includes officers and faculty to 1940.

TEXAS A & M UNIVERSITY (1871, as Agricultural & Mechanical College of Texas; 1963, present name).

Perry, George S. THE STORY OF TEXAS A & M. New York: McGraw-Hill, 1951. xiv, 264 p. Appendix, illus.

> The story of the Morrill (Land Grant) Act college of Texas, the oldest state institution of higher learning in the state. Written in an informal style, unlike most institutional histories. School songs with music are included. The appendix has an extensive chronology with officers and football scores over the years.

TEXAS, UNIVERSITY OF (1881).

Lane, John J. HISTORY OF THE UNIVERSITY OF TEXAS. Austin: Henry Hutchings, 1891. viii, 322 p. Illus.

> The earliest history of this university. There is much on the discussions and legislation leading up to the establishment of the institution. Names and backgrounds of the first faculty are listed. The work is not indexed.

Long, Walter E. FOR ALL TIME TO COME. Austin: n.p., 1964. xv, 111 p. Illus.

> The most recent work on the University of Texas. The book may have been a limited edition as it was issued boxed in a slip cover.

UTAH

BRIGHAM YOUNG UNIVERSITY (1875, as an academy; 1903, present name).

Wilkinson, Ernest L., ed. BRIGHAM YOUNG UNIVERSITY: THE FIRST ONE HUNDRED YEARS. 4 vols. Provo: Brigham Young University Press, 1975-76. Illus.

> The volumes give a very complete story of the development and subsequent growth of this university, founded as an academy by Brigham Young, president of the Church of Jesus Christ of Later-Day Saints (Mormons).

UTAH, UNIVERSITY OF (1850, as University of Deseret; 1892, present name).

Chamberlin, Ralph V. THE UNIVERSITY OF UTAH: A HISTORY OF ITS FIRST ONE HUNDRED YEARS, 1850-1950. Salt Lake City: University of Utah Press, 1960. xix, 616 p. Appendixes, illus.

> The institution was first opened when Utah was the territory of Deseret, but it failed in support and patronage. A new charter was issued under Utah which led to the growth of this thriving western university. Extensive appendixes include the important documents, courses of study, lists and biographies of officers, and a chronology of the university's history.

VERMONT

BENNINGTON COLLEGE (1932).

Jones, Barbara. BENNINGTON COLLEGE: THE DEVELOPMENT OF AN
EDUCATIONAL IDEA. New York: Harper, 1946. xviii, 239 p.

A work devoted to the unique general education program at this progressive women's college. The relatively short history is covered in
the preface. The exploration of the Bennington idea began in 1923.

MIDDLEBURY COLLEGE (1800).

Lee, William S. FATHER WENT TO COLLEGE: THE STORY OF MIDDLEBURY.
New York: Wilson-Erickson, 1936. xii, 249 p. Illus.

The book is written in a biographical and narrative style rather than
the usual chronological approach. The college had its roots in the
Addison County Grammar School chartered in 1797. President Timothy
Dwight of Yale was instrumental in the establishment of Middlebury.

NORWICH UNIVERSITY (1819, as American Literary, Scientific, and Military
Academy; 1834, chartered as Norwich University).

Dodge, Grenville M., and Ellis, William A., eds. NORWICH UNIVERSITY,
1819-1911. 3 vols. Montpelier, Vt.: Capital City Press, 1911. Illus.

This college with a military affiliation began as an academy in
Norwich, Vermont, and moved to Middletown, Connecticut, in
1825. The Middletown buildings became the campus for Wesleyan
University in 1833. The academy was reopened in Vermont in
1829 and Norwich University evolved from this institution. Volume
1 contains history. Volumes 2 and 3 list trustees, officers, faculty, and alumni with extensive biographical material.

VERMONT, UNIVERSITY OF (1791).

Lindsay, Julian I. TRADITION LOOKS FORWARD: THE UNIVERSITY OF
VERMONT, A HISTORY, 1791-1909. Burlington: University of Vermont and
State Agricultural College, 1954. 285 p. Illus.

First college instruction was given in 1800. The university was
merged with Vermont Agricultural College in 1865. It is the
oldest state university in New England.

VIRGINIA

HAMPTON INSTITUTE (1868, as Hampton Normal and Agricultural Institute;
1930, present name).

Armstrong, Samuel C., et al. MEMORIES OF OLD HAMPTON. Hampton,
Va.: Institute Press, 1909. 136 p. Illus.

A work by the founder and published by the Armstrong League of
Hampton Workers. A valuable source on the early history of Hampton.

Schall, Keith L., ed. STONY THE ROAD: CHAPTERS IN THE HISTORY OF
HAMPTON INSTITUTE. Charlottesville: University Press of Virginia, 1977.
xx, 183 p. Illus.

Seven essays by various authors relating to the history of this predominantly black college. Some American Indians were among the
early students at the institute. College-level work began in 1920.

HAMPDEN-SYDNEY COLLEGE (1776).

Grigsby, Hugh B. DISCOURSE ON THE LIVES AND CHARACTERS OF THE
EARLY PRESIDENTS OF HAMPDEN-SYDNEY COLLEGE. Richmond, Va.:
Hermitage Press, 1913. x, 46 p.

The college was not chartered until 1783 although it opened for instruction earlier. Samuel Stanhope Smith, later to be the head of
Princeton, was the first president, from 1775 to 1779. This brief work
was an address delivered in 1876 for the centenary of the founding.

HOLLINS COLLEGE (1842, as Valley Union Seminary; 1910, present name).

Niederer, Frances J. HOLLINS COLLEGE: AN ILLUSTRATED HISTORY.
Charlottesville: University Press of Virginia, 1973. 221 p. Illus.

The profusely illustrated history of one of the oldest women's colleges.
The name was changed in 1910 in honor of Mr. and Mrs. John Hollins who had earlier made large financial donations. The architecture of the college ranges from Greek Revival to a 1960s modern style.

RANDOLPH-MACON COLLEGE (1830).

Irby, Richard. HISTORY OF RANDOLPH-MACON COLLEGE, VIRGINIA.
Richmond, Va.: Whittet and Shepperson, [c. 1899]. 331 p.

The history of the oldest Methodist college in the United States through
1898. Classes began in 1832 but were suspended during the Civil War.

RANDOLPH-MACON WOMAN'S COLLEGE (1891).

Cornelius, Roberta D. THE HISTORY OF RANDOLPH-MACON WOMAN'S COL-
LEGE. Chapel Hill: University of North Carolina Press, 1951. xviii, 428 p. Illus.

The college had its origin with the parent foundation, the Randolph-
Macon Board of Trustees of the earlier men's institution. Classes
began in 1893. This work was prepared for the fiftieth anniversary.

VIRGINIA MILITARY INSTITUTE (1839).

Couper, William. ONE HUNDRED YEARS AT VMI. 4 vols. Richmond, Va.:
Garrett and Massie, 1939. Illus.

A very detailed history of this early military academy. Much
biographical material. General George Marshall was graduated
from the class of 1901.

VIRGINIA POLYTECHNIC INSTITUTE AND STATE UNIVERSITY (1872, as
Virginia Agricultural and Mechanical College; 1970, present name).

Kinnear, Duncan L. THE FIRST ONE HUNDRED YEARS: A HISTORY OF
VIRGINIA POLYTECHNIC INSTITUTE AND STATE UNIVERSITY. Blacksburg:
Virginia Polytechnic Institute Educational Foundation, 1972. xiv, 498 p.

The history of the land-grant college of Virginia. For some
years, it was known as Virginia Polytechnic Institute. First degrees were granted in 1885. The story of the college is presented
by presidential administrations.

VIRGINIA, UNIVERSITY OF (1819).

Adams, Herbert B. THOMAS JEFFERSON AND THE UNIVERSITY OF VIRGINIA.
Contributions to American Education History Series, vol. 2. Edited by Herbert
Adams. Washington, D.C.: Government Printing Office, 1888. 308 p. Illus.

The university—its organization, buildings, philosophy of education, and curriculum—was the creation of Thomas Jefferson.

Bruce, Philip A. HISTORY OF THE UNIVERSITY OF VIRGINIA, 1819-1919.
5 vols. New York: Macmillan, 1922l. illus.

A large and important work which divides the history of the university
into nine periods. The years after 1842 have extensive treatment.

O'Neal, William B. PICTORIAL HISTORY OF THE UNIVERSITY OF VIRGINIA.
Charlottesville: University Press of Virginia, 1968. viii, 177 p. Illus.

The high points of the institution's history are brought up through the
1960s. The illustrations begin with the buildings of Jefferson's time.

WASHINGTON AND LEE UNIVERSITY (1749, as Augusta Academy; 1813, as
Washington College; 1867, present name).

Crenshaw, Ollinger. GENERAL LEE'S COLLEGE: THE RISE AND GROWTH
OF WASHINGTON AND LEE UNIVERSITY. New York: Random House, 1969.
xvi, 366 p. Illus.

The story of a university that has evolved from an eighteenth-
century academy that had George Washington's patronage.
General Robert E. Lee became president in 1865.

WILLIAM AND MARY, COLLEGE OF (1693).

Adams, Herbert B. THE COLLEGE OF WILLIAM AND MARY: A CONTRI-
BUTION TO THE HISTORY OF HIGHER EDUCATION WITH SUGGESTIONS

FOR ITS NATIONAL PROMOTION. U.S. Bureau of Education, Circulars of Information, no. 1. Washington, D.C.: Government Printing Office, 1887. 89 p. Illus.

> The early relationship of George Washington with the college is presented in detail. At the time of the writing of this work, the college was at a low point in its history.

Hartwell, Henry; Blair, James; et al. THE PRESENT STATE OF VIRGINIA AND THE COLLEGE. Williamsburg, Va.: Colonial Williamsburg, 1940. lxxiii, 105 p. Illus.

> This work was first published in London in 1727, authored by Hartwell, one of the first trustees, and Blair, the long-time first president. It is a most important work for the earliest period in the college's history. A long preface gives much background information.

Morpurgo, J.E. THEIR MAJESTIES' ROYALL COLLEDGE: WILLIAM AND MARY IN THE SEVENTEENTH AND EIGHTEENTH CENTURY. Williamsburg, Va.: Endowment Association of College of William and Mary, 1976. xix, 247 p. Illus.

> A thoroughly researched and well-illustrated history of the college from its founding through the eighteenth century.

WASHINGTON

WASHINGTON STATE UNIVERSITY (1890, as Washington State Agricultural College and School of Science; 1959, present name).

Bryan, Enoch A. HISTORICAL SKETCH OF THE STATE COLLEGE OF WASHINGTON, 1890-1925. Spokane, Wash.: Alumni Association and the Associated Students, 1928. 556 p.

> The first degrees were awarded in 1897 and the institution became the State College of Washington in 1905. This history was written by the president from 1893 to 1916, one who reorganized and upgraded this land-grant college.

WASHINGTON, UNIVERSITY OF (1861).

Gates, Charles M. THE FIRST CENTENNIAL AT THE UNIVERSITY OF WASHINGTON, 1861-1961. Seattle: University of Washington Press, 1961. iv, 252 p. Illus.

> An attractive and well-illustrated volume written for the one-hundredth anniversary of the establishment of this northwestern territorial university.

WEST VIRGINIA

MARSHALL UNIVERSITY (1837, as Marshall Academy; 1858, present name).

ONE HUNDRED YEARS OF MARSHALL COLLEGE. Huntington, W. Va.: Centennial Committee of Marshall College, 1937. 167 p. Illus.

> Named for Chief Justice John Marshall. The institution had early ties with the Methodist Church. This is an account of the centennial celebration and the history of the college is treated in one article.

WISCONSIN

WISCONSIN, UNIVERSITY OF (1848).

Bogue, Allan G., and Taylor, Robert. THE UNIVERSITY OF WISCONSIN: ONE HUNDRED AND TWENTY-FIVE YEARS. Madison: University of Wisconsin Press, 1975. x, 289 p. Illus.

> This volume contains the earlier two-volume history by Curti and Carstensen (1949) and brings the chronicle of the university up to 1974.

Curti, Merle, and Carstensen, Vernon. THE UNIVERSITY OF WISCONSIN: A HISTORY, 1848-1925. 2 vols. Madison: University of Wisconsin Press, 1949. Illus.

> Volume 1 deals with the university's beginnings under the territory of Wisconsin through the nineteenth century. Volume 2 carries the history into the twentieth century to the 1920s. Curti was a distinguished American historian.

WYOMING

WYOMING, UNIVERSITY OF (1886).

Clough, Wilson O. A HISTORY OF THE UNIVERSITY OF WYOMING, 1887-1937. Laramie: Laramie Print Co., 1937. 199 p. Illus.

> The university received its charter from the territorial legislature and opened for classes in 1887. This history covers the first fifty years.

_____. THE THIRD QUARTER: THE UNIVERSITY OF WYOMING. Laramie: University of Wyoming, 1962. 132 p.

> The university's history is brought up through the Depression, World War II, and the postwar years, the latter period being one of the greatest growth.

Sources of Information

BARRON'S PROFILES OF AMERICAN COLLEGES. 12th ed. 2 vols. Woodbury, N.Y.: Barron's Educational Series, 1980.

> Especially helpful for perspective college students. Volume 1 is arranged by state with critical observations of each institution. A preliminary section, "Most Competitive," "Less Competitive," is a special feature. Volume 2 comprises an index to major areas of study.

Blaze, Wayne, et al. GUIDE TO ALTERNATIVE COLLEGES AND UNIVER-
SITIES. Boston: Beacon Press, 1974. xv, 141 p.

> Alternative programs at traditional colleges as well as innovative
> colleges (e.g., College of the Atlantic).

Cass, James, and Birnbaum, Max. COMPARATIVE GUIDE TO AMERICAN
COLLEGES. 8th ed. New York: Harper and Row, 1977. xxxiii, 749 p.

> Designed especially for students and parents. A "Selectivity
> Index," a key to admission difficulty, is included.

THE COLLEGE BLUE BOOK. 16th ed. 3 vols. New York: Macmillan
Information, 1977.

> A very comprehensive and detailed work. A sourcebook that has
> been published since 1923. Volume 1 has tabular data. Volume
> 2 has narrative descriptions. Volume 3 lists degrees and subjects
> offered by colleges.

Furniss, W. Todd, ed. AMERICAN UNIVERSITIES AND COLLEGES. 11th ed.
Washington, D.C.: American Council on Education, 1973. xiv, 1,879 p.

> The most comprehensive and valuable guide to American institutions
> of higher education. Important data (history, admissions, programs,
> etc.) presented on each institution arranged by state.

Harris, Sherry S., ed. ACCREDITED INSTITUTIONS OF POSTSECONDARY
EDUCATION, 1980-1981. Washington, D.C.: American Council on Education,
1980. 392 p.

> A directory of accredited institutions, professionally accredited
> programs, and candidates for accreditation.

Lovejoy, Clarence E. LOVEJOY'S COLLEGE GUIDE. New York: Simon
and Schuster, 1979. 386 p.

> A popular, quick-reference college guide that has been published
> since 1940. Coverage is concise but important data are presented.
> There is a section on "Career Curricula and Special Programs."

THE NATIONAL FACULTY DIRECTORY, 1982. 2 vols. Detroit: Gale Research Co., 1981.

> About 496,400 college faculty members with their universities are
> listed. This work was first published in 1970.

YEARBOOK OF HIGHER EDUCATION, 1980-1981. 12th ed. Chicago:
Marquis Academic Media, 1980. x, 787 p.

> Part 1 is a directory of institutions of higher education with brief
> data. Part 2 contains statistics and resource information.

HISTORY OF AMERICAN EDUCATION

Bibliographies

Cordasco, Francesco, and Brickman, William W., eds. A BIBLIOGRAPHY OF AMERICAN EDUCATIONAL HISTORY. New York: AMS Press, 1975. 394 p.

Over three thousand annotated entries arranged both in categories and chronologically.

Herbst, Jurgen. THE HISTORY OF AMERICAN EDUCATION. American History Series. Edited by Arthur S. Link. Northbrook, III.: AHM Publishing Corp., 1973. xv, 153 p.

A very complete treatment of the subject from book and article sources. Listing is under the major historical subtopics. Not annotated.

General Works

Bailyn, Bernard. EDUCATION IN THE FORMING OF AMERICAN SOCIETY. Chapel Hill: University of North Carolina Press, 1960. xvi, 147 p.

A most significant work on early American educational history, one that has received much attention and is frequently quoted. First part of book comprises an essay on the many facets to the study of the history of learning. The second part consists of a bibliographical essay on American educational history.

Bayles, Ernest E., and Hook, Bruce L. GROWTH OF AMERICAN EDUCATIONAL THOUGHT AND PRACTICE. New York: Harper and Row, 1966. x, 305 p. Illus.

This work presents the philosophy as well as the history of American education.

Boone, Richard G. HISTORY OF EDUCATION IN THE UNITED STATES. International Education Series, vo. 2. Edited by William T. Harris. New York: D. Appleton, 1889. xv, 402 p.

The work covers the period from the earliest settlement up to publication date in the nineteenth century. It went through several reprintings up to 1914.

Brubacher, John S. A HISTORY OF THE PROBLEMS OF EDUCATION. 2d ed. New York: McGraw-Hill, 1966. 637 p.

A historical approach around persistent educational problems (e.g., aims, politics, religious issues, and teacher training).

Butler, Nicholas M. EDUCATION IN THE UNITED STATES. 2 vols. Albany: J.B. Lyon Co., 1900. Illus.

> A significant review of the status of U.S. education at all levels
> in the late nineteenth century. Prepared for the U.S. exhibit
> at Paris Exhibition of 1900. Butler was the long-time president
> of Columbia University (1901 to 1945). A one-volume edition
> of this work appeared in 1910 from American Book Company.

Butts, R. Freeman. PUBLIC EDUCATION IN THE UNITED STATES: FROM
REVOLUTION TO REFORM. New York: Holt, Rinehart and Winston, 1978.
xi, 436 p.

> The work begins in the late eighteenth century, when roots of
> the American public schools took form, and the story is carried
> into the 1970s. The focus is on the role of the public school as
> a sort of backlash to much of the recent revisionist writing on
> the subject.

Butts, R. Freeman, and Cremin, Lawrence A. A HISTORY OF EDUCATION
IN AMERICAN CULTURE. New York: Henry Holt, 1953. x, 628 p.

> A comprehensive view of the American education historical story
> (not just public and elementary and secondary schools). Much
> on the twentieth century is included. One of the most important
> works in the field published to 1953.

Calam, John. PARSONS AND PEDAGOGUES. New York: Columbia University Press, 1971. xi, 249 p.

> The work of the Society for the Propagation of the Gospel in
> Foreign Parts (established 1701), especially in the schooling of
> Negro, American Indian, and poor white children during the
> colonial period.

Church, Robert L. EDUCATION IN THE UNITED STATES: AN INTERPRETIVE
HISTORY. New York: Free Press, 1976. x, 489 p. Illus.

> This work begins with "Education in the New Nation, 1776-1820,"
> with no presentation of the colonial epoch. A special strength
> is the coverage of more recent educational history, from 1940 to
> 1975, a time of volatility and change.

Cohen, Sheldon. A HISTORY OF COLONIAL EDUCATION, 1607-1776.
New York: John Wiley, 1974. vii, 228 p.

> Chapters deal with European antecedents, and with New England,
> middle, and southern colonies' developments. A bibliographical
> essay and a time line of colonial education are included.

Cohen, Sol, ed. EDUCATION IN THE UNITED STATES: A DOCUMENTARY
HISTORY. 5 vols. New York: Random House, 1974.

> An array of more than one thousand documents going beyond the
> narrow subject of pedagogy to the many areas included under
> "American education."

Cremin, Lawrence A. AMERICAN EDUCATION: THE COLONIAL EXPER-
IENCE, 1607-1783. New York: Harper and Row, 1970. xvi, 688 p.

> The most complete treatment to date of the history of American
> education in the colonial period. Written by a distinguished
> scholar in educational history and president of Teachers College,
> Columbia University.

_____. AMERICAN EDUCATION: THE NATIONAL EXPERIENCE, 1783-1876.
New York: Harper and Row, 1980. xii, 607 p.

> The second volume of a comprehensive history of American educa-
> tion (see above). The time span encompassed is from the end of
> the Revolution to the period of southern Reconstruction. Awarded
> 1981 Pulitzer Prize for history.

_____. TRADITIONS OF AMERICAN EDUCATION. New York: Basic
Books, 1977. 172 p.

> How American educational institutions evolved through history and
> the part they have played in the national culture.

Cubberley, Ellwood P. PUBLIC EDUCATION IN THE UNITED STATES.
Boston: Houghton Mifflin, 1919. xxv, 517 p. Illus.

> A classic and important textbook by the dean of the School of
> Education at Stanford. Went through many editions through the
> 1940s. A limitation was its narrow view of education as essen-
> tially public schooling.

Curti, Merle E. THE SOCIAL IDEAS OF AMERICAN EDUCATORS. New York:
Charles Scribner's Sons, 1935. xxii, 613 p.

> The work and ideas of B.T. Washington, W.T. Harris, F.W.
> Parker, G.S. Hall, H. Mann, and Dewey.

Dabney, Charles W. UNIVERSAL EDUCATION IN THE SOUTH. 2 vols.
Chapel Hill: University of North Carolina Press, 1936. Illus.

> Volume 1 begins in colonial America and continues through the
> nineteenth century. Volume 2 presents the development of public
> education in the southern states into the 1930s.

Dexter, Edwin G. A HISTORY OF EDUCATION IN THE UNITED STATES.
New York: Macmillan, 1904. xxi, 656 p.

> A factualized account presented through topics. Author was dean
> at the University of Illinois and later commissioner of education
> in Puerto Rico. It was a popular text in normal schools and
> went through several editions by the 1920s.

Edwards, Newton, and Richey, Herman G. THE SCHOOL IN THE AMERICAN
SOCIAL ORDER. Boston: Houghton Mifflin, 1947. xiv, 880 p. Illus.

> Social, political, and economic factors are emphasized in this
> history from the colonial period to mid-twentieth century.

Finney, Ross L. THE AMERICAN PUBLIC SCHOOL. New York: Macmillan, 1921. xiv, 335 p. Illus.

Public schools are discussed. The history begins with colonial times and ends with conclusion of World War I, with the problems facing public schools in that latter period. European influences upon American schools are noted.

Good, H.G. A HISTORY OF AMERICAN EDUCATION. 2d ed. New York: Macmillan, 1962. x, 610 p.

A popular textbook in the history of American education. A strength is a section on issues that have been critical in the twentieth century.

Greer, Colin. THE GREAT SCHOOL LEGEND: A REVISIONIST INTERPRE-TATION OF AMERICAN PUBLIC EDUCATION. New York: Viking Press, 1972. 224 p.

A revisionist challenge to the accepted consensus history of American public schooling. Author claims that the school system has always failed the poor.

Hansen, Allen O. LIBERALISM AND AMERICAN EDUCATION IN THE EIGHTEENTH CENTURY. New York: Macmillan, 1926. xxv, 317 p.

Presents nine plans (Rush, Coram, Sullivan, Smith, duCourteil, Chip-man, Knox, duPont de Nemours, and Webster) for an American national system of education published between 1785 and 1800.

Kandel, I.L. AMERICAN EDUCATION IN THE TWENTIETH CENTURY. Cambridge, Mass.: Harvard University Press, 1957. 247 p.

Public school education in the first half of the twentieth century based upon the concept of educational opportunity for all. The last book of a distinguished scholar in the historical and compara-tive foundations of education.

Knight, Edgar W., ed. A DOCUMENTARY HISTORY OF EDUCATION IN THE SOUTH BEFORE 1860. 5 vols. Chapel Hill: University of North Carolina Press, 1949-53.

Development of education (private, public, elementary, secondary, and higher education) from the colonial to the pre-Civil War period. A very extensive presentation of documents.

_____. EDUCATION IN THE UNITED STATES. Rev. ed. Boston: Ginn, 1951. xvi, 753 p.

First published in 1929. Some emphasis on developments in the South.

_____. PUBLIC EDUCATION IN THE SOUTH. Boston: Ginn, 1922. xii, 482 p.

For some years, the definitive work on education in the South by the distinguished professor of education history at the University of North Carolina. The coverage is to the early twentieth century.

Krug, Edward A. SALIENT DATES IN AMERICAN EDUCATION, 1635-1964. New York: Harper and Row, 1966. ix, 159 p.

A brief chronology, with explanations, of thirty-five of the most significant events in American education from the establishment of the Boston Latin School to the Economic Opportunity Act of the Lyndon Johnson administration.

Meyer, Adolphe E. AN EDUCATIONAL HISTORY OF THE AMERICAN PEOPLE. 2d ed. New York: McGraw-Hill, 1967. 489 p. Illus.

European background of American education leading to colonial patterns. The truly American nature of institutions is stressed as the twentieth century arrived. First published in 1957.

Monroe, Paul. FOUNDING OF THE AMERICAN PUBLIC SCHOOL SYSTEM. New York: Macmillan, 1940. xiv, 520 p.

The coverage is to the Civil War period. One of the most complete accounts up to its time. A second volume was intended to bring the work up to the 1940s. It exists in microfilm from the typescript.

Moore, Ernest C. FIFTY YEARS OF AMERICAN EDUCATION: A SKETCH OF THE PROGRESS OF EDUCATION IN THE UNITED STATES FROM 1867 TO 1917. Boston: Ginn, 1917. 96 p.

A memento published for the fiftieth anniversary of Ginn and Company, publishers.

Nassaw, David. SCHOOLED TO ORDER: A SOCIAL HISTORY OF PUBLIC SCHOOLING IN THE UNITED STATES. New York: Oxford University Press, 1979. 320 p.

A revisionist history of American public schooling. It stresses periods when large numbers of nontraditional students came to school. Both the students and the institutions were transformed.

Noble, Stuart G. A HISTORY OF AMERICAN EDUCATION. New York: Rinehart, 1954. xx, 552 p. Illus.

A college textbook, first published in 1938 and popular through the 1960s, dividing the epochs of American educational history into five periods from "Colonial Beginnings" to "First Half of Twentieth Century." Much on curriculum and methodology through the years.

Potter, Robert E. THE STREAM OF AMERICAN EDUCATION. New York: American Book Co., 1967. vii, 552 p.

A well-documented chronological analysis of the currents in American education against the background of other social and historical events.

Pulliam, John D. HISTORY OF EDUCATION IN AMERICA. 2d ed. Columbus: Charles E. Merrill, 1976. 192 p.

History of American education presented within the framework of five periods. A chronological organization. Relationship is shown between the present and past educational issues.

Rippa, S. Alexander. EDUCATION IN A FREE SOCIETY: AN AMERICAN HISTORY. 2d ed. New York: David McKay, 1971. 392 p.

An educational history with much emphasis on developments since 1919.

Rudolph, Frederick, ed. ESSAYS ON EDUCATION IN THE EARLY REPUBLIC. Cambridge, Mass.: Harvard University Press, 1965. xxv, 389 p.

The proposals for a national school system put forth by Benjamin Rush, Noah Webster, Robert Coram, Simeon Doggett, Samuel Smith, Samuel Knox, and Amable-Louis-Rose de Lafitte duCourteil.

Slosson, Edwin E. THE AMERICAN SPIRIT IN EDUCATION: A CHRONICLE OF GREAT TEACHERS. Chronicles of America Series, vol. 33. New Haven, Conn.: Yale University Press, 1921. x, 309 p. Illus.

The work is a history of American education to the early twentieth century.

Thwing, Charles F. A HISTORY OF EDUCATION IN THE UNITED STATES SINCE THE CIVIL WAR. Boston: Houghton Mifflin, 1910. 348 p.

This work, by a president of Western Reserve University, and a Congregational Church minister, was long a standard reference on American educational history for the late nineteenth century. The emphasis is essentially on schooling below the collegiate level.

Tyack, David B., ed. TURNING POINTS IN AMERICAN EDUCATIONAL HISTORY. Waltham, Mass.: Blaisdell Publishing Co., 1967. xiv, 488 p.

A combination of essays by the author and reading selections arranged in eleven chapters on significant topics in educational history (e.g., "Becoming an American: The Education of the Immigrant").

Welter, Rush. POPULAR EDUCATION AND DEMOCRATIC THOUGHT IN AMERICA. New York: Columbia University Press, 1962. xiii, 473 p. Bibliog.

Colonial precedents, Jacksonian democracy, Civil War atmosphere, and several themes in twentieth-century thought through the 1930s.

HISTORY, TEACHING OF

Ballard, Martin, ed. NEW MOVEMENTS IN THE STUDY AND TEACHING OF HISTORY. Bloomington: Indiana University Press, 1970. vi, 234 p.

Essays by a number of authors, some noted historians (e.e., Arnold Toynbee), on the teaching of history.

Fink, Lawrence A. HONORS TEACHING IN AMERICAN HISTORY. New York: Teachers College Press, 1969. vii, 65 p.

Teaching history through source materials. Suggestions for giving history honors courses in a secondary school.

Hinsdale, Burke A. HOW TO STUDY AND TEACH HISTORY. New York: D. Appleton, 1894. xxiii, 346 p.

An early work on the subject by one who had served as president of Hiram College and superintendent of schools in Cleveland.

Johnson, Henry. TEACHING OF HISTORY IN ELEMENTARY AND SECONDARY SCHOOLS. New York: Macmillan, 1949. xv, 467 p.

This is the last edition of a classic work on the teaching of history which first appeared in 1908. A widely used college textbook in history methods' courses.

Roucek, Joseph S., ed. THE TEACHING OF HISTORY. New York: Philosophical Library, 1967. 282 p.

Sixteen essays on many aspects of the subject (from the regional, "African History," to the psychological, "Children's Historical Mindedness." Encompasses elementary, secondary, and higher education.

HOME ECONOMICS EDUCATION

Bevier, Isabel. HOME ECONOMICS IN EDUCATION. Philadelphia: J.B. Lippincott, 1924. 226 p.

A history of the home economics movement from the earliest times. The author was one of the pioneer writers on the teaching of home economics and it was her belief that it was a part of liberal education as well as a professional field.

Cooley, Anna M. DOMESTIC ART IN WOMAN'S EDUCATION. New York: Charles Scribner's Sons, 1911. xi, 274 p.

An early work designed for those studying the teaching of domestic science and its place in the school curriculum.

Fleck, Henrietta. TOWARD BETTER TEACHING OF HOME ECONOMICS. New York: Macmillan, 1974. viii, 470 p. Illus.

An up-to-date text reflecting changes in family life-style. A general treatment of all areas encompassed within the field under such items as group processes, methods, resources, creativity, and evaluation.

Lee, Jeanette A., and Dressel, Paul L. LIBERAL EDUCATION AND HOME ECONOMICS. New York: Teachers College, Columbia University, 1963. xii, 108 p.

The relationship of the home economics component to liberal education.

McGrath, Earl J., and Johnson, Jack T. THE CHANGING MISSION OF HOME ECONOMICS: A REPORT ON HOME ECONOMICS IN THE LAND GRANT COLLEGES AND STATE UNIVERSITIES. New York: Teachers College Press, 1968. xv, 121 p.

A modern statement on the role and scope of home economics in higher education.

Williamson, Maude, and Lyle, Mary S. HOMEMAKING EDUCATION IN THE HIGH SCHOOL. 4th ed. New York: Appleton-Century-Crofts, 1962. 351 p. Illus.

A very complete overview of the elements involved in home economics education, even a chapter on "Homemaking Education for Boys." The work, addressed to teachers in training as well as in service, was first published in 1934.

HUMANISTIC EDUCATION

Patterson, C.H. HUMANISTIC EDUCATION. Englewood Cliffs, N.J.: Prentice-Hall, 1973. xi, 239 p.

Goal of humanistic education is to develop self-actualizing people. The work of Maslow is cited. In historic survey, the author clears up the confusion between humanism in the Renaissance and modern usage of the term in educational practice.

Read, Donald A., and Simon, Sidney B., eds. HUMANISTIC EDUCATION SOURCEBOOK. Englewood Cliffs, N.J.: Prentice-Hall, 1975. xiv, 482 p.

Collected essays on several pertinent topics in humanistic education (e.g., "Teaching with Feeling," "Sensitivity Education").

Simpson, Elizabeth L. HUMANISTIC EDUCATION: AN INTERPRETATION. Cambridge, Mass.: Ballinger Publishing Co., 1976. xi, 328 p. Bibliog.

Roots of the movement are found in mental health education movement which began in 1930s. Hallmarks of humanistic education include the blending of emotion and behavior into positive values. The work was originally a Ford Foundation study.

Weller, Richard H., ed. HUMANISTIC EDUCATION: VISIONS AND REALITIES. Berkeley, Calif.: McCutchan Publishing Corp., 1977. xx, 377 p.

Papers from a symposium on humanistic education sponsored by Phi Delta Kappa in Greensboro, North Carolina, in January 1976.

IMMIGRANTS, EDUCATION OF

Berkson, Isaac B. THEORIES OF AMERICANIZATION: A CRITICAL STUDY. New York: Arno Press, 1969. viii, 226 p.

An early work on cultural pluralism. The author's concern was primarily with Jewish immigrants in New York City. First published by Teachers College, Columbia University, 1920.

Thompson, Frank V. SCHOOLING OF THE IMMIGRANT. New York: Harper, 1920. xxiv, 408 p.

Written when European immigrant children were being schooled in large numbers. Stresses the importance of the school in process of Americanization.

INDEPENDENT SCHOOLS

Heely, Allan V. WHY THE PRIVATE SCHOOL? New York: Harper, 1951. x, 208 p.

Observations on the role of the independent school by a headmaster of Lawrenceville School in New Jersey.

Kraushaar, Otto F. AMERICAN NONPUBLIC SCHOOLS: PATTERNS OF DIVERSITY. Baltimore: Johns Hopkins University Press, 1972. xv, 387 p.

A study of independent schools describing goals, finances, philosophies, faculty, leadership, and readiness for change. A general treatment though much emphasis on religious denominational schools.

McLachlan, James. AMERICAN BOARDING SCHOOLS: A HISTORICAL STUDY. New York: Charles Scribner's Sons, 1970. x, 381 p. Illus.

American private secondary schools presented historically in three groups: "Federalist" (e.g., New England academies), "Victorian" (e.g., St. Paul's), and "Progressive" (e.g., many more recent prep schools).

Prescott, Peter S. A WORLD OF OUR OWN: NOTES ON LIFE AND LEARNING IN A BOYS' PREPARATORY SCHOOL. New York: Coward-McCann, 1970. 400 p.

> The inner workings of an independent preparatory school (Choate). Not favorable toward such institutions.

Sargent, Porter E. THE HANDBOOK OF PRIVATE SCHOOLS. 62d ed. Boston: Porter Sargent Publishers, 1981. 1,448 p.

> An annual descriptive survey of American independent elementary and secondary schools. First appeared in 1914.

INDUSTRIAL ARTS EDUCATION

Barlow, Melvin L. HISTORY OF INDUSTRIAL EDUCATION IN THE UNITED STATES. Peoria, Ill.: Charles A. Bennett Co., 1967. 512 p. Illus.

> The most up-to-date history of the industrial arts movement in the United States. There is a chapter on "Women in Industrial Education."

Bennett, Charles A. HISTORY OF MANUAL AND INDUSTRIAL EDUCATION UP TO 1870. Peoria, Ill.: Industrial Arts Press, 1926. 461 p. Illus.

> The history begins with the roots of the movement before the Renaissance and continues to the development of art education in relation to industry.

_____. HISTORY OF MANUAL AND INDUSTRIAL EDUCATION, 1870-1917. Peoria, Ill.: Manual Arts Press, 1936. 566 p. Chronology. Illus.

> This is a continuation of the above volume. The vocational education movement is covered. The chronology is brought to the Smith-Hughes Vocational Education Act in 1917.

Bonser, Frederick G., and Russell, James E. INDUSTRIAL EDUCATION. New York: Teachers College, Columbia University, 1914. 50 p.

> Concern is with the fundamental values in industrial education. Bonser promoted the general shop concept and is known as the father of industrial arts education.

Fisher, Berenice M. INDUSTRIAL EDUCATION: AMERICAN IDEALS AND INSTITUTIONS. Madison: University of Wisconsin Press, 1967. xiii, 267 p.

> A work that explores the scope and structure of industrial education using sociology and history in the approach.

Silvius, G. Harold, and Curry, Estell H. TEACHING SUCCESSFULLY IN INDUSTRIAL EDUCATION. 2d ed. Bloomington, Ind.: McKnight and McKnight, 1967. xx, 645 p. Illus.

A very complete work which includes lesson planning, classroom management, safety, instructional material, and student evaluation.

Woodward, Calvin M. THE MANUAL TRAINING SCHOOL. Boston: D.C. Heath, 1887. vii, 366 p. Illus.

Essays on the origins and aims of manual training by one of the early leaders in the movement. A good historical source.

INNOVATIONS IN EDUCATION

de Grazia, Alfred, and Sohn, David A., eds. REVOLUTION IN TEACHING: NEW THEORY, TECHNOLOGY, AND CURRICULA. New York: Bantam Books, 1964. vi, 310 p. Illus.

Collection of essays on new developments, beginning with the early 1960s, that sought to revolutionize teaching.

Gross, Ronald, and Murphy, Judith. THE REVOLUTION IN THE SCHOOLS. New York: Harcourt, Brace and World, 1964. vi, 250 p.

Fifteen reports on controversial developments (team teaching, programmed instruction, nongraded classes, etc., by some noted authorities (e.g., Bruner, Skinner, Ashton-Warner, and Murphy).

Miles, Matthew B., ed. INNOVATIONS IN EDUCATION. New York: Teachers College Press, 1964. xii, 689 p. Illus.

Chapters by members of the Horace-Mann Lincoln Institute at Teachers College coming from a seminar on innovation and change. The papers represent the thinking of the early 1960s regarding the new departures in education.

Oettinger, Anthony G. RUN, COMPUTER, RUN: THE MYTHOLOGY OF EDUCATIONAL INNOVATION. Cambridge, Mass.: Harvard University Press, 1969. xx, 302 p. Illus.

Author claims that much of the application of computer technology to schools is fund oriented and politically oriented. He is less than enthusiastic about some methods in individualized instruction: without other forms of education, student may believe there always exists a correct answer to every question.

Rich, John M., ed. INNOVATIONS IN EDUCATION: REFORMERS AND THEIR CRITICS. New York: Allyn and Bacon, 1975. viii, 363 p.

Articles by educational innovators on most of the new departures of the 1960s and 1970s: accountability, career education, open classrooms, free schools, and others.

Toffler, Alvin, ed. LEARNING FOR TOMORROW: THE ROLE OF THE FUTURE IN EDUCATION. New York: Random House, 1974. xxvi, 421 p.

A collection of futurist projections by several authors. Much more than methodology is discussed.

Turner, Joseph. MAKING NEW SCHOOLS: THE LIBERATION OF LEARNING. New York: David McKay, 1971. xii, 302 p.

Explores reforms and innovations coming out of the 1960s at all levels of education.

JEWISH EDUCATION

Dushkin, Alexander N. JEWISH EDUCATION IN NEW YORK CITY. New York: Bureau of Jewish Education, 1918. ix, 596 p. Map. Illus.

A historical and statistical treatment of the Jewish educational establishment in New York. A map of the city shows the location of Jewish schools in 1918.

Gamoran, Emmanuel. CHANGING CONCEPTS IN JEWISH EDUCATION. 2 vols. New York: Macmillan, 1924. Reprint. New York: Arno Press, 1975. xiii, 239 p. viii, 186 p.

In two books bound as one volume. The first part deals with the historical background, the second with the principles of Jewish education.

Gartner, Lloyd P., ed. JEWISH EDUCATION IN THE UNITED STATES: A DOCUMENTARY HISTORY. New York: Teachers College Press, 1969. xv, 224 p.

Documents and selective writings from the engagement of a schoolmaster by Shearith Israel Congregation (New York) in 1760 to the Jewish day schools of the 1960s.

Winter, Nathan H. JEWISH EDUCATION IN A PLURALISTIC SOCIETY. New York: New York University Press, 1966. xvi, 262 p.

The work of Samson Benderly, a pioneer in American Jewish education, is presented. Essentially, his contribution was the introduction of supplementary, after-school programs.

JUNIOR HIGH SCHOOL

Briggs, Thomas H. THE JUNIOR HIGH SCHOOL. New York: Houghton Mifflin, 1920. x, 350 p.

One of the earliest works on the junior high school by a professor at Teachers College, Columbia University, who was influential in the development of such institutions.

Conant, James B. RECOMMENDATIONS FOR EDUCATION IN THE JUNIOR HIGH SCHOOL YEARS. Princeton, N.J.: Education Testing Service, 1960. 46 p.

A monograph presenting a critical examination of grades seven, eight, and nine by a leading educator of the time.

Gruhn, William T., and Douglass, Harl R. THE MODERN JUNIOR HIGH SCHOOL. 3d ed. New York: Ronald Press, 1971. vi, 424 p.

An up-to-date edition of a work first published in 1947. The organization is around four parts: history and philosophy, instruction, guidance, and organization.

Koos, Leonard V. THE JUNIOR HIGH SCHOOL. Enl. ed. New York: Ginn and Co., 1927. xiv, 506 p. Illus.

First published in 1920. The special functions, organizational pattern, program of studies, methodology, and physical plant of the junior high school are featured.

_____. JUNIOR HIGH SCHOOL TRENDS. New York: Harper, 1955. x, 171 p.

Reviews developments in the junior high school through the 1950s.

KINDERGARTEN

Baylor, Ruth M. ELIZABETH PALMER PEABODY: KINDERGARTEN PIONEER. Philadelphia: University of Pennsylvania Press, 1965. 228 p. Illus.

In 1860 Elizabeth Peabody (1804-94) opened the first English-speaking kindergarten in the United States.

Blow, Susan. LETTERS TO A MOTHER ON THE PHILOSOPHY OF FROEBEL. New York: D. Appleton, 1899. xix, 311 p. Illus.

An explanation of the ideas of Friedrich Froebel, founder of the kindergarten, written by one of the leaders of the kindergarten movement in the United States.

Cohen, Dorothy H., and Rudolph, Marguerita. KINDGARTEN AND EARLY SCHOOLING. Englewood Cliffs, N.J.: Prentice-Hall, 1977. xv, 432 p. Illus.

This is a revised edition of an earlier work, KINDERGARTEN: A YEAR OF LEARNING (1964), by the same authors. There is a chapter on the importance of parents in early childhood education. There are suggestions for activities in the several curriculum areas.

Headley, Neith E. FOSTER AND HEADLEY'S EDUCATION IN THE KINDER-GARTEN. 4th ed. New York: American Book Co., 1966. xii, 564 p. Illus.

A revision of a classic text first published in 1936. An overview
of the learning areas, records and reports, and background information on five-year olds. "Readiness for First-Grade Living" is
the final chapter.

Kraus-Boelte, Maria, and Kraus, John. THE KINDERGARTEN GUIDE: AN
ILLUSTRATED HANDBOOK DESIGNED FOR THE SELF-INSTRUCTION OF
KINDERGARTNERS, MOTHERS AND NURSES. 2 vols. New York: E.
Steiger, 1882. Illus.

Mrs. Kraus had worked with the kindergarten in England for
several years, and with her husband organized the Normal Training Kindergarten in New York in 1873.

Mann, Mary, and Peabody, Elizabeth P. MORAL CULTURE OF INFANCY
AND KINDERGARTEN GUIDE. Boston: T.O.P. Burnham, 1863. v, 10 p.

The earliest publication in America on the kingergarten.

Ramsey, Marjorie E., and Bayless, Kathleen M. KINDERGARTEN: PROGRAMS
AND PRACTICES. St. Louis: C.V. Mosby, 1980. xiii, 320 p. Appendixes,
illus.

An attractive and comprehensive handbook for kindergarten teachers.
Appendixes include forms, books, and other source materials.

LEARNING DISABILITIES

Brueckner, Leo J., and Bond, Guy L. THE DIAGNOSIS AND TREATMENT
OF LEARNING DISABILITIES. New York: Appleton-Century-Crofts, 1955.
ix, 424 p. Illus.

Overview of the nature and diagnoses of learning problems. Curriculum areas emphasized are reading, spelling, language, handwriting, and arithmetic.

Goodman, Libby, and Mann, Lester. LEARNING DISABILITIES IN THE
SECONDARY SCHOOL: ISSUES AND PRACTICES. New York: Grune and
Stratton, 1976. ix, 256 p. Bibliog.

Identification of learning troubles and suggested program for
remediation.

Lynn, Roa, et al. LEARNING DISABILITIES: AN OVERVIEW OF THEORIES,
APPROACHES, AND POLITICS. New York: Free Press, 1979. xii, 195 p.
Illus.

Much of the book is based upon interviews. Author suffered from
dyslexia. An important chapter is "The LD (learning disabilities)
Establishment."

LEGAL EDUCATION

Allen, Francis A. LAW, INTELLECT AND EDUCATION. Ann Arbor: University of Michigan Press, 1979. viii, 123 p.

> Papers on several aspects of legal education (e.g., "The New Anti-Intellectualism in American Legal Education").

Epstein, Elliot, et al. BARRON'S GUIDE TO LAW SCHOOLS. Woodbury, N.Y.: Barron's Educational Series, 1978. vi, 212 p.

> Concise descriptions of over 160 American law schools. First published in 1967.

Haber, Donald, and Cohen, Julius, eds. THE LAW SCHOOL OF TOMORROW: THE PROJECTION OF AN IDEAL. New Brunswick, N.J.: Rutgers University Press, 1968. 240 p.

> Seminar papers delivered in 1966 at the opening of a new building at Rutgers Law School. Robert M. Hutchins, former chancellor, University of Chicago, was one of the contributors.

Johnson, William R. SCHOOLED LAWYERS: A STUDY IN THE CLASH OF PROFESSIONAL CULTURES. New York: New York University Press, 1978. xvii, 215 p. Illus.

> A study of the development of legal education in the United States from the early nineteenth century.

LYCEUM MOVEMENT

Bode, Carl. THE AMERICAN LYCEUM: TOWN MEETING OF THE MIND. Carbondale: Southern Illinois University Press, 1968. xii, 275 p.

> The pre-Civil War lyceum movement, an early model of adult education, is described in detail.

Holbrook, Josiah. AMERICAN LYCEUM OR SOCIETY FOR THE IMPROVEMENT OF SCHOOLS AND DIFFUSION OF USEFUL KNOWLEDGE. Boston: Perkins and Marvin, 1829. 24 p.

> The basic work on the American lyceum movement by its founder. Holbrook was active in popularizing knowledge through lectures in towns and villages.

Mead, David. YANKEE ELOQUENCE IN THE MIDDLE WEST: THE OHIO LYCEUM, 1850-1870. East Lansing: Michigan State College Press, 1951. viii, 273 p.

> The popular lecture series began in New England in the 1820s and spread to the Midwest by the 1950s. Here the extent of the movement in Ohio is examined.

MAGNET SCHOOLS

Estes, Nolan, and Waldrip, Donald R. MAGNET SCHOOLS: LEGAL AND PRACTICAL IMPLICATIONS. Piscataway, N.J.: New Century Education Corp., 1978. 149 p. Illus.

> Addresses made at the first international conference on magnet schools held in 1977 in Dallas.

Missal, Gerald E., ed. SCHOOLS AND PROGRAMS OF CHOICE: VOLUNTARY DESEGREGATION IN MASSACHUSETTS. Boston: Massachusetts Department of Education, 1977. 86 p. Illus.

> A description of the magnet school program in Boston from its beginnings in 1969.

MATHEMATICS, TEACHING OF

Butler, Charles, et al. TEACHING OF SECONDARY MATHEMATICS. 5th ed. New York: McGraw-Hill, 1970. vi, 597 p. Illus.

> A widely used text (since 1941) made current to reflect newer methodology. The second part of the text deals with the teaching of selected topics (e.g., trigonometry, calculus, probability).

Cajori, Florian. THE TEACHING AND HISTORY OF MATHEMATICS IN THE UNITED STATES. U.S. Bureau of Education Circular of Information, no. 8. Washington, D.C.: Government Printing Office, 1890. 400 p.

> Author was the first American professor of the history of mathematics. The work includes a list of mathematics textbooks printed in the United States up to 1890.

Copeland, Richard W. MATHEMATICS AND THE ELEMENTARY TEACHER. 2d ed. Philadelphia: W.B. Saunders, 1972. ix, 336 p. Illus.

> The learning theories of Bruner, as applied to quantitative learning.

Grossnickle, Foster E., and Brueckner, Leo J. DISCOVERING MEANINGS IN ELEMENTARY SCHOOL MATHEMATICS. 4th ed. New York: Holt, Rinehart and Winston, 1963. x, 468 p. Illus.

> On the study and teaching of arithmetic. These two authors first published in the field in 1947. This book reflects the work of the school mathematics study group--"modern mathematics."

MEDICAL EDUCATION

Cordasco, Francesco, with Alloway, David N., eds. MEDICAL EDUCATION IN THE UNITED STATES: A GUIDE TO INFORMATION SERVICES. Education Information Guide Series, vol. 8. Detroit: Gale Research Co., 1980. xx, 393 p.

> Books and periodicals covering a wide scope in American medical education. References in biography, health policies, hospitals, as well as in history of medicine and medical education are included. A list of medical schools and biomedical and related journals are among the features. Some annotations.

Davis, Nathan S. HISTORY OF MEDICAL EDUCATION AND INSTITUTIONS IN THE UNITED STATES. Chicago: S.C. Griggs, 1851. x, 228 p.

> An early history of medical education by the father of the American Medical Association. The treatment is from the colonial period to 1850.

Flexner, Abraham. MEDICAL EDUCATION IN THE UNITED STATES AND CANADA. New York: Arno Press, 1972. xvii, 346 p.

> A reprint of the significant Flexner Report, first published in 1910, which brought about a fundamental transformation in medical education.

Kaufman, Martin. AMERICAN MEDICAL EDUCATION: THE FORMATIVE YEARS, 1765-1919. Westport, Conn.: Greenwood Press, 1976. x, 210 p.

> The schooling given to physicians and the practice of medicine in the years before the Flexner reforms (see entry above).

Norwood, William F. MEDICAL EDUCATION IN THE UNITED STATES BEFORE THE CIVIL WAR. Philadelphia: University of Pennsylvania Press, 1944. xvi, 487 p.

> A study of the rise and progress of medical instruction in America from the colonial days up to the 1860s.

METHODOLOGY, PRINCIPLES OF TEACHING

Nineteenth Century

Alcott, William A. A WORD TO TEACHERS: OR, TWO DAYS IN A PRIMARY SCHOOL. Boston: Allen and Ticknor, 1833. xvi, 84 p.

> Author was a Connecticut schoolmaster. Book is divided into two parts, "The Girls' School" and "The Boys' School," and relates the actual work of two days in a school in Hartford. The work was intended for "female teachers" of primary schools.

Baldwin, Joseph. ART OF SCHOOL MANAGEMENT. New York: D. Appleton, 1881. xiii, 504 p.

> A text for normal school students and a reference for beginning teachers.

Fowle, William B. THE TEACHERS' INSTITUTE: OR, FAMILIAR HINTS FOR YOUNG TEACHERS. Boston: William B. Fowle, 1847. ix, 258 p.

> Each of the common branch subjects is treated. The author had been a teacher in Boston for twenty-one years. This work grew out of lectures given at teachers' institutes.

Hall, Samuel R. LECTURES ON SCHOOL-KEEPING. Boston: Richardson, Lord, and Holbrook, 1829. xi, 135 p.

> The first American treatise on teaching written in English. Hall opened a normal school in Concord, Vermont, in 1823, and his lectures were the basis for this work.

Hewett, Edwin C. A TREATISE ON PEDAGOGY FOR YOUNG TEACHERS. New York: American Book Co., 1884. 228 p.

> Author states that it is not a book of methods (but some methodology is found), but a presentation of the principles that underlie methods. By the president of Illinois State Normal University.

McMurry, Charles A., and Frank, M. THE METHOD OF THE RECITATION. Bloomington, Ill.: Public School Publishing Co., 1897. 319 p.

> Based on inductive-deductive thought processes and on the teaching of Herbart, the German educationist. Several editions of this work appeared to 1916.

Northend, Charles. THE TEACHER AND THE PARENT: A TREATISE UPON COMMON-SCHOOL EDUCATION. Boston: Jenks, Hickling and Swan, 1853. x, 327 p.

> Contains practical suggestions on school procedures for teachers. It also has a message for parents.

Page, David P. THEORY AND PRACTICE OF TEACHING: OR, THE MOTIVES AND METHODS OF GOOD SCHOOL-KEEPING. Syracuse, N.Y.: Hall and Dickson, 1847. 349 p.

> The first principal of the State Normal School at Albany, New York, was the author. It was the authoritative work on the principles of teaching for many years in the nineteenth century.

Parker, Francis W. NOTES OF TALKS ON TEACHING. New York: E.L. Kellogg and Co., 1883. xxi, 182 p.

> Talks give by Colonel Parker at Martha's Vineyard summer institute in 1882. His methodology stressed the cultivation of freedom and informality in the classroom. The author was later superintendent of schools in Quincy, Massachusetts, and principal of Cook County Normal School in Chicago.

Potter, Alonzo, and Emerson, George B. THE SCHOOL AND THE SCHOOLMASTER. New York: Harper and Brothers, 1842. 552 p. Illus.

A popular manual for teachers and administrators. Part 1 deals
with education in general and, in particular, common schools
are treated. Part 2 deals with the management of schools.

Raub, Albert N. SCHOOL MANAGEMENT: INCLUDING A FULL DISCUS-
SION OF SCHOOL ECONOMY, SCHOOL ETHICS, SCHOOL GOVERNMENT
AND THE PROFESSIONAL RELATIONS OF THE TEACHER. Philadelphia:
Raub and Co., 1882. 285 p.

Author believed that teaching was a science based upon principles
firmly fixed.

Twentieth Century to 1940

Bagley, William C. CLASSROOM MANAGEMENT: ITS PRINCIPLES AND
TECHNIQUES. New York: Macmillan, 1907. xvii, 322 p.

Presents routines necessary for the teacher (beginning with the
first day of school). The book also includes instructional methods,
professional ethics, and other practical items especially for a beginning teacher.

Boone, Richard G. SCIENCE OF EDUCATION. New York: Charles Scribner's
Sons, 1904. xiii, 407 p.

Education proceeds under some generally accepted systematized
of knowledge. Author had been a superintendent of schools, the
principal of a normal school in Michigan, and professor of education at the University of California.

Charters, Werrett W. TEACHING THE COMMON BRANCHES: A TEXTBOOK
FOR TEACHERS IN RURAL AND GRADED SCHOOLS. Rev. ed. Boston:
Houghton Mifflin, 1917. x, 369 p.

Teaching methods for all elementary school subjects. Work was
first published in 1913, a time when there was attention given to
improvement of rural school teaching.

Dutton, Samuel T. SCHOOL MANAGEMENT: PRACTICAL SUGGESTIONS
CONCERNING THE CONDUCT AND LIFE OF THE SCHOOL. New York:
Charles Scribner's Sons, 1903. xv, 278 p.

The emphasis on school keeping continues into the early twentieth
century. The author had been a superintendent of schools and
later a professor of school administration at Teachers College,
Columbia University.

Kilpatrick, William H. FOUNDATION OF METHOD: INFORMAL TALKS
ON TEACHING. New York: Macmillan, 1925. xi, 388 p. Illus.

The author, a leader in the progressive education movement,
writes of purposeful schoolroom activities, especially the project
method.

McMurry, Charles A. THE ELEMENTS OF GENERAL METHOD, BASED ON THE PRINCIPLES OF HERBART. Rev. ed. New York: Macmillan, 1903. 331 p.

> The aims of education, values of studies, and factors of interest correlation, induction, and apperception form the content. The work was first published in 1892.

Rice, Joseph M. SCIENTIFIC MANAGEMENT IN EDUCATION. New York: Hinds, Noble and Eldredge, 1913. xxi, 282 p.

> The principles of teaching along the lines of the new "science" of education. Rice (1857-1934), a physician and writer on education, was an early proponent of the·scientific method in educational practice and research.

Since 1940

Bayles, Ernest E. THE THEORY AND PRACTICE OF TEACHING. New York: Harper and Brothers, 1950. x, 362 p.

> General theory and practice in teaching at all levels, from elementary school to university. Psychological emphasis on the Gestalt--the whole student goes to school.

Burton, William H. THE GUIDANCE OF LEARNING ACTIVITIES. New York: D. Appleton-Century, 1944. xiv, 601 p.

> Teaching principles based upon the psychological principles of learning. The author taught the principles of teaching at Harvard Graduate School of Education from 1939 to 1955, and this was his principal work.

Davis, Robert H., et al. LEARNING SYSTEM DESIGN: AN APPROACH TO THE IMPROVEMENT OF INSTRUCTION. New York: McGraw-Hill, 1974. x, 342 p.

> Describes a systematic approach to teaching based upon learning systems designs used in industry and the military. Text applies to a wide range of instructional modes, from the lecture to the newest forms of instructional technology.

Duke, Daniel L., ed. CLASSROOM MANAGEMENT. 78th Yearbook, National Society for the Study of Education. Chicago: University of Chicago Press, 1971. xxi, 447 p.

> A collection of thirteen papers on one of the oldest topics of concern in schooling. Half of the essays are by authors who are identified with educational psychology. Classroom management is defined as the procedure necessary to maintain an environment in which teaching and learning can take place.

Haskew, Laurence D. THIS IS TEACHING: AN INTRODUCTION TO EDU-
CATION IN AMERICA. New York: Scott, Foresman, 1956. xv, 336 p.
Illus.

> An introduction to education textbook that has much on what
> teachers and learners do in the classroom.

Haugh, John B., and Duncan, James K. TEACHING: DESCRIPTION AND
ANALYSIS. Reading, Mass.: Addison-Wesley, 1970. xv, 445 p. Illus.

> Teaching as a rational, humane, and professional activity. The
> principal divisions of the work are curriculum planning, instruction,
> and evaluation.

Joyce, Bruce, and Weil, Marsha. MODELS OF TEACHING. 2d ed. Englewood Cliffs, N.J.: Prentice-Hall, 1980. xiv, 499 p.

> Alternative patterns of teaching are described. Four models are
> presented as approaches to teaching. "A book for the present
> and for the future," the preface states.

Kelner, Bernard G. HOW TO TEACH IN THE ELEMENTARY SCHOOL. New
York: McGraw-Hill, 1958. 343 p.

> A comprehensive treatment of teaching methods used in the late
> 1950s in elementary schools. Designed for the student in training
> and the beginning teacher.

Rivlin, Harry N. TEACHING ADOLESCENTS IN SECONDARY SCHOOLS:
THE PRINCIPLES OF EFFECTIVE TEACHING IN JUNIOR AND SENIOR HIGH
SCHOOLS. New York: Appleton-Century-Crofts, 1948. xi, 516 p.

> Secondary school teaching presenting the "new" methods of the
> late 1940s.

MIDDLE SCHOOLS

Kindred, Leslie, et al. THE INTERMEDIATE SCHOOL. Englewood Cliffs,
N.J.: Prentice-Hall, 1968. viii, 531 p. Illus.

> An overview of the characteristics of the intermediate or middle
> school, which began in the 1960s to replace the junior high
> school.

Moss, Theodore C. MIDDLE SCHOOL. Boston: Houghton Mifflin, 1969.
xiv, 283 p. Illus.

> The evolution of the movement is presented and several chapters
> deal with curriculum areas.

Popper, Samuel H. THE AMERICAN MIDDLE SCHOOL: AN ORGANIZATION-
AL ANALYSIS. Waltham, Mass.: Blaisdell, 1967. xxii, 378 p. Illus.

One of the first works on the middle school organization in which there is much content on the historical background of the movement.

MINORITY GROUPS, EDUCATION OF

Weinberg, Meyer. A CHANCE TO LEARN: A HISTORY OF RACE AND EDUCATION IN THE UNITED STATES. New York: Cambridge University Press, 1977. viii, 471 p.

An examination of four minority groups: blacks, Chicanos, Puerto Ricans, and American Indians. The work covers elementary, secondary, and higher education from the nineteenth century to the present.

_____. THE EDUCATION OF THE MINORITY CHILD: A COMPREHENSIVE BIBLIOGRAPHY OF 10,000 SELECTED ENTRIES. Chicago: Integrated Education Associates, 1970. xii, 530 p.

Most American minorities are covered in this extensive bibliography. Not annotated.

MODERN LANGUAGES, TEACHING OF

Allen, Edward D., and Valette, Rebecca M. MODERN LANGUAGE CLASS-ROOM TECHNIQUES: A HANDBOOK. New York: Harcourt Brace Jovanovich, 1972. ix, 306 p.

For teachers of French, Spanish, and German. Practice rather than theory is emphasized.

Finocchiaro, Mary. TEACHING CHILDREN FOREIGN LANGUAGES. New York: McGraw-Hill, 1964. 210 p.

The strengths and limitations of several currently used approaches are discussed. Sample lessons are given for Italian, French, Spanish, German, Russian, and Hebrew.

Grittner, Frank M. LEARNING A SECOND LANGUAGE. 79th Yearbook, National Society for the Study of Education. Chicago: University of Chicago Press, 1980. xii, 241 p.

Eleven papers by various authors. Bilingual education is included. Historical background of foreign-language study is presented.

Pillet, Roger A. FOREIGN LANGUAGE STUDY: PERSPECTIVE AND PRO-SPECT. Chicago: University of Chicago Press, 1973. x, 194 p.

Author provides evidences of the need to develop a new philosophy of foreign-language study. The earlier bases for studying languages were undergoing changes by the 1970s.

MONTESSORI TEACHING

Kilpatrick, William H. THE MONTESSORI SYSTEM EXAMINED. Boston: Houghton Mifflin, 1914. viii, 71 p.

> The author found the Montessori methods wanting. This monograph had influence in setting back the time when Montessori teaching would spread to any large degree in the United States.

Lillard, Paula P. MONTESSORI, A MODERN APPROACH. New York: Schocken Books, 1972. xvii, 174 p. Illus.

> An introduction to the history and philosophy of the method and its application to teaching reading and writing.

Rambusch, Nancy M. LEARNING HOW TO LEARN: AN AMERICAN AP-PROACH TO MONTESSORI. Baltimore: Helicon Press, 1962. x, 180 p. Illus.

> Presents factors affecting the child, environment, and teacher. Contains a bibliography (1909-61) of Montessori methodology in English.

Ward, Florence E. THE MONTESSORI METHOD AND THE AMERICAN SCHOOL. New York: Macmillan, 1913. xvi, 243 p. Reprint. New York: Arno Press, 1971. Illus.

> An early supportive work of the system of schooling developed by Dr. Maria Montessori, the Italian physician and educator.

MORAL EDUCATION

Adler, Felix. THE MORAL INSTRUCTION OF CHILDREN. New York: D. Appleton, 1892. xiii, 270 p.

> The philosophic basis of the moral views of the founder of the Ethical Culture Society and the Ethical Culture School in New York City.

Hall, Robert T., and Davis, John U. MORAL EDUCATION IN THEORY AND PRACTICE. Buffalo: Prometheus Books, 1975. 189 p.

> By a philosopher and an educational psychologist. Case studies depicting moral problems are suggested for use with students.

McCluskey, Neil G. PUBLIC SCHOOLS AND MORAL EDUCATION: THE INFLUENCE OF HORACE MANN, WILLIAM TORREY HARRIS, AND JOHN DEWEY. New York: Columbia University Press, 1958. 315 p.

> A treatment of three strong voices (Mann, Harris, and Dewey) on moral education in public schools.

MUSIC EDUCATION

Damrosch, Frank H. SOME ESSENTIALS IN THE TEACHING OF MUSIC. New York: G. Schirmer, 1916. 101 p.

> An early work on the teaching of music by the supervisor of music in the public schools of New York from 1897 to 1905.

Dykema, Peter W., and Cundiff, Hannah H. SCHOOL MUSIC HANDBOOK: A GUIDE FOR MUSIC EDUCATORS. Boston: C.C. Birchard, 1955. xx, 669 p.

> Designed to meet the needs of classroom teachers as well as music teachers in elementary through high schools.

Gelineau, R. Phyllis. EXPERIENCES IN MUSIC. New York: McGraw-Hill, 1970. xv, 375 p.

> Basic procedures for teaching music from kindergarten through grade six. Songs, listening activities, music games, harmony, transparency masters for teaching aids, and rhythm band orchestration are featured.

Harris, Ernest H., ed. MUSIC EDUCATION: A GUIDE TO INFORMATION SOURCES. Education Information Guide Series, vol. 1. Detroit: Gale Research Co., 1978. xvii, 566 p.

> The large and broad field of music education is covered in annotations for books, monographs, catalogs, theses, and articles.

Land, Lois R., and Vaughan, Mary Ann. MUSIC IN TODAY'S CLASSROOM: CREATING, LISTENING, PERFORMING. New York: Harcourt Brace Jovanovich, 1973. viii, 200 p.

> Designed especially for a one-semester course in music education for prospective elementary teachers. Listening skills, composing, and creative musical involvement are features.

OPEN CLASSROOMS

Carswell, Evelyn M., and Roubinek, Darrel L. OPEN SESAME: A PRIMER IN OPEN EDUCATION. Pacific Palisades, Calif.: Goodyear Publishing Co., 1974. xiv, 287 p.

> Many ideas are presented along with humor and a good understandinf of children.

Hertzberg, Alvin, and Stone, Edward F. SCHOOLS ARE FOR CHILDREN: AN AMERICAN APPROACH TO THE OPEN CLASSROOM. New York: Schocken Books, 1971. 232 p. Illus.

After visits to many British open classrooms, the authors present how the method can be implemented in American schools.

Kohl, Herbert R. THE OPEN CLASSROOM: A PRACTICAL GUIDE TO A NEW WAY OF TEACHING. New York: New York Review Book, 1969. 116 p.

A brief work emphasizing some practical aspects of open education (e.g., beginning the school year, discipline).

Sabaroff, Rose, and Hanna, Maryann. THE OPEN CLASSROOM: A PRACTICAL GUIDE FOR THE TEACHER OF THE ELEMENTARY GRADES. Metuchen, N.J.: Scarecrow Press, 1976. iii, 145 p. Illus.

Concrete examples for the open classroom: suggested activities, games, and charts for recording progress.

Silberman, Charles E. THE OPEN CLASSROOM READER. New York: Random House, 1973. xxiii, 789 p. Illus.

Over seventy-five contributions on all aspects of open education including materials to use.

Stephens, Lillian S. GUIDE TO OPEN EDUCATION. New York: Holt, Rinehart and Winston, 1974. xii, 377 p. Illus.

Gives details of beginning and conducting an open classroom. The work also traces the historical and philosophical basis for open education.

Weber, Lillian. THE ENGLISH INFANT SCHOOL AND INFORMAL EDUCATION. New York: Prentice-Hall, 1971. xii, 276 p.

Although this book is about the English infant school, out of which came many of the ideas of open education, the author, in a final chapter, concentrates on the differences between American and English early childhood education.

PERIODICALS ON EDUCATION

Camp, William L., and Schwark, Bryan L. GUIDE TO PERIODICALS IN EDUCATION AND ITS ACADEMIC DISCIPLINES. 2d ed. Metuchen, N.J.: Scarecrow Press, 1975. x, 552 p.

Journals are alphabetically listed by major topic. Many data concerning each are included. Many regional and state periodicals, and those no longer published, are not included.

Hamilton, Malcolm C. EDUCATIONAL JOURNALS: A UNION LIST. Cambridge, Mass.: Gutman Library, Harvard Graduate School of Education, 1974. viii, 247 p.

Lists the Harvard holdings and those in thirty-four other libraries in the Northeast. The work also provides a history of American educational journals.

Krepel, Wayne J., and DuVall, Charles R. EDUCATION AND EDUCATION-RELATED SERIALS. Littleton, Colo.: Libraries Unlimited, 1977. 255 p.

An alphabetical descriptive listing of 510 current American journals on education.

Thursfield, Richard E. HENRY BARNARD'S AMERICAN JOURNAL OF EDUCATION. Baltimore: Johns Hopkins Press, 1945. 359 p.

Barnard (1811-1900) founded the AMERICAN JOURNAL OF EDUCATION, a great source of educational literature. It began in 1855 and ran to 1882.

PESTALOZZIAN PRACTICE IN AMERICA

Calkins, Norman A. PRIMARY OBJECT LESSONS FOR A GRADUATED COURSE OF DEVELOPMENT. New York: Harper and Brothers, 1861. x, 362 p. Illus.

The author interpreted the Pestalozzian movement through several books on object recognition. Calkins was an assistant superintendent of schools in New York and later an instructor at the Normal School of New York City (Hunter College).

Dearborn, Ned H. THE OSWEGO MOVEMENT IN AMERICAN EDUCATION. New York: Arno Press, 1969. ix, 189 p.

The work of Edward Sheldon (1823-97) at Oswego, New York, State Normal School, in interpreting the methodology of Pestalozzi. The book was first issued in 1925 by Teachers College, Columbia University.

Gutek, Gerald C. JOSEPH NEEF: THE AMERICANIZATION OF PESTALOZZI. University: University of Alabama Press, 1978. viii, 159 p.

Author compares the methodology of Pestalozzi with his American exponent Neef.

Monroe, Will S. HISTORY OF THE PESTALOZZIAN MOVEMENT IN THE UNITED STATES. New York: C.W. Bardeen, 1907. Reprint. New York: Arno Press, 1969. 244 p.

An account of such American proponents of Pestalozzi as Neef, Russell, Carter, Barnard, and Sheldon.

Neef, Joseph. SKETCH OF A PLAN AND METHOD OF EDUCATION. Philadelphia: 1808. 168 p.

Neef did much to introduce the thought and practice of the Swiss educator, Pestalozzi, to America. This volume is often considered the first pedagogical work published in English in the United States.

PHILOSOPHY OF EDUCATION

General Works

Baatz, Charles Albert, ed. THE PHILOSOPHY OF EDUCATION: A GUIDE TO INFORMATION SOURCES. Education Information Guide Series, vol. 6. Detroit: Gale Research Co., 1980. 344 p.

> An information guide for the beginner and specialist of the philosophy of education and its related fields.

Baatz, Charles Albert, and Baatz, Olga K., eds. THE PSYCHOLOGICAL FOUNDATIONS OF EDUCATION: A GUIDE TO INFORMATION SOURCES. Education Information Guide Series, vol. 10. Detroit: Gale Research Co., 1981. 441 p.

> A scientific study of human personality, on the congnitive, moral, emotional, and poietic actualization of the human person, and on the singular relationship of personality study and self-actualization to the education of every person.

Broudy, Harry S., et al., eds. PHILOSOPHY OF EDUCATION: AN ORGANIZATION OF TOPICS AND SELECTED SOURCES. Urbana: University of Illinois Press, 1967. xii, 287 p.

> An extensive annotated treatment of books and dissertations under various topics included in the philosophy of education. The organization of topics includes two factors: the types of educational problems (e.g., teaching-learning), and the sources of philosophical materials (e.g., philosophy of religion).

Brubacher, John S. MODERN PHILOSOPHIES OF EDUCATION. 4th ed. New York: McGraw-Hill, 1969. 393 p.

> A classic work since 1939. It consists of an introduction to a range of viewpoints in educational philosophy. The literature published since 1900 was heavily drawn upon.

Ozman, Howard, and Craver, Sam. PHILOSOPHICAL FOUNDATIONS OF EDUCATION. Columbus: Charles E. Merrill, 1976. xi, 239 p.

> An overview of idealism, realism, pragmatism, reconstructionism, behaviorism, existentialism, and the newer analytic movement and their relationships to education.

Smith, Christiana M., and Broudy, Harry S., eds. PHILOSOPHY OF EDUCATION: AN ORGANIZATION OF TOPICS AND SELECTED SOURCES. SUPPLEMENT, 1969. Urbana: University of Illinois Press, 1969. 139 p.

> A supplement to the 1967 volume edited by Broudy and others (see above).

Thwing, Charles F. WHAT EDUCATION HAS THE MOST WORTH? New York: Macmillan, 1924. x, 235 p.

A study in educational values, conditions, methods, forces, and results by a former president of Western Reserve University.

Essentialism

Bagley, William C. EDUCATION AND EMERGENT MAN: A THEORY OF EDUCATION WITH PARTICULAR APPLICATION TO PUBLIC EDUCATION IN THE UNITED STATES. New York: T. Nelson and Sons, 1934. xiv, 238 p.

A major theme is that tested and ordered experience should be the basis of school instruction. The author, an essentialist, was a critic of extreme tendencies in progressive education.

_____. THE EDUCATIVE PROCESS. New York: Macmillan, 1905. xix, 358 p.

The first work by a foremost essentialist in educational philosophy and practice. The principal function of the educative process is to transmit to each generation the experiences of the human race.

Demiashkevich, Michael J. AN INTRODUCTION TO THE PHILOSOPHY OF EDUCATION. New York: American Book Co., 1935. xiii, 440 p.

By a Russain-American who was an important proponent of the philosophy of essentialism in education.

Existentialism

Greene, Maxine. TEACHER AS STRANGER: EDUCATIONAL PHILOSOPHY FOR THE MODERN AGE. Belmont, Calif.: Wadsworth Publishing Co., 1973. 308 p. Illus.

An existentialist approach to the philosophy of education. The author urges teachers to "do" philosophy in confronting educational problems.

Perennialism

Johnston, Herbert. A PHILOSOPHY OF EDUCATION. New York: McGraw-Hill, 1963. 362 p. Illus.

The principal theme is that the development of virtues should constitute man's education, and the school should be concerned with that kind of knowledge. The work of Thomas Aquinas is cited.

Maritain, Jacques. THE EDUCATION OF MAN: EDUCATIONAL PHILOSOPHY. Garden City, N.Y.: Doubleday, 1962. 191 p.

An anthology of writings of Maritain in which he brings out the Christian-perennialist philosophy of education.

Pragmatism

Bayles, Ernest E. PRAGMATISM IN EDUCATION. New York: Harper and Row, 1966. x, 146 p.

> The principle behind progressive education, the philosophy of pragmatism, is applied here to educational practice.

Child, John L. EDUCATION AND THE PHILOSOPHY OF EXPERIMENTALISM. Foreword by William Kilpatrick. New York: Century, 1931. 264 p.

> The exposition of experimentalism as a philosophical creed for education.

Dewey, John. DEMOCRACY AND EDUCATION. New York: Macmillan, 1916. xiv, 434 p.

> Dewey's early and important work wherein he stated his philosophy of education. He connected the growth of democracy with the development of experimental methods.

Kilpatrick, William H. PHILOSOPHY OF EDUCATION. New York: Macmillan, 1951. x, 465 p.

> A comprehensive presentation of Kilpatrick's philosophy of the educative process. He was a prominent disciple of Dewey and did much to extend that philosopher's teachings to the elementary and secondary school classrooms.

Wynne, John P. PHILOSOPHIES OF EDUCATION FROM THE STANDPOINT OF THE PHILOSOPHY OF EXPERIMENTALISM. New York: Prentice-Hall, 1947. xiv, 427 p.

> Intended as a textbook, but also serves the general reader in clearly delineating the progressive philosophy of education.

Realism

Broudy, Harry S. BUILDING A PHILOSOPHY OF EDUCATION. New York: Prentice-Hall, 1954. 480 p.

> The author was an exponent of the classical realist viewpoint in philosophy of education.

Reconstructionism

Brameld, Theodore. PATTERNS OF EDUCATIONAL PHILOSOPHY: A DEMOCRATIC INTERPRETATION. Yonkers, N.Y.: World Book Co., 1950. xxiv, 824 p.

> A presentation of the educational philosophy of reconstructionism by one of its principal proponents.

_____. TOWARD A RECONSTRUCTED PHILOSOPHY OF EDUCATION.

New York: Dryden Press, 1956. xiv, 417 p.

> The work includes a dialog on reconstructionism and its critics.
> It also deals with how educational practice has retreated from
> the goals of progressivism.

Shimahara, Nobuo. EDUCATIONAL RECONSTRUCTION: PROMISE AND
CHALLENGE. Columbus: Charles E. Merrill, 1973. xi, 433 p.

> A collection of readings on the need for and approaches to a
> more radical pattern of educational direction.

PHYSICAL EDUCATION

Anderson, William G. LIGHT GYMNASTICS: A GUIDE TO SYSTEMATIC
INSTRUCTION IN PHYSICAL TRAINING. New York: E. Maynard, 1889.
234 p. Illus.

> A nineteenth-century work written at a time when more attention
> began to be paid to physical education (especially gymnastics) in
> the schools. Author was the organizer of the American Associa-
> tion for the Advancement of Physical Education.

Bancroft, Jessie H. GAMES FOR THE PLAYGROUND, HOME, SCHOOL AND
GYMNASIUM. Rev. ed. New York: Macmillan, 1967. ix, 685 p. Illus.

> Bancroft's GAMES is one of the most long-lasting (since 1909),
> useful publications in the field. Author was first American woman
> to publish a considerable amount of literature on physical educa-
> tion.

Daughtrey, Greyson. EFFECTIVE TEACHING IN PHYSICAL EDUCATION FOR
SECONDARY SCHOOLS. 2d ed. Philadelphia: W.B. Saunders, 1973. xii,
632 p. Illus.

> Primarily a methods text consolidating concepts from kinesiology,
> measurement, and curriculum. Seventy-five lesson plans in indivi-
> dual and team activities are included.

Gerber, Ellen W. INNOVATORS AND INSTITUTIONS IN PHYSICAL EDUCA-
TION. Philadelphia: Lea and Febiger, 1971. xvii, 452 p. Illus.

> A historical work dealing with individuals and institutions that
> have been influential in some important aspect of physical educa-
> tion. The scope covers from ancient days into the twentieth
> century.

Mackenzie, Marlin M. TOWARD A NEW CURRICULUM IN PHYSICAL EDU-
CATION. New York: McGraw-Hill, 1969. xiv, 203 p.

> A textbook but also a statement as to how physical education
> might be reconstructed. Among other things considered is more
> emphasis on kinesthetics.

Means, Richard K. A HISTORY OF HEALTH EDUCATION IN THE UNITED STATES. Philadelphia: Lea and Febiger, 1962. 412 p. Illus.

> The history includes physical, health, and recreational education.

Root, Nathaniel W.T. SCHOOL AMUSEMENT: OR, HOW TO MAKE THE SCHOOL INTERESTING. EMBRACING SIMPLE RULES FOR MILITARY AND GYMNASTIC EXERCISES. New York: A.S. Barnes, 1857. xvi, 225 p. Illus.

> An early work on physical education. The plates illustrate gymnastics and drilling.

Vannier, Maryhelen, and Gallahue, David L. TEACHING PHYSICAL EDUCATION IN ELEMENTARY SCHOOLS. 6th ed. Philadelphia: W.B. Saunders, 1978. xiii, 708 p. Illus.

> A well-known methods textbook with graded physical activities for children. Physical education for special education students is included.

Vannier, Maryhelen; Gallahue, David L.; and Fait, Hollis F. TEACHING PHYSICAL EDUCATION IN SECONDARY SCHOOLS. 4th ed. Philadelphia: W.B. Saunders, 1975. xvii, 580 p. Illus.

> The contribution that physical education can make in the schooling of adolescents. For physical education majors, beginning teachers, or graduate students in the field. All secondary school physical activities and sports are covered.

Weston, Arthur. THE MAKING OF AMERICAN PHYSICAL EDUCATION. New York: Appleton-Century-Crofts, 1962. xiv, 319 p.

> Five historical chapters and then forty-three selections from the writings of leaders in the field.

Williams, Jesse F. ADMINISTRATION OF HEALTH AND PHYSICAL EDUCATION. 6th ed. Philadelphia: W.B. Saunders, 1964. ix, 349 p. Illus.

> A work that has been almost a handbook on the subject since its first appearance in 1934. The author, one of the leaders in the field, adopted the educational philosophy of Dewey and Kilpatrick to the methodology of physical education.

PROFESSIONAL ASSOCIATIONS

Emerson, George B. HISTORY AND DESIGN OF THE AMERICAN INSTITUTE OF INSTRUCTION. Boston: Ticknor, Reed, and Fields, 1849. 12 p.

> The American Institute of Instruction, the first professional society of teachers, was established in 1830, largely through the efforts of Emerson.

NEA HANDBOOK, 1980-81. Washington, D.C.: National Education Association, 1980. 340 p.

>An annual listing of NEA data with state and local affiliations.

Wesley, Edgar B. NEA: THE FIRST HUNDRED YEARS. New York: Harper and Row, 1957. 419 p.

>Published on the occasion of the centennial of the largest professional association of educators, an organization largely responsible for building school-teaching as a profession.

PROGRAMMED INSTRUCTION

Fry, Edward. TEACHING MACHINES AND PROGRAMMED INSTRUCTION: AN INTRODUCTION TO AUTOINSTRUCTION. New York: McGraw-Hill, 1963. 244 p. Illus.

>Describes, explains, and pictures all major types of teaching machines to that date.

Lange, Phil, ed. PROGRAMMED LEARNING. 66th Yearbook, National Society for the Study of Education. Prepared by Committee on Programmed Instruction. Chicago: University of Chicago Press, 1967. xii, 334 p., cxiii.

>The book has three sections: foundations (antecedents), programs, and issues and problems.

Lumsdaine, Arthur A., and Glaser, Robert, eds. TEACHING MACHINES AND PROGRAMMED LEARNING. 2 vols. Washington, D.C.: National Education Association, 1960-65. Illus.

>A sourcebook of research reports and articles on teaching machines and programmed learning, beginning with a paper published by Sidney Pressey in 1926.

O'Day, Edward F., et al. PROGRAMMED INSTRUCTION: TECHNIQUES AND TRENDS. New York: Appleton-Century-Crofts, 1971. viii, 214 p. Illus.

>A basic work on programmed learning. Authors are from San Diego State College and research is based upon practices in junior and senior colleges and in a military installation.

Skinner, B.F. THE TECHNOLOGY OF TEACHING. New York: Appleton-Century-Crofts, 1968. ix, 271 p. Illus.

>A milestone in the history of programmed instruction and other aspects of the newer technology in education by a distinguished psychologist and one who was responsible for much of the early work in these areas.

PROGRESSIVE EDUCATION MOVEMENT

Aikin, Wilford. THE STORY OF THE EIGHT-YEAR STUDY. New York: Harper and Row, 1942. x, 158 p.

Conclusions and recommendations based on the Commission on the Relation of School and College, which started in 1933. Selected students were admitted to college without the traditional entrance requirements.

Bode, Boyd H. MODERN EDUCATIONAL THEORIES. New York: Macmillan, 1927. xiv, 351 p.

An early statement on the "newer" theories of education. Experience, democracy, scientific management of teaching, curriculum making, and other topics are discussed.

_____. PROGRESSIVE EDUCATION AT THE CROSSROADS. New York: Newson, 1938. 128 p.

Work by an early proponent of the progressive education movement. Bode is critical of some developments in its practice.

Cohen, Ronald D., and Mohl, Raymond. THE PARADOX OF PROGRESSIVE EDUCATION: THE GARY PLAN AND URBAN SCHOOLING. Port Washington, N.Y.: Kennikat Press, 1979. viii, 216 p.

The contradictions and tensions that developed in progressive education are examined. The Gary Plan was a platoon-school organization that originated in Gary, Indiana.

Counts, George S. DARE THE SCHOOL BUILD A NEW SOCIAL ORDER? New York: John Day, 1932. 56 p.

Counts originally raised this question in papers given before education societies. He pointed out a weakness of progressive education: that it had set forth no theory of social welfare.

Cremin, Lawrence A. THE TRANSFORMATION OF THE SCHOOL: PROGRESSIVISM IN AMERICAN EDUCATION, 1876-1957. New York: Alfred A. Knopf, 1961. xiv, 387 p. xxiv.

The work traces the rise of progressive education from its roots at the Centennial Exposition of 1876 to the demise of the movement (as an organization) in 1955.

Dewey, John. EXPERIENCE AND EDUCATION. New York: Macmillan, 1938. xvi, 116 p.

A look-back on progressive education: how it differed from traditional schooling and why some progressive educators failed in achieving their goal. Written when Dewey was nearly eighty.

Graham, Patricia A. PROGRESSIVE EDUCATION: FROM ARCADY TO ACADEME. New York: Teachers College Press, 1967. x, 193 p. Appendix.

The development of the progressive education movement with focus on the Progressive Education Association from its incorporation in 1931 to its demise in 1955. Appendix includes a bibliographical essay.

Kilpatrick, William H. EDUCATION FOR A CHANGING CIVILIZATION. New York: Macmillan, 1926. v, 143 p.

School curriculum and methods of teaching must be dynamic rather than static in the light of changing economic and social conditions. By a leading advocate of progressive education.

Rugg, Harold O., and Shumaker, Ann. THE CHILD-CENTERED SCHOOL: AN APPRAISAL OF THE NEW EDUCATION. New York: World Book, 1928. xiv, 359 p.

An early evaluation of progressive education. Criticism of such schools is given with conclusion that proof of their value rests in the cultivation of creativity.

Washburn, Carleton W. WHAT IS PROGRESSIVE EDUCATION? New York: John Day, 155 p.

An exposition of the principal characteristics of progressive education intended for parents "and others." It is contrasted with traditional schooling. Author was superintendent of schools in Winnetka, Illinois, and president of the Progressive Education Association.

Washburn, Carleton, and Marland, Sidney P., Jr. WINNETKA: THE HISTORY AND SIGNIFICANCE OF AN EDUCATIONAL EXPERIMENT. Englewood Cliffs, N.J.: Prentice-Hall, 1963. xiv, 402 p.

Story of an education innovation, the Winnetka Plan, in the 1920s and 1930s. The plan stressed self-instruction, group projects, and individual creativity.

PUBLIC RELATIONS

Bortner, Doyle M. PUBLIC RELATIONS FOR TEACHERS. New York: Simmons-Boardman Publishing Corp., 1959. 166 p. Bibliog.

Intended for a text in a graduate, teacher-training program.

Fine, Benjamin. EDUCATIONAL PUBLICITY. New York: Harpers, 1951. xi, 561 p.

A practical volume offering tested suggestions on publicity for educational institutions and organizations, by the then education editor of the NEW YORK TIMES.

Jones, James J., and Stout, Irving W. SCHOOL PUBLIC RELATIONS: ISSUES AND CASES. New York: G.P. Putnam's Sons, 1960. xii, 195 p.

> Cases of educational issues dealing with school boards and community groups.

Reeder, Ward G. AN INTRODUCTION TO PUBLIC-SCHOOL RELATIONS. Rev. ed. New York: Macmillan, 1953. 284 p. Illus.

> An early work on the subject (revision of 1937 edition) and a very comprehensive treatment. A handbook which still is useful in spite of its date.

RACIAL INTEGRATION, SEGREGATION OF SCHOOLS

Ashmore, Harry S. THE NEGRO AND THE SCHOOLS. 2d ed. Chapel Hill: University of North Carolina Press, 1954. xv, 239 p.

> The legal history of racial segregation in schools. Includes the full text of 1954 Supreme Court decision on segregation.

Mack, Raymond W., ed. OUR CHILDREN'S BURDEN: STUDIES OF DESEGREGATION IN NINE AMERICAN COMMUNITIES. New York: Random House, 1968. xiii, 473 p.

> The communities studied include Chicago, Los Angeles, and Savannah among smaller places, both urban and suburban.

Muse, Benjamin. TEN YEARS OF PRELUDE: THE STORY OF INTEGRATION SINCE THE SUPREME COURT'S 1954 DECISION. New York: Viking Press, 1964. ix, 308 p.

> Based upon the 1954 Brown decision and other cases. Comprehensive and fully documented.

Rist, Ray C., ed. DESEGREGATED SCHOOLS: APPRAISALS OF AN AMERICAN EXPERIMENT. New York: Academic Press, 1979. 264 p.

> The "Southern Experience" and the "Northern Experience" are among the parts of this book. A collection of writings on many phases of racial integration of schools since the 1954 Supreme Court Brown decision.

Sullivan, Neil V., and Stewart, Evelyn S. NOW IS THE TIME: INTEGRATION IN THE BERKELEY SCHOOLS. Bloomington: Indiana University Press, 1970. xvii, 205 p.

> Berkeley, California, in September 1968, became the first large American city to racially integrate its schools. The procedures and new programs for those schools are set forth.

Wilkinson, J. Harvie, III. FROM BROWN TO BAKKE: THE SUPREME COURT AND SCHOOL INTEGRATION, 1954-1978. New York: Oxford University Press, 1979. viii, 368 p.

An informative presentation of the several levels involved in integration cases: courts, school boards, classrooms, and agitators.

READING, TEACHING OF

Betts, Emmett A. FOUNDATIONS OF READING INSTRUCTION, WITH EMPHASIS ON DIFFERENTIATED GUIDANCE. New York: American Book Co., 1957. 757 p. Illus.

The author has supported the cause of reading instruction based upon the needs of children rather than a rigid curriculum. From the 1930s, he has been a leader in the teaching of reading.

Briggs, Thomas H., and Coffman, Lotus D. READING IN PUBLIC SCHOOLS. Chicago: Row, Peterson, 1908. 274 p.

One of the first textbooks on reading instruction.

Chall, Jeanne S. LEARNING TO READ: THE GREAT DEBATE. New York: McGraw-Hill, 1967. 372 p. Illus.

Fifty years (1910–60) of research was evaluated and much of it found wanting. An important work on the teaching of reading.

Fry, Edward B. ELEMENTARY READING INSTRUCTION. New York: McGraw-Hill, 1977. x, 339 p. Illus.

Part 1 covers the basis of reading (with a detailed chapter on phonics); part 2, readiness and methods; and part 3, evaluation.

Gates, Arthur I. THE IMPROVEMENT OF READING: A PROGRAM OF DIAGNOSTIC AND REMEDIAL METHODS. 3d ed. New York: Macmillan, 1951. xix, 657 p. Illus.

The author, an educational psychologist, brought a factual foundation to the teaching of reading. This work first appeared in 1927.

Harris, Albert J., and Sipay, Edward R. HOW TO INCREASE READING ABILITY: A GUIDE TO DEVELOPMENTAL AND REMEDIAL METHODS. 6th ed. New York: David McKay, 1975. xix, 713 p. Illus.

A classic text in the field since 1940. Revised to include the latest research.

_____. HOW TO TEACH READING: A COMPETENCY-BASED PROGRAM. New York: Longman, 1979. xviii, 631 p. Illus.

A competency-based course is organized into segments called modules. Each module has learning objectives and an instructional pattern.

Huey, Edmund B. PSYCHOLOGY AND PEDAGOGY OF READING. New York: Macmillan, 1908. xvi, 469 p. Illus.

The history of the teaching of reading and an early work on
methodology in reading instruction. The work was republished
up until 1924.

Kohl, Herbert R. READING: HOW TO. New York: E.P. Dutton, 1973.
xiii, 224 p.

Author claims there isn't a reading problem, only problem teachers
and problem schools. Techniques are presented to help teachers
reach all students.

Roswell, Florence G., and Natchez, Gladys. READING DISABILITY: A
HUMAN APPROACH TO LEARNING. 3d ed. New York: Basic Books,
1977. xiv, 306 p.

Methods for diagnosing various kinds of reading problems and remedial techniques to use.

Schantz, Marie E., and Brunner, Joseph F., eds. READING IN AMERICAN
SCHOOLS: A GUIDE TO INFORMATION SOURCES. Education Information
Guide Series, vol. 5. Detroit: Gale Research Co., 1980. xii, 266 p.

Annotated listing of books and periodical references in a number
of subtopics. A noteworthy feature is a listing by decade (the
"1930s") of published research.

RELIGION AND EDUCATION

Bower, William C. CHURCH AND STATE IN EDUCATION. Chicago: University of Chicago Press, 1944. vi, 103 p.

The problem of the historic relation of church and state dealt
with and solution offered for the church and school problem.

Brickman, William W., and Lehrer, Stanley, eds. RELIGION, GOVERNMENT,
AND EDUCATION. New York: Society for the Advancement of Education,
1961. 292 p.

Ten essays on several controversial areas of church-school relations
with documents. A chronology of American church-state relations
is provided.

Butts, R. Freeman. THE AMERICAN TRADITION IN RELIGION AND EDU-
CATION. Boston: Beacon Press, 1950. xiv, 230 p.

The long struggle for separation of church and state (and education)
in America.

Drouin, Edmond G., ed. THE SCHOOL QUESTION: A BIBLIOGRAPHY ON
CHURCH-STATE RELATIONSHIPS IN AMERICAN EDUCATION. Washington,
D.C.: Catholic University of America, 1963. xxi, 261 p.

Bibliography covers only the years 1940 to 1960. The issue of church and state is subdivided into pertinent subtopics. Books, pamphlets, periodicals, court case material, and dissertations are included. For most book listings, references to published reviews are given.

Duker, Sam. THE PUBLIC SCHOOLS AND RELIGION: THE LEGAL CONTEXT. New York: Harper and Row, 1966. xiii, 238 p.

Contains portions of important Supreme Court decisions on religion and public schools, including the important 1963 Abington v. Schempp case outlawing prayers and Bible reading.

Dunn, William K. WHAT HAPPENED TO RELIGIOUS EDUCATION? Baltimore: Johns Hopkins Press, 1958. 346 p.

A study of the decline of religious teaching in public elementary schools from 1776 to 1861.

Hay, Clyde L. THE BLIND SPOT IN AMERICAN PUBLIC EDUCATION. New York: Macmillan, 1950. xviii, 110 p.

A plea for provisions of religious instruction in public schools. The work appeared thirteen years before the 1963 Supreme Court decision.

Kliebard, Herbert M., ed. RELIGION AND EDUCATION IN AMERICA: A DOCUMENTARY HISTORY. Scranton, Pa.: International Textbook Co., 1969. x, 251 p.

Relationship between education and religion with citations from pertinent documents.

Stowe, Calvin E. THE RELIGIOUS ELEMENT IN EDUCATION. Boston: W.D. Tecknor, 1844. 34 p.

An address before the American Institute of Education by a strong supporter of public education and the husband of Harriet Beecher Stowe.

Swomley, John M., Jr. RELIGION, THE STATE AND THE SCHOOLS. New York: Pegasus, 1968. ix, 220 p.

The church-state situation in the United States with several practices and proposals concerning the teaching of religion.

RESEARCH IN EDUCATION

Brickman, William W. RESEARCH IN EDUCATIONAL HISTORY. Norwood, Pa.: Norwood Editions, 1973. ix, 254 p.

A reprint of Professor Brickman's 1949 work, GUIDE TO RESEARCH IN EDUCATIONAL HISTORY.

COMPLETE GUIDE AND INDEX TO ERIC REPORTS THRU DECEMBER 1969. Englewood Cliffs, N.J.: Prentice-Hall, 1970. 1,338 p.

The Educational Resources Information Center (ERIC) of the U.S. Office of Education indexes articles, government publications, conference reports, and other items, in the field of education.

Grant, W. Vance, and Lind, C. George. DIGEST OF EDUCATION STATISTICS, 1979. Washington, D.C.: National Center for Educational Statistics, 1979. xvii, 216 p.

Published more or less yearly since 1962.

Hamilton, Malcom C. DIRECTORY OF EDUCATIONAL STATISTICS: A GUIDE TO SOURCES. Ann Arbor, Mich.: Pierian Press, 1974. xiv, 71 p.

Sources of educational statistics, both current and historical, on a wide range of topics.

Manheim, Theodore, et al. SOURCES IN EDUCATIONAL RESEARCH: A SELECTED AND ANNOTATED BIBLIOGRAPHY. Detroit: Wayne State University Press, 1969. viii, 20 p.

A handbook to the sources of research literature available in the fields of education. The volume has ten parts, each paged separately.

RESOURCES IN EDUCATION. Washington, D.C.: Educational Resources Information Center, 1975-- .

Formerly known as RESEARCH IN EDUCATION and also referred to as ERIC RESOURCES IN EDUCATION. An abstract that lists articles, government publications, conference reports, and other items, in education.

Tuckman, Bruce W. CONDUCTING EDUCATIONAL RESEARCH. 2d ed. New York: Harcourt Brace Jovanovich, 1978. xvi, 479 p.

Each step in research process stated, including data analysis by computer.

Woodbury, Marda L. A GUIDE TO SOURCE OF EDUCATIONAL INFORMATION. Washington, D.C.: Information Resources Press, 1976. xvi, 371 p.

Contains a helpful beginning section, "The Research Process." Work deals with four sources of information: printed, information centers, organizations and government agencies, and special search and bibliographic services.

ROMAN CATHOLIC EDUCATION

Burns, James A. THE CATHOLIC SCHOOL SYSTEM IN THE UNITED STATES: ITS PRINCIPLES, ORIGIN, AND ESTABLISHMENT. New York: Benziger, 1908. 415 p.

Volume brings the church schools up to 1840, the beginning of the great immigration period. Author was a Roman Catholic educational historian and was president of Notre Dame from 1919 to 1922.

_____. THE GROWTH AND DEVELOPMENT OF THE CATHOLIC SCHOOL SYSTEM. New York: Benziger, 1912. 421 p.

A continuation of the 1908 edition (above). Immigration resulted in a rapid growth of Roman Catholic education.

Greeley, Andrew M., et al. CATHOLIC SCHOOLS IN A DECLINING CHURCH. Kansas City: Sheed and Ward, 1976. ix, 483 p.

The demography of American Roman Catholicism, and other items, in relation to the schools of the church. The volume reports on a 1974 National Opinion Research Center survey of adult Roman Catholics.

Hassenger, Robert, ed. THE SHAPE OF CATHOLIC HIGHER EDUCATION. Chicago: University of Chicago Press, 1967. 378 p.

Essays on topics concerning Roman Catholic undergraduate collegiate education (e.g., "Some Effects of Jesuit Education," "Some Problem Areas in Catholic Higher Education").

McCluskey, Neil G., ed. CATHOLIC EDUCATION IN AMERICA: A DOCUMENTARY HISTORY. New York: Teachers College Press, 1964. xii, 205 p.

Documents are included which trace the development of Roman Catholic education in America from 1792 to the early 1960s.

Power, Edward J. CATHOLIC HIGHER EDUCATION IN AMERICA: A HISTORY. New York: Appleton-Century-Crofts, 1972. ix, 493 p.

Work is divided into three sections: formative years, period of development (nineteenth century to 1940), and the modern period (1940--). Within these divisions, topics such as governance, faculties, curriculum, and students are discussed.

Schuster, George N. CATHOLIC EDUCATION IN A CHANGING WORLD. New York: Holt, Rinehart and Winston, 1968. x, 241 p.

Argument is made for the preservation of Roman Catholic schools and a prediction is offered that their future will be decided by laymen. Author was a Roman Catholic lay scholar and former president of Hunter College.

RURAL SCHOOLS

Burton, Warren. THE DISTRICT SCHOOL AS IT WAS: BY ONE WHO WENT TO IT. Boston: Carter, Hendee, 1833. x, 156 p.

A classic on the rural district school as it was in the early 1800s. Author was a Congregational clergyman and sought social reform through education.

Butterworth, Julian E., and Dawson, Howard A. THE MODERN RURAL SCHOOL. New York: McGraw-Hill, 1952. xii, 494 p.

One of the more recent works on rural education, still a reality in many places in the 1950s. Sociological and economic backgrounds of rural life are included.

Foght, Harold W. AMERICAN RURAL SCHOOL: ITS CHARACTERISTICS, ITS FUTURE, AND ITS PROBLEMS. New York: Macmillan, 1910. xxi, 361 p. Illus.

A textbook intended for rural teachers, superintendents, board members, and teachers in training. An extensive overview of organization, supervision, teaching methods, buildings, and curriculum areas (especially agriculture and manual training). The last chapter deals with school district consolidation.

Kennedy, Millard F. SCHOOLMASTER OF YESTERDAY. New York: Whittlesey House, 1940. viii, 359 p. Illus.

A three-generation story (1820-1919) of rural education in Kentucky and Indiana.

Lutes, Della T. COUNTRY SCHOOLMA'AM. New York: Little, Brown, 1941. 328 p.

The experiences of a rural school teacher in Michigan.

Weber, Julia. MY COUNTRY SCHOOL DIARY. New York: Harper, 1946. xvi, 270 p. Illus.

An adventure in creative teaching. It consists of a diary kept for over four years while teaching in a rural school in New Jersey.

Wofford, Kate V. MODERN EDUCATION IN THE SMALL RURAL SCHOOL. New York: Macmillan, 1938. xiii, 582 p. Appendixes, illus.

An introduction to the rural child, school, and teacher. Appendixes include suggested multiple-grade programs, forms for record keeping, and equipment.

SCHOOL BOARDS

Counts, George S. THE SOCIAL COMPOSITION OF BOARDS OF EDUCATION. Chicago: University of Chicago, 1927. Reprint. New York: Arno Press, 1969. ix, 100 p.

Counts was affiliated with Teachers College, Columbia University.

Gittell, Marilyn, ed. SCHOOL BOARDS AND SCHOOL POLICY: AN EVAL-
UATION OF DECENTRALIZATION IN NEW YORK CITY. New York: Praeger,
1973. xii, 169 p.

New York City's public schools were decentralized in 1970 (but
still under a central board). This is an evaluation made two
years afterwards. One of the conclusions: decentralization failed
to grant community boards enough power over personnel.

SCIENCE, TEACHING OF

Hone, Elizabeth B., et al. A SOURCEBOOK FOR ELEMENTARY SCIENCE.
2d ed. New York: Harcourt Brace Jovanovich, 1971. 475 p.

Demonstrations of the major concepts covered in a science program for elementary grades. Over fifteen hundred demonstrations
and experiments.

Morhalt, Evelyn, et al. TEACHING HIGH SCHOOL SCIENCE: A SOURCE-
BOOK FOR THE BIOLOGICAL SCIENCES. New York: Harcourt, Brace,
1958. 506 p. Illus.

Both content and method presented, and there are suggested out-
lines and syllabi.

Schmidt, Victor E., and Rockcastle, Verne N. TEACHING SCIENCE WITH
EVERYDAY THINGS. New York: McGraw-Hill, 1968. xii, 167 p. Illus.

An elementary school science sourcebook on using common items
for science activities. Especially useful in schools that have
little science equipment.

Smith, Alexander, and Hall, Edwin H. THE TEACHING OF CHEMISTRY
AND PHYSICS IN THE SECONDARY SCHOOL. New York: Longmans,
Green, 1902. xiii, 377 p. Illus.

One of the first works on the teaching of these sciences in the
high schools.

Underhill, Orra E. THE ORIGINS AND DEVELOPMENT OF ELEMENTARY
SCHOOL SCIENCE. Chicago: Scott, Foresman, 1941. xii, 347 p. Illus.

History of the teaching of science in the elementary grades.

Victor, Edward. SCIENCE FOR THE ELEMENTARY SCHOOL. 3d ed. New
York: Macmillan, 1975. ix, 774 p. Illus.

Goals and methods of science education as well as science content for teachers.

Washton, Nathan S. TEACHING SCIENCE IN ELEMENTARY AND MIDDLE
SCHOOLS. New York: David McKay, 1974. xxvi, 482 p. Illus.

Concise guide to organizing, teaching, and evaluating science instruction from kindergarten through grade eight. Piaget's theory of concept development is its methodological basis.

SECONDARY EDUCATION

General Works and Issues

Bremer, John, and Von Moschzisker, Michael. THE SCHOOL WITHOUT WALLS: PHILADELPHIA'S PARKWAY PROGRAM. New York: Holt, Rinehart and Winston, 1971. xi, 295 p.

One of the best models for a new departure in secondary education of the 1960s known as the "alternative secondary school."

Caswell, Hollis L., et al., eds. THE AMERICAN HIGH SCHOOL: ITS RESPONSIBILITY AND OPPORTUNITY. 8th Yearbook, John Dewey Society. New York: Harper, 1946. viii, 264 p.

A general work on the secondary school of the 1940s.

Conant, James B. THE AMERICAN HIGH SCHOOL TODAY. New York: McGraw-Hill, 1959. xiii, 140 p.

A study of the comprehensive (nonspecialized) high school, advocated by Conant, with twenty-one recommendations. Guidelines are given on class size, staffing, and course requirements.

_____. THE COMPREHENSIVE HIGH SCHOOL. New York: McGraw-Hill, 1967. vii, 95 p.

Conant's second work on the high school wherein he promotes the concept of a secondary school that would have most of those of that school age under one roof (as opposed to the separate, specialized schools).

Eurich, Alvin C., ed. HIGH SCHOOL 1980: THE SHAPE OF THE FUTURE IN AMERICAN SECONDARY EDUCATION. New York: Pitman Publishing Corp., 1970. 304 p.

Twenty-four educators (among them Conant, Howe, Postman) contributed essays on topics which ranged from student militancy to technological research. Strengths and weaknesses of secondary schools in the late 1960s are stated, and there is a futuristic look at the decade to follow.

Inglis, Alexander J. PRINCIPLES OF SECONDARY EDUCATION. Boston: Houghton Mifflin, 1918. xvi, 741 p.

An early work on this area of schooling by a Harvard professor of education, and one who contributed to the 1918 Cardinal Principles of Secondary Education.

Keyes, Ralph. IS THERE LIFE AFTER HIGH SCHOOL? Boston: Little, Brown, 1976. xii, 240 p. Illus.

> The self-image that is developed in high school influences one's adult life. Secondary education experiences are one of the most meaningful common denominators of American society.

Morrison, Henry C. THE PRACTICE OF TEACHING IN THE SECONDARY SCHOOL. Chicago: University of Chicago Press, 1926. viii, 661 p.

> By a professor of education and director of the Laboratory School at the University of Chicago from 1919 to 1937. He devised the Morrison Unit Plan as a substitute for lesson assignments in high school.

National Commission on the Reform of Secondary Education. THE REFORM OF SECONDARY EDUCATION: A REPORT OF THE NATIONAL COMMISSION ON THE REFORM OF SECONDARY EDUCATION. New York: McGraw-Hill, 1973. xviii, 188 p.

> Examination of goals, programs, and future directions. There was input from eight hundred educators. Sponsored by the Charles Kettering Foundation.

Owen, David. HIGH SCHOOL. New York: Viking Press, 1981. 262 p.

> An outsider infiltrates the senior class of an upstate New York high school and delivers a very candid report on teachers and teaching, and students and their world. The work serves as an informal report on public secondary schooling at the end of the 1970s.

Smith, Frederick R., and Cox, C. Benjamin. SECONDARY SCHOOLS IN A CHANGING SOCIETY. New York: Holt, Rinehart and Winston, 1976. xv, 201 p.

> Essentially a textbook. It contains a survey of the history of American education, and discusses the social forces influencing today's schools, especially the adolescent subculture.

Stiles, Lindley J., et al. SECONDARY EDUCATION IN THE UNITED STATES. New York: Harcourt, Brace and World, 1962. xii, 528 p. Illus.

> A general treatment of the objectives, organization, program, and concerns of the American high school.

Van Til, William, ed. ISSUES IN SECONDARY EDUCATION. 75th Yearbook, National Society for the Study of Education. Chicago: University of Chicago Press, 1976. xiii, 350 p.

> Twelve papers by various authors on a variety of pertinent topics ending with "The Future, Social Decisions, and Educational Change in Secondary Schools."

History

Adams, Oscar F. SOME FAMOUS AMERICAN SCHOOLS. Boston: D. Estes, 1903. xiv, 341 p. Illus.

> Nazareth Hall, Phillips Andover, Phillips Exeter, Lawrenceville, St. Paul's, St. Mark's, Shattuc, Groton, and Belmont are featured.

Brown, Elmer E. THE MAKING OF OUR MIDDLE SCHOOLS. New York: Longmans, Green, 1903. xii, 547 p.

> "Middle Schools" are secondary schools. The author traces these institutions back to the Latin grammar schools of England, and then shows the development of the American secondary school through the nineteenth century.

Grizzell, Emit D. ORIGIN AND DEVELOPMENT OF THE HIGH SCHOOL IN NEW ENGLAND BEFORE 1865. New York: Macmillan, 1923. xv, 428 p.

> This work examines the pre-high school forms of secondary education (Latin grammar schools and academies) and treats the spread of the public high school movement, starting with the first one in Boston in 1821, to other states.

Kandel, Isaac L. HISTORY OF SECONDARY EDUCATION: A STUDY IN THE DEVELOPMENT OF LIBERAL EDUCATION. Boston: Houghton Mifflin, 1930. xvii, 577 p.

> Part 1 deals with educational foundations from the ancient world, and part 2 with Europe and America.

Krug, Edward. THE SHAPING OF THE AMERICAN HIGH SCHOOL. New York: Harper and Row, 1964. xvii, 485 p.

> The origin of the public high school, the report of the Committee of Ten in 1892, and subsequent changes up to 1920.

Middlekauff, Robert. ANCIENTS AND AXIOMS: SECONDARY EDUCATION IN EIGHTEENTH CENTURY NEW ENGLAND. New Haven, Conn.: Yale University Press, 1963. 218 p.

> A treatment of several kinds of secondary schools (especially Latin grammar schools, private classical schools, and academies) that were found in eighteenth-century America.

Sizer, Theodore R. SECONDARY SCHOOLS AT THE TURN OF THE CENTURY. New Haven, Conn.: Yale University Press, 1964. xiv, 304 p.

> Two traditions of the secondary school, the practical and the classical, are examined. The recommendations and influence of the Committee of Ten are well covered.

Small, Walter H. EARLY NEW ENGLAND SCHOOLS. Boston: Ginn, 1914. ix, 401 p.

> Latin grammar schools, English schools, early private schools, are among the early secondary schools discussed. The time span covered is essentially the seventeenth and eighteenth centuries.

Institutional Histories by State

CONNECTICUT

CHOATE ROSEMARY HALL (1896)

St. John, George. FORTY YEARS AT SCHOOL. New York: Henry Holt, 1959. 303 p. Illus.

> The memoirs of the long-time headmaster (1908-47) includes much history of Choate School, coeducational with Rosemary Hall (1890) since 1977.

THE GUNNERY (1849)

Korpalski, Adam. THE GUNNERY, 1850-1975: A DOCUMENTARY HISTORY. Washington, Conn.: Adam Korpalski, 1977. 308 p. Illus.

> An attractive, well-illustrated, and documented volume on this school, named for Frederick W. Gunn, its founder.

HOPKINS GRAMMAR SCHOOL (1660)

Bacon, Leonard W. AN HISTORICAL DISCOURSE ON THE TWO-HUNDREDTH ANNIVERSARY OF THE FOUNDING OF THE HOPKINS GRAMMAR SCHOOL. New Haven, Conn.: T.J. Stafford, 1860. 70 p. Appendix.

> The text of original documents is given in the appendix.

HOTCHKISS SCHOOL (1892)

Wertenbaker, Lael T., and Basserman, Maude. THE HOTCHKISS SCHOOL: A PORTRAIT. Lakeville: Hotchkiss School, 1966. 185 p. Illus.

> Independent secondary school for boys named for its benefactor, Maria Bissell Hotchkiss.

TAFT SCHOOL (1890)

Taft, Horace D. MEMORIES AND OPINIONS. New York: Macmillan, 1942. 336 p. Illus.

> The founder of the school (and a brother of President William Howard Taft) relates the history of the institution in his memoirs.

DISTRICT OF COLUMBIA

DUNBAR HIGH SCHOOL (1870)

Hundley, Mary G. THE DUNBAR STORY (1870-1955). New York: Vantage Press, 1965. 179 p. Illus.

> The history of the distinguished Negro public high school in Washington, D.C., known at its opening as the Preparatory High School for Colored Youth.

HAWAII

PUNAHOU SCHOOL (1841)

Potter, Norris W. THE PUNAHOU STORY. Palo Alto, Calif.: Pacific Books, 1969. 224 p. Illus.

> The history of Honolulu's oldest secondary school, founded by Congregational church missionaries from the mainland. It is now a coeducational (grades K to 12) day school.

MAINE

BERWICK ACADEMY (1791)

A MEMORIAL OF THE ONE HUNDREDTH ANNIVERSARY OF THE FOUNDING OF BERWICK ACADEMY, SOUTH BERWICK, MAINE, JULY FIRST, 1891. Cambridge, Mass.: Riverside Press, 1891. 118 p.

> A historical account of Maine's first academy.

BRIDGTON ACADEMY (1808)

Stevens, Ernest N. A BRIEF HISTORY OF BRIDGTON ACADEMY. 1808-1957. Bridgton, Maine: n.p., 1958. x, 195 p. Illus.

> Academy was organized by a local group of citizens. A boarding and day secondary school for boys.

HEBRON ACADEMY (1804)

Hall, Harold E. HISTORY OF HEBRON ACADEMY, HEBRON, MAINE, 1804-1972. Hebron, Maine: Trustees of Hebron Academy, 1979. 308 p. Illus.

> Deacon William Barrows and a group of local Baptists founded this school in a small village in the then district of Maine. It is now an independent, coeducational secondary school.

MARYLAND

BALTIMORE CITY COLLEGE (1839)

Leonhart, James C. ONE HUNDRED YEARS OF THE BALTIMORE CITY COL-LEGE. Baltimore: H.G. Roebuch and Son, 1939. 308 p. Illus.

> A very complete record of events, faculty, and students of the third oldest public high school in the United States.

MASSACHUSETTS

ABBOT ACADEMY (1828)

Lloyd, Susan M. A SINGULAR SCHOOL: ABBOT. Hanover, Mass.: University Press of New England, 1979. 642 p. Illus.

> Abbot has been affiliated with Phillips Academy since 1973.

BOSTON ENGLISH HIGH SCHOOL (1821)

ONE HUNDRED YEARS OF THE ENGLISH HIGH SCHOOL OF BOSTON. Boston: Centenary Committee, 1924. v, 87 p. Illus.

> Established as the Boston English Classical School, the first public school in the United States.

BOSTON LATIN SCHOOL (1635)

Holmes, Pauline. A TERCENTENARY HISTORY OF THE BOSTON PUBLIC LATIN SCHOOL, 1635-1935. Cambridge, Mass.: Harvard University Press, 1935. xxiv, 541 p. Illus.

> America's oldest secondary school. Written for the three hundredth anniversary.

DEERFIELD ACADEMY (1797)

McPhee, John. THE HEADMASTER: FRANK L. BOYDEN OF DEERFIELD. New York: Farrar, Straus and Giroux, 1966. 149 p. Illus.

> Although the academy was chartered in 1797, the long headmaster-ship of Frank Boyden constitutes the most significant history of the institution.

GOVERNOR DUMMER ACADEMY (1763)

Ragle, John W. GOVERNOR DUMMER ACADEMY HISTORY. South Byfield, Mass.: Governor Dummer Academy, 1963. xvi, 187 p. Illus.

> Institution claims to be the oldest boys' boarding school in the United States and the oldest academy in New England. History was written for the school's two hundredth anniversary.

GROTON SCHOOL (1884)

Ashburn, Frank D. PEABODY OF GROTON, A PORTRAIT. New York:
Coward-McCann, 1944. xii, 444 p. Illus.

Endicott Peabody was the school's founder and long-time headmaster. Much is included on the early history of the institution.

MILTON ACADEMY (1798)

Hale, Richard W., Jr. MILTON ACADEMY, 1798-1948. Milton, Mass:
Milton Academy, 1948. x, 185 p.

The academy opened for students in 1807 (boys only at outset;
girls in 1816). Written for the one hundred and fiftieth anniversary of the school's incorporation.

NORTHFIELD MOUNT HERMON SCHOOL (1879)

Mabie, Janet. THE YEARS BEYOND: THE STORY OF NORTHFIELD, D.L.
MOODY, AND THE SCHOOLS. East Northfield, Mass: Northfield Bookstore,
1960. 239 p. Illus.

Dwight Moody, Christian evangelist, founded Northfield Young
Ladies' Seminary in 1879 and Mount Hermon Boys' School in 1881.
They were combined into a single institution in 1970.

PHILLIPS ACADEMY (1778)

Allis, Frederick S. YOUTH FROM EVERY QUARTER: A BICENTENNIAL
HISTORY OF PHILLIPS ACADEMY, ANDOVER. Hanover, Mass.: University
Press of New England, 1979. xxvii, 770 p. Illus.

The most recent history of this venerable New England academy
founded by Samuel Phillips, Jr. It was the model for a number
of schools of its type.

ROXBURY LATIN SCHOOL (1645)

Hale, Richard W., Jr. TERCENTENARY HISTORY OF THE ROXBURY LATIN
SCHOOL, 1645-1945. Cambridge, Mass.: Riverside Press, 1946. v, 170 p.
Illus.

Massachusetts' second oldest Latin grammar school. Now an independent boys' school.

SAINT MARK'S SCHOOL (1865)

Hall, Edward T. SAINT MARK'S SCHOOL: A CENTENNIAL HISTORY.
Lunenburg, Vt.: Stinehour Press, 1967. xiii, 290 p. Illus.

The history of the years since 1924 of this independent boys' preparatory school which follows the doctrine and discipline of the
Episcopal Church.

SPRINGFIELD CLASSICAL HIGH SCHOOL (1828)

Orr, William. THE HISTORY OF THE CLASSICAL HIGH SCHOOL OF
SPRINGFIELD, MASSACHUSETTS. Springfield, Mass.: Classical High School
Alumni Association, 1936. 257 p. Illus.

> The story of the beginnings and subsequent growth of this early
> public high school.

NEW HAMPSHIRE

PHILLIPS EXETER ACADEMY (1781)

Echols, Edward C., ed. THE PHILLIPS EXETER ACADEMY: A PICTORIAL
HISTORY. Exeter, N.H.: Phillips Exeter Press, 1970. viii, 110 p. Illus.

> A most attractive and well-illustrated volume which brings the
> history of New Hampshire's oldest academy to 1963.

SAINT PAUL'S SCHOOL (1855)

Heckscher, August. ST. PAUL'S: THE LIFE OF A NEW ENGLAND SCHOOL.
New York: Charles Scribner's Sons, 1980. xv, 398 p. Illus.

> An Episcopal church school built on the British pattern of a
> secondary boarding school. A passionate history by one of its
> graduates.

NEW JERSEY

Bole, Robert D., and Johnson, Laurence B. THE NEW JERSEY HIGH SCHOOL:
A HISTORY. Princeton, N.J.: D. Van Nostrand, 1964. xvi, 174 p. Illus.

> Some early independent secondary schools are mentioned, but es-
> sentially this work covers the development of public high school in
> the state from the mid-nineteenth century.

BLAIR ACADEMY (1848)

Sharpe, John C. MEMORIES OF BLAIR. Blairstown, N.J.: n.p., 1939. ix,
228 p. Illus.

> The history of the academy from 1892 to 1927 written by its
> headmaster from 1898 to 1927.

LAWRENCEVILLE SCHOOL (1808)

Mulford, Roland J. HISTORY OF THE LAWRENCEVILLE SCHOOL, 1810-1935.
Princeton, N.J.: Princeton University Press, 1935. xx, 358 p. Illus.

> Part 1 covers history from 1810 to 1883; part 2 from 1883 to 1935;
> and parts 3 and 4 are devoted to student activities and athletics.

PINGRY SCHOOL (1861)

THE BEGINNINGS OF WISDOM: THE STORY OF PINGRY SCHOOL, ELIZABETH, NEW JERSEY, 1861-1961. Elizabeth, N.J.: Board of Trustees, 1961. 338 p. Illus.

> The school was founded by John Francis Pingry whose personality dominated the institution for many years.

RUTGERS PREPARATORY SCHOOL (1766)

Sperduto, Frank V. A HISTORY OF RUTGERS PREPARATORY SCHOOL. Somerset, N.J.: Rutgers Preparatory School, 1967. xiii, 189 p.

> Founded as Queen's College Grammar School. Ties with Rutgers University ended in 1957 when the school became an independent, coeducational elementary and secondary school.

ST. MARY'S HALL (1837)

Shaw, Helen L. THE FIRST HUNDRED YEARS OF ST. MARY'S HALL ON THE DELAWARE. Yardley, Pa.: Cook Printers, 1936. xv, 167 p. Illus.

> A girls' school founded by Bishop George Washington Doane of the Episcopal Diocese of New Jersey.

NEW YORK

ALBANY ACADEMY (1813)

CELEBRATION OF THE SEMI-CENTENNIAL ANNIVERSARY OF THE ALBANY ACADEMY, ALBANY, JUNE 23, 1863. Albany, N.Y.: J. Munsell, 1863. 188 p.

> The proceedings of the fiftieth anniversary include a historical discourse.

COLLEGIATE SCHOOL (1638)

Waterbury, Jean P. A HISTORY OF COLLEGIATE SCHOOL, 1638-1963. New York: Clarkson N. Potter, 1965. 160 p.

> The history of New York's oldest school, founded by the Dutch West India Company and the Dutch Reformed Church.

COLUMBIA GRAMMAR SCHOOL (1763)

Sullivan, McDonald, and Dixon, Ross, eds. THE COLUMBIA GRAMMAR SCHOOL, 1764-1964: A HISTORICAL LOG. New York: Columbia Grammar School, 1965. xiv, 58 p. Illus.

> School was established by King's College (Columbia) but severed its connection with the college in 1833. It is an independent, coeducational elementary and secondary school.

EMMA WILLARD SCHOOL (1814)

Fairbanks, A.W. EMMA WILLARD AND HER PUPILS, OR FIFTY YEARS OF TROY FEMALE SEMINARY, 1822-1872. New York: Mrs. Russell Sage, 1898. 895 p. Illus.

A concise, early history of the school with a complete biographical record of students to 1898. Emma Willard began her seminary in Middlebury, Vermont, in 1814 and moved it to Troy in 1821. The present name dates from 1892.

ERASMUS HALL HIGH SCHOOL (1787)

Boughton, Willis. CHRONICLES OF ERASMUS HALL, 1787-1896. Brooklyn: Erasmus Hall High School, 1906. 229 p. Illus.

The institution was the second oldest academy in New York state. It became a public high school in 1896.

HORACE MANN SCHOOL (1887)

HORACE MANN AFTER 50 YEARS. New York: Horace Mann School for Boys, 1937. 75 p.

A history prepared for the fiftieth anniversary of this pioneer New York country day school.

PACKER COLLEGIATE INSTITUTE (1845)

Nickerson, Marjorie L. A LONG WAY FORWARD: THE FIRST HUNDRED YEARS OF THE PACKER COLLEGIATE INSTITUTE. Brooklyn: Packer Collegiate Institute, 1945. xiii, 284 p. Illus.

Opened as Brooklyn Female Academy. A junior college division began in 1919, the first in New York state. The school encompasses elementary, secondary, and junior college levels and is now coeducational.

XAVIER HIGH SCHOOL (1847)

THE COLLEGE OF ST. FRANCIS XAVIER: A MEMORIAL AND A RETROSPECT, 1847-1897. New York: Meany Printing Co., 1897. 273 p. Illus.

The early history of a New York Roman Catholic boys' secondary school which began as a college and continued as such until 1912.

PENNSYLVANIA

Mulhern, James. A HISTORY OF SECONDARY EDUCATION IN PENNSYLVANIA. Philadelphia: By the author, 1933. xv, 714 p. Bibliog.

A detailed and documented study of the development of secondary schools in the state.

CENTRAL HIGH SCHOOL OF PHILADELPHIA (1836)

Edmonds, Franklin S. HISTORY OF THE CENTRAL HIGH SCHOOL OF
PHILADELPHIA. Philadelphia: J.B. Lippincott, 1902. xiv, 394 p. Illus.

The oldest public high school outside of New England.

GEORGE SCHOOL (1893)

HISTORY OF GEORGE SCHOOL, 1893-1943. George School, Pa.: Alumni
Association, 1943. 158 p. Illus.

The will of John M. George, a Quaker, left a bequest which
resulted in the establishment of the school. George L. Maris was
influential in its opening.

GERMANTOWN ACADEMY (1759)

A HISTORY OF THE GERMANTOWN ACADEMY. Philadelphia: S.H. Burbank,
1910. xvi, 321 p. Illus.

Published on its one hundred and fiftieth anniversary.

GIRARD COLLEGE (1832)

HISTORY OF GIRARD COLLEGE. Philadelphia: Girard College, 1927. xi,
390 p. Illus.

A school for orphan boys founded by the will of Stephen Girard,
Philadelphia merchant and banker.

MERCERSBURG ACADEMY (1832)

Klein, H.M.J. A CENTURY OF EDUCATION AT MERCERSBURG. Lancaster,
Pa.: Lancaster Press, 1936. xiv, 683 p. Illus.

The roots of the academy can be traced to a classical school attached to York Theological Seminary. The school moved to
Mercersburg in 1835 and Marshall College (later Franklin and
Marshall) was organized. William M. Irvine reorganized the
classical school into Mercersburg Academy in 1893.

MORAVIAN ACADEMY (1742)

Richel, William C. HISTORY OF THE RISE, PROGRESS, AND PRESENT CON-
DITION OF THE BETHLEHEM FEMALE SEMINARY. 2d ed. Philadelphia:
J.B. Lippincott, 1870. 570 p.

This institution joined the Moravian Preparatory School (also
founded in 1742) in 1971 to form the Moravian Academy.

WESTTOWN SCHOOL (1799)

Dewees, Watson W., and Dewees, Sarah B. HISTORY OF WESTTOWN BOARDING

SCHOOL. Philadelphia: Sherman and Co., 1899. viii, 204 p. Illus.

> Founded by the Society of Friends. New a coeducational elementary and secondary school.

WILLIAM PENN CHARTER SCHOOL (1689)

THE WILLIAM PENN CHARTER SCHOOL. Philadelphia: n.p., 1917. 32 p. Photos., Illus.

> A brief historical statement, description of courses of study, and several photographs of the institution.

RHODE ISLAND

MOSES BROWN SCHOOL (1819)

Kelsey, Rayner W. CENTENNIAL HISTORY OF MOSES BROWN SCHOOL, 1819-1919. Providence, R.I.: Moses Brown School, 1919. xviii, 178 p. Illus.

> Established by members of the Society of Friends. Named for Moses Brown (1738-1836), a Friend and philanthropist.

VIRGINIA

EPISCOPAL HIGH SCHOOL (1839)

Kinsolving, Arthur B. THE STORY OF A SOUTHERN SCHOOL: THE EPISCOPAL HIGH SCHOOL OF VIRGINIA. Baltimore: Norman, Remington Co., 1922. 335 p. Illus.

> A boarding school for boys established by the Episcopal diocese of Virginia and located in Alexandria.

SEX EDUCATION

Burt, John J., and Meeks, Linda B. EDUCATION FOR SEXUALITY: CONCEPTS AND PROGRAMS FOR TEACHING. 2d ed. Philadelphia: W.B. Saunders, 1975. xiii, 537 p. Illus.

> Topical outlines suggested for courses. Material on abortion, contraception, and homosexuality are included.

Schulz, Esther D., and Williams, Sally R. FAMILY LIFE AND SEX EDUCATION: CURRICULUM AND INSTRUCTION. New York: Harcourt, Brace and World, 1969. xiv, 281 p.

> A methods book for teachers in training and/or beginning teachers. Background material included can be useful from kindergarten through high school.

Seruya, Flora C., et al. SEX AND SEX EDUCATION: A BIBLIOGRAPHY. New York: Bowker, 1972. xiii, 336 p.

A most comprehensive compilation on sexuality and an invaluable contribution to sex education.

SOCIAL STUDIES, TEACHING OF

Banks, James A., and Joyce, William W., eds. TEACHING SOCIAL STUDIES TO CULTURALLY DIFFERENT CHILDREN. Reading, Mass.: Addison-Wesley, 1971. xiv, 396 p.

"Culturally different" relates to race and ethnicity. Contributors write of teaching strategies for dealing with these students in social studies classes.

Jarolimek, John. SOCIAL STUDIES IN ELEMENTARY EDUCATION. 5th ed. New York: Macmillan, 1977. xi, 369 p. Illus.

A popular textbook in social studies methods used since 1959.

Mayer, Martin. WHERE, WHEN, AND WHY: SOCIAL STUDIES IN AMERICAN SCHOOLS. New York: Harper and Row, 1963. xvi, 207 p.

Based on three years of classroom visits at both elementary and secondary levels. Much dialog quoted from actual class observations. Social studies textbooks, with few exceptions, were found wanting when this item was published.

Michaelis, John U. SOCIAL STUDIES FOR CHILDREN IN A DEMOCRACY: RECENT TRENDS AND DEVELOPMENTS. 5th ed. Englewood Cliffs, N.J.: Prentice-Hall, 1972. xv, 592 p. Illus.

This edition of a methods' textbook that first appeared in 1950 utilizes the most recent research on teaching in the area (e.g., the method of inquiry).

Tryon, Rolla M. THE SOCIAL STUDIES AS SCHOOL SUBJECTS. New York: Charles Scribner's Sons, 1935. xiii, 541 p.

A report of the Commission on the Social Studies of the American Historical Association.

Wesley, Edgar B., and Wronski, Stanley P. TEACHING SOCIAL STUDIES IN HIGH SCHOOLS. 5th ed. Boston: D.C. Heath, 1964. x, 628 p. Illus.

This work had its beginnings in 1937 with Wesley's first work on teaching social studies. New materials include a guide to student teaching and an analysis of a social studies unit.

SOCIOLOGY OF EDUCATION

Adams, Donald K. SCHOOLING AND SOCIAL CHANGE IN MODERN AMERICA. New York: David McKay, 1972. ix, 304 p.

The relationship between societal change and educational change. Schooling and social stratification and attempts to equalize educational opportunity are focused upon.

Brown, Francis J. EDUCATIONAL SOCIOLOGY. 2d ed. New York: Prentice-Hall, 1954. xvi, 677 p. Illus.

A standard educational sociology text first published in 1947 and in use for some years. Rapid changes since the 1950s have made it a period piece to some degree.

Coleman, James S., et al. EQUALITY OF EDUCATIONAL OPPORTUNITY. Washington, D.C.: Government Printing Office, 1966. vi, 737 p.

A summary report of the significant Coleman Report which examined a very large population sample of public school children in attempting to evaluate the equality of schooling that black and white students had in the 1960s.

Cordasco, Francesco, and Alloway, David N., eds. SOCIOLOGY OF EDUCATION: A GUIDE TO INFORMATION SOURCES. Education Information Guide Series, vol. 2. Detroit: Gale Research Co., 1979. xiii, 266 p.

Annotations on books about many topics within educational sociology beginning with the 1960s. Over fifteen hundred entries.

Davis, Allison. SOCIAL-CLASS INFLUENCES UPON LEARNING. Cambridge, Mass.: Harvard University Press, 1948. 100 p.

An important and early study on class and school success. It was the 1948 Inglis lecture at Harvard.

Finney, Ross L. A SOCIOLOGICAL PHILOSOPHY OF EDUCATION. Modern Teacher Series. Edited by W.C. Bagley. New York: Macmillan, 1928. xi, 563 p.

An early work on the subject by a prolific writer on many fields within education during the early twentieth century.

Gordon, C. Wayne, ed. USES OF THE SOCIOLOGY OF EDUCATION. 73d Yearbook, National Society for the Study of Education. Chicago: University of Chicago Press, 1974. xviii, 518 p., cxii.

Sixteen papers by various authors on sociological problems confronting those involved in the profession of education.

Havighurst, Robert J., and Levine, Daniel U. SOCIETY AND EDUCATION. 5th ed. Boston: Allyn and Bacon, 1979. xii, 617 p. Illus.

A popular college text in the field since 1957.

Jencks, Christopher, et al. INEQUALITY: A REASSESSMENT OF THE EFFECT OF FAMILY AND SCHOOLING IN AMERICA. New York: Basic Books, 1972. xxi, 399 p. Illus.

> Jencks and a team of researchers viewed inequality from the social and economic structures of society. The relationship of family and success in schooling is shown.

Lortie, Dan C. SCHOOLTEACHER: A SOCIOLOGICAL STUDY. Chicago: University of Chicago Press, 1975. xii, 284 p.

> The best recent work on the social portrait of the teaching profession. Over five thousand teachers were questioned. Three traits found: conservative (doing things the way they have been done), presentist (few plan to teach for a long time), and individualistic (no single type of personality).

Sexton, Patricia C. EDUCATION AND INCOME: INEQUALITIES IN OUR PUBLIC SCHOOLS. New York: Viking Press, 1961. 298 p.

> Based on a study of a midwestern city school system. The limitations of a child's educational opportunities are related to parents' income.

Swift, David W., ed. AMERICAN EDUCATION: A SOCIOLOGICAL VIEW. Boston: Houghton Mifflin, 1976. xv, 473 p. Illus.

> Contributions by twelve writers in field of educational sociology. Main topics include structure, function, and minority education.

Warner, William L., et al. WHO SHALL BE EDUCATED? THE CHALLENGE OF UNEQUAL OPPORTUNITIES. New York: Harper, 1944. xii, 190 p.

> A factual statement of the extent to which public schools offer equality of opportunity. One of the papers is "The Negro in the American Caste System."

SPECIAL EDUCATION

General Works

Anderson, Robert M., et al. INSTRUCTIONAL RESOURCES FOR TEACHERS OF THE CULTURALLY DISADVANTAGED AND EXCEPTIONAL. Springfield, Ill.: Charles C Thomas, 1969. xii, 304 p.

> A resource book especially designed for librarians and teachers of disadvantaged children (defined as those with diverse handicapping conditions or impoverished environmental backgrounds). All curriculum areas are covered.

Baker, Harry J. INTRODUCTION TO EXCEPTIONAL CHILDREN. 3d ed. New York: Macmillan, 1959. 523 p. Illus.

The gifted as well as the mentally and physically handicapped
are included.

THE DIRECTORY FOR EXCEPTIONAL CHILDREN. 9th ed. Boston: Porter
Sargent Publishers, 1981. 1,382 p.

A listing of educational and training facilities by state.

Dunn, Lloyd M., ed. EXCEPTIONAL CHILDREN IN THE SCHOOL: SPECIAL
EDUCATION IN TRANSITION. 2d ed. New York: Holt, Rinehart and
Winston, 1973. xiii, 600 p. Illus.

A general textbook covering the gifted, behavioral problems,
learning disabilities, and several physical disabilities.

Gowan, John C., et al., eds. THE GUIDANCE OF EXCEPTIONAL CHILDREN:
A BOOK OF READINGS. 2d ed. New York: David McKay, 1972. xi,
465 p.

Articles on all divisions of special education: gifted, emotionally
disturbed, mentally retarded, blind, deaf, underachievers, and
the physically handicapped.

Thompson, Glen R., ed. YEARBOOK OF SPECIAL EDUCATION, 1980-81.
6th ed. Chicago: Marquis Academic Media, 1980. 442 p.

Articles by authorities on new developments in the several divisions
of special education.

The Emotionally Disturbed

Bettelheim, Bruno. LOVE IS NOT ENOUGH: THE TREATMENT OF EMOTION-
ALLY DISTURBED CHILDREN. New York: Avon Books, 1972. 415 p. Illus.

A report by a distinguished psychologist on day-to-day life at a
special school in Chicago. Work first published in 1950.

Haring, Norris G., and Phillips, E. Lakin. EDUCATING EMOTIONALLY
DISTURBED CHILDREN. New York: McGraw-Hill, 1962. 322 p.

A structured method of running a classroom for the emotionally
disturbed.

Hewett, Frank M. THE EMOTIONALLY DISTURBED CHILD IN THE CLASS-
ROOM. Boston: Allyn and Bacon, 1968. x, 373 p.

Presents a developmental strategy for use with children with mal-
adaptive behavior.

Strain, Phillip S., et al. TEACHING EXCEPTIONAL CHILDREN: ASSESSING
AND MODIFYING SOCIAL BEHAVIOR. New York: Academic Press, 1976.
viii, 152 p.

A work directed toward those who are concerned with accelerating positive social interaction among socially isolated children. For advanced students of the subject.

Learning Disabilities

Brueckner, Leo J., and Bond, Guy L. THE DIAGNOSIS AND TREATMENT OF LEARNING DISABILITIES. New York: Appleton-Century-Crofts, 1955. ix, 424 p. Illus.

Overview of the nature and diagnoses of learning problems. Curriculum areas emphasized are reading, spelling, language, handwriting, and arithmetic.

Ellingson, Careth, and Cass, James. DIRECTOR OF FACILITIES FOR THE LEARNING-DISABLED AND HANDICAPPED. New York: Harper and Row, 1972. xii, 624 p.

Public and private diagnostic facilities are listed by state.

Faas, Larry A. CHILDREN WITH LEARNING PROBLEMS: A HANDBOOK FOR TEACHERS. Boston: Houghton Mifflin, 1980. xii, 418 p. Illus.

Chapters on diagnosis and specific learning problems.

Farnham-Diggory, Sylvia. LEARNING DISABILITIES: A PSYCHOLOGICAL PERSPECTIVE. Cambridge, Mass.: Harvard University Press, 1978. vi, 154 p. Illus.

A clearly written work on recent advances in the treatment of learning disabilities.

Goodman, Libby, and Mann, Lester. LEARNING DISABILITIES IN THE SECONDARY SCHOOL: ISSUES AND PRACTICES. New York: Grune and Stratton, 1976. ix, 256 p. Bibliog.

Identification of learning troubles and suggested program for remediation.

Johnson, Doris J., and Mykleburst, Helmer R. LEARNING DISABILITIES: EDUCATIONAL PRINCIPLES AND PRACTICES. New York: Grune and Stratton, 1967. xii, 336 p. Illus.

A wealth of practical suggestions and exercises to be used in working with students with learning disorders.

Loehner, Conrad A. LEARNING DISABILITIES AND THE EDUCATIONALLY-HANDICAPPED CHILD. Upland, Calif.: Phalarope Publishing Co., 1971. 183 p.

The child, family, and school are dealt with. The schizophrenic and the brain-damaged receive considerable treatment. Pertinent questions and answers appear at the end of the work.

Lynn, Roa, et al. LEARNING DISABILITIES: AN OVERVIEW OF THEORIES, APPROACHES, AND POLITICS. New York: Free Press, 1979. xii, 195 p. Illus.

> Much of the book is based upon interviews. Author suffered from dyslexia. An important chapter is "The LD (learning disabilities) Establishment."

Ross, Alan O. LEARNING DISABILITY: THE UNREALIZED POTENTIAL. New York: McGraw-Hill, 1977. xviii, 202 p.

> A general and comprehensive treatment of learning-disabled children. Extensive coverage of the role of testing. There are annotated references to each topic.

Sapir, Selma G., and Nitzburg, Ann C. CHILDREN WITH LEARNING PROBLEMS: READINGS IN A DEVELOPMENTAL INTERACTION APPROACH. New York: Brunner, Mazel, 1973. xvi, 709 p. Illus.

> Essays, addresses, and lectures on diagnosing and treating disorders that block learning, from hyperkinetic children to the retarded.

Mainstreaming

Blankenship, Colleen, and Lilly, M. Stephen. MAINSTREAMING STUDENTS WITH LEARNING AND BEHAVIOR PROBLEMS: TECHNIQUES FOR THE CLASSROOM TEACHER. New York: Holt, Rinehart and Winston, 1981. xi, 353 p.

> The assimilation of students with mild handicaps into regular classrooms is known as mainstreaming. This book deals with the process as it concerns sutdents with learning and behavior problems, and physical and sensory impairments.

Siegel, Ernest. SPECIAL EDUCATION IN THE REGULAR CLASSROOM. New York: John Day, 1969. xv, 171 p.

> Teaching minimally handicapped children with others in regular classes.

The Mentally Retarded

Ayers, Leonard P. LAGGARDS IN OUR SCHOOLS: A STUDY OF RETARDATION AND ELIMINATION IN CITY SCHOOL SYSTEMS. New York: Russell Sage Foundation, 1909. xv, 236 p.

> A pioneer work in the identification of mentally retarded students in public schools.

Hutt, Max L., and Gibby, Robert G. THE MENTALLY RETARDED CHILD: DEVELOPMENT, EDUCATION, AND TREATMENT. 3d ed. Boston: Allyn and Bacon, 1976. ix, 513 p. Illus.

Latest research findings incorporated into this revised comprehensive book, a work that first appeared in 1958.

Perry, Natalie. TEACHING THE MENTALLY RETARDED CHILD. 2d ed. New York: Columbia University Press, 1974. xiv, 751 p.

This book, a revision of a 1960 work, has been enlarged to cover "trainable retardates" and their school needs.

Rivera, Geraldo. WILLOWBROOK: A REPORT ON HOW IT IS AND WHY IT DOESN'T HAVE TO BE. New York: Random House, 1972. 147 p. Illus.

A startling expose of the inadequacy of New York's Willowbrook State School, a resident institution for the severely mentally retarded, presented in the form of a journal.

Robinson, Nancy M., and Halbert, R. THE MENTALLY RETARDED CHILD: A PSYCHOLOGICAL APPROACH. 2d ed. New York: McGraw-Hill, 1976. xvi, 592 p.

The subject is approached from standpoint of etiology, psychological theory, behavioral evaluation, and testing. Not a book on methodology of teaching.

Seguin, Edward. IDIOCY AND ITS TREATMENT BY THE PHYSIOLOGICAL METHOD. New York: W. Wood and Co., 1866. xi, 457 p. Reprint. New York: A.M. Kelley, 1971.

The foundation work on the education of the mentally retarded. Seguin (1812-80) came to America from France in 1850.

Smith, Robert M. CLINICAL TEACHING: METHODS OF INSTRUCTION FOR THE RETARDED. 2d ed. New York: McGraw-Hill, 1974. viii, 366 p. Illus.

Educational problems of the retarded from preschool through post school. Curriculum and techniques of instruction are included.

Talbot, Mabel E. EDWARD SEGUIN: A STUDY OF AN EDUCATIONAL APPROACH TO THE TREATMENT OF MENTALLY DEFECTIVE CHILDREN. New York: Teachers College, Columbia University, 1964. xiii, 150 p. Illus.

A review of the work of Seguin, who systematically developed the methodology for teaching the mentally retarded.

Witty, Paul A., ed. THE EDUCATIONALLY RETARDED AND DISADVANTAGED. 66th Yearbook, National Society for the Study of Education. Chicago: University of Chicago Press, 1967. xiii, 384 p., lxii.

Articles cover the mentally and socially disadvantaged.

The Physically Handicapped

Bigge, June L., and O'Donnell, Patrick A. TEACHING INDIVIDUALS WITH PHYSICAL AND MULTIPLE DISABILITIES. Columbus: Charles E. Merrill, 1976. viii, 279 p. Illus.

> Task analysis (options and steps necessary to accomplish a task) is the framework of this detailed work on the physically and multiple handicapped.

Bleck, Eugene E., and Nagel, Donald A., eds. PHYSICALLY HANDICAPPED CHILDREN: A MEDICAL ATLAS FOR TEACHERS. New York: Grune and Stratton, 1975. xiv, 304 p. Illus.

> Illustrations and text on amputations, asthma, cerebral palsy, cystic fibrosis, muscular dystrophy, and other physical disorders found in young people.

Love, Harold D., and Walthall, Joe E. A HANDBOOK OF MEDICAL, EDUCA-TIONAL, AND PSYCHOLOGICAL INFORMATION FOR TEACHERS OF PHYSICAL-LY HANDICAPPED CHILDREN. Springfield, Ill.: Charles C Thomas, 1977. xii, 219 p.

> Diseases, physical and sensory disabilities, and school problems of students with such handicaps.

SPEECH, TEACHING OF

Ogilvie, Mardel. TEACHING SPEECH IN THE HIGH SCHOOL: PRINCIPLES AND PRACTICES. New York: Appleton-Century-Crofts, 1961. 434 p.

> Fundamentals of speaking along with public address, drama, story-telling, radio and television.

Pronovost, Wilbert. THE TEACHING OF SPEAKING AND LISTENING IN THE ELEMENTARY SCHOOL. New York: Longmans, Green, 1959. ix, 338 p.

> Principles of articulation along with such activities as group dis-cussion, oral reading, and dramatics. A chapter is included on the speech and hearing handicapped child in the classroom.

Rochmis, Lyda N., and Doob, Dorothy. SPEECH THERAPY: A GROUP AP-PROACH FOR SCHOOLS AND CLINICS. New York: John Day, 1970. xiv, 236 p.

> Material is best suited for upper elementary grades and secondary schools. The exercises are for groups of students in need of therapy.

Wallace, Karl R., et al. HISTORY OF SPEECH EDUCATION IN AMERICA. New York: Appleton-Century-Crofts, 1954. x, 687 p. Illus.

> Essays on rhetoric, the elocution movement, literary societies, and theatricals in educational history. Prepared under the auspices of the Speech Association of America.

STATE AND CITY EDUCATION SYSTEMS

Alabama

Clark, Willis G. HISTORY OF EDUCATION IN ALABAMA, 1702-1889. Bureau of Education, Circular of Information, no. 3. Washington, D.C.: Government Printing Office, 1889. 281 p.

> First comprehensive history of schooling in Alabama.

Weeks, Stephen B. HISTORY OF PUBLIC SCHOOL EDUCATION IN ALABAMA. Washington, D.C.: Government Printing Office, 1915. 290 p.

> The development of public elementary and secondary schools.

Alaska

REPORT ON THE WORK OF THE BUREAU OF EDUCATION FOR THE NATIVES OF ALASKA, 1914-1915. U.S. Department of the Interior. Bureau of Education, Bulletin no. 47, 1916. Washington, D.C.: Government Printing Office, 1917. 85 p. Illus.

> Reports from teachers and superintendents in the several school districts. A large folding map shows public schools for natives in Alaska. Subsequent bulletins continue the reports for these early twentieth-century years.

Arizona

Weeks, Stephen B. HISTORY OF PUBLIC SCHOOL EDUCATION IN ARIZONA. U.S. Bureau of Education, Bulletin no. 17. Washington, D.C.: Government Printing Office, 1918. 141 p.

> Begins with the territorial schools in the 1860s and continues to the development of state administration of schools after 1912.

Arkansas

Shinn, Josiah H. HISTORY OF EDUCATION IN ARKANSAS. U.S. Bureau of Education, Circular of Information, no. 1. Washington, D.C.: Government Printing Office, 1900. 121 p. Illus.

Treatment is in two parts: before the Civil War and after the war. Common schools, academies, and the development of the city high schools are covered. There are two chapters on higher education.

Weeks, Stephen B. HISTORY OF PUBLIC SCHOOL EDUCATION IN ARKAN-SAS. U.S. Bureau of Education, Bulletin no. 27. Washington, D.C.: Government Printing Office, 1912. 131 p.

Development of schools in the territory and state from 1827 up to early twentieth century.

California

Cloud, Roy W. EDUCATION IN CALIFORNIA. Stanford, Calif.: Stanford University Press, 1952. xiv, 296 p. Illus.

One hundred years of leaders, organizations, and accomplishments. Much on teachers' professional organizations.

Swett, John. PUBLIC EDUCATION IN CALIFORNIA: ITS ORIGIN AND DEVELOPMENT. New York: American Book Co., 1911. 320 p. Reprint. New York: Arno Press, 1961. Illus.

One of California's earliest superintendent of public education presents his autobiography and memoirs portraying the early schools of the state.

Colorado

Colorado Education Association. 1861-1885. EDUCATION IN COLORADO: A BRIEF HISTORY OF THE EARLY EDUCATIONAL INTERESTS OF COLORADO. Compiled by the State Teachers Association. Denver: News Printing Co., 1885. 99 p.

Both public and independent efforts in schooling are included.

Risley, James H. HOW IT GREW: A HISTORY OF THE PUEBLO PUBLIC SCHOOLS. Denver: University of Denver Press, 1953. xiv, 335 p. Illus.

A detailed history of the development of a small city school system in the American West.

Connecticut

James, May H. THE EDUCATIONAL HISTORY OF OLD LYME, CONNECTICUT, 1635-1935. New Haven, Conn.: Yale University Press, 1939. vii, 259 p. Illus.

A three-hundred year history of schooling in a Connecticut town. The volume might serve as a model for writing local educational history.

Steiner, Bernard C. THE HISTORY OF EDUCATION IN CONNECTICUT. U.S. Bureau of Education, Circular of Information, no. 2. Washington, D.C.: Government Printing Office, 1893. 300 p. Illus.

> How education developed from colonial days to 1890s with a considerable coverage of Yale, Trinity, and Wesleyan.

Delaware

Powell, Lyman P. HISTORY OF EDUCATION IN DELAWARE. U.S. Bureau of Education, Circular of Information, no. 3. Washington, D.C.: Government Printting Office, 1893. 186 p. Illus.

> Colonial education under the Swedes, Dutch, and English. Under the republic, later private education, academies, Delaware College, and the nineteenth-century growth of public education.

Weeks, Stephen B. HISTORY OF PUBLIC SCHOOL EDUCATION IN DELAWARE. U.S. Bureau of Education, Bulletin no. 18. Washington, D.C.: Government Printing Office, 1917. 181 p. Illus.

> A very complete treatment of Delaware schooling into the early twentieth century. Several statistical tables of school data are included.

Florida

Bush, George G. HISTORY OF EDUCATION IN FLORIDA. U.S. Bureau of Education, Circular of Information, no. 7. Washington, D.C.: Government Printing Office, 1889. 54 p. Illus.

> A brief monograph with a large part devoted to secondary education.

Pyburn, Nita K., ed. DOCUMENTARY HISTORY OF EDUCATION IN FLORIDA, 1822-1860. Tallahassee: Florida State University Press, 1951. xiv, 196 p.

> Significant documents providing the framework of education in Florida before 1860.

Georgia

Jones, Charles E. EDUCATION IN GEORGIA. U.S. Bureau of Education, Circular of Information, no. 4. Washington, D.C.: Government Printing Office, 1889. 154 p. Illus.

> An overview of elementary, secondary, and higher education with chapters on denominational schools, charitable institutions, and schools for black people.

Orr, Dorothy. HISTORY OF EDUCATION IN GEORGIA. Chapel Hill: University of North Carolina Press, 1950. xiv, 463 p. Appendix, illus.

Appendix has biographical sketches of prominent leaders in Georgia education.

Hawaii

A SURVEY OF EDUCATION IN HAWAII. U.S. Bureau of Education, Bulletin no. 16. Washington, D.C.: Government Printing Office, 1920. 171 p.

Provisions for and problems of schooling the several cultural groups, especially the Japanese.

Wist, Benjamin O. A CENTURY OF PUBLIC EDUCATION IN HAWAII. Honolulu: Hawaiian Educational Review, 1940. xi, 221 p. Illus.

Schooling in the kingdom and territory from 1840 to 1940.

Illinois

Cook, John W. EDUCATIONAL HISTORY OF ILLINOIS. Chicago: Henry O. Shepard, 1912. 744 p. Illus.

Includes biographies of early educational leaders.

Herrick, Mary J. THE CHICAGO SCHOOLS: A SOCIAL AND POLITICAL HISTORY. Beverly Hills, Calif.: Sage Publications, 1971. 464 p.

History of the Chicago public school system with much detail on the present century. Several chapters deal with the fiscal, racial, and political issues since the 1950s.

Indiana

Boone, Richard G. A HISTORY OF EDUCATION IN INDIANA. New York: D. Appleton, 1892. xi, 454 p.

Published lectures that were given annually to the department of pedagogy at Indiana University.

Bourne, Randolph S. THE GARY SCHOOLS. Boston: Houghton Mifflin, 1916. xiii, 204 p. Illus.

Gary schools early attracted the attention of progressive educations. The "whole child" and other modern concepts were practiced in that city's public schools. An important work by a social critic of note.

Iowa

Aurner, Clarence R. HISTORY OF EDUCATION IN IOWA. 5 vols. Iowa City: State Historical Society of Iowa, 1914.

A very detailed history by an author who has written several books on the history and government of Iowa.

Kentucky

McVey, Frank L. THE GATES OPEN SLOWLY: A HISTORY OF EDUCATION IN KENTUCKY. Lexington: University of Kentucky Press, 1949. viii, 321 p.

By the president of the University of Kentucky from 1917 to 1940.

Louisiana

Cline, Rodney. EDUCATION IN LOUISIANA: HISTORY AND DEVELOPMENT. Baton Rouge: Claitor's Publishing Division, 1974. xi, 215 p. Bibliog., illus.

Educational history brought up to the 1970s.

Fay, Edwin W. THE HISTORY OF EDUCATION IN LOUISIANA. U.S. Bureau of Education, Circular of Information, no. 1, 1898. Washington, D.C.: Government Printing Office, 1898. 264 p. Illus.

Educational history presented in three periods to 1890, beginning with the days of French rule.

Maine

Chadbourne, Ava H. A HISTORY OF EDUCATION IN MAINE: A STUDY OF A SECTION OF AMERICAN EDUCATIONAL HISTORY. Lancaster, Pa.: Science Press, 1936. xiii, 544 p. Illus.

Common schools, academies, normal schools, and colleges from the late eighteenth century to the 1930s. An extension of Chadbourne's earlier work, THE BEGINNINGS OF EDUCATION IN MAINE (New York: Teachers College, Columbia University, 1928).

Maryland

Steiner, Bernard C. HISTORY OF EDUCATION IN MARYLAND. Washington, D.C.: Government Printing Office, 1894. 331 p. Illus.

Common and secondary schools are covered in chapters 1 and 2, written by Basil Sollers. The remaining deal with higher education.

Massachusetts

Brayley, Arthur W. SCHOOLS AND SCHOOLBOYS OF OLD BOSTON: AN HISTORICAL CHRONICLE OF THE PUBLIC SCHOOLS OF BOSTON FROM 1636 TO 1844. Boston: L.P. Hager, 1894. 439 p. Illus.

Historical account of early Boston schools with biographical sketches of some early students.

Emerson, George B. EDUCATION IN MASSACHUSETTS: EARLY LEGISLATION AND HISTORY. Boston: J. Wilson and Son, 1869. 36 p.

Lectures given before the Lowell Institute by the founder of the American Institute of Instruction.

Kaestle, Carl F., and Vinovski, Maris A. EDUCATION AND SOCIAL CHANGE IN NINETEENTH-CENTURY MASSACHUSETTS. New York: Cambridge University Press, 1980. xxi, 349 p.

Massachusetts used as a case study in how schooling affected social change. Two communities, Boxford (rural) and Lynn (city) were the focal points. Extensive statistical references.

Kozol, Jonathan. DEATH AT AN EARLY AGE. Boston: Houghton Mifflin, 1967. xii, 240 p.

The author attacks the Boston public school system as destructive to black students.

Martin, George H. THE EVOLUTION OF THE MASSACHUSETTS PUBLIC-SCHOOL SYSTEM: A HISTORICAL SKETCH. New York: D. Appleton, 1894. xx, 284 p.

Six lectures including ones on early legislation, colonial schools, the academy, and the work of Horace Mann.

Schultz, Stanley K. THE CULTURE FACTORY: BOSTON PUBLIC SCHOOLS, 1789-1860. New York: Oxford University Press, 1973. 394 p. Illus.

How Boston schools coped with the problem of immigrant children to the time of the Civil War.

Michigan

Dain , Floyd R. EDUCATION IN THE WILDERNESS. Vol. 1 of A HISTORY OF EDUCATION IN MICHIGAN. Lansing: Michigan Historical Commission, 1968. xviii, 346 p. Illus.

Schooling chronicled from early days in the territory to 1850.

Disbrow, Donald W. SCHOOLS FOR AN URBAN SOCIETY. Vol. 3 of A HISTORY OF EDUCATION IN MICHIGAN. Lansing: Michigan Historical Commission, 1968. xiv, 338 p. Illus.

School growth in the twentieth century.

Moehlman, Arthur B. PUBLIC EDUCATION IN DETROIT. Bloomington, Ind.: Public School Publishing Co., 1925. 263 p. Illus.

Book is structured around three periods in the history of schools

in this city: French and English colonial period; the formative
period (1796+); and the period of public free schools (1824+).

Starring, Charles R., and Knauss, James O. THE MICHIGAN SEARCH FOR
EDUCATIONAL STANDARDS. Vol. 2 of A HISTORY OF EDUCATION IN
MICHIGAN. Lansing: Michigan Historical Commission, 1969. xii, 226 p.
Illus.

School history through the early 1900s.

Minnesota

Greer, John N. THE HISTORY OF EDUCATION IN MINNESOTA. U.S.
Bureau of Education, Circular of Information, no. 2, 1902. Washington, D.C.:
Government Printing Office, 1902. 223 p. Illus.

Common schools, high schools, and the University of Minnesota.

Mississippi

Mayes, Edward. HISTORY OF EDUCATION IN MISSISSIPPI. Washington, D.C.:
Government Printing Office, 1899. 290 p. Illus.

Common schools covered briefly. Most attention on higher education
with a chapter on the institutions for black students.

Noble, Stuart G. FORTY YEARS OF THE PUBLIC SCHOOLS IN MISSISSIPPI
WITH SPECIAL REFERENCE TO THE EDUCATION OF THE NEGRO. New York:
Teachers College, Columbia University, 1918. ix, 142 p.

Much information on the segregated schooling of black students.

Missouri

Phillips, Claude A. A HISTORY OF EDUCATION IN MISSOURI. Jefferson City,
Mo.: Hugh Stephens Printing Co., 1911. x, 292 p.

The essential facts concerning the history and organization of Missouri's
schools.

Troen, Selwyn. THE PUBLIC AND THE SCHOOLS: SHAPING THE ST. LOUIS
SYSTEM, 1838-1920. Columbus: University of Missouri Press, 1975. xi, 248 p.

Such leaders as William Harris, Susan Blow, and Calvin Woodward
were associated with schools in St. Louis and that city system attracted
national interest.

Nebraska

Caldwell, Howard W. EDUCATION IN NEBRASKA. U.S. Bureau of Education,

Circular of Information, no. 3, 1902. Washington, D.C.: Government Printing Office, 1902. 268 p. Illus.

> Only one chapter on public schools with the others on higher education.

New Hampshire

Bouton, Nathaniel. THE HISTORY OF EDUCATION IN NEW HAMPSHIRE. Concord, N.H.: Marsh, Capen, and Lyon, 1833. 36 p.

> A discourse delivered before the New Hampshire Historical Society.

Bush, George G. HISTORY OF EDUCATION IN NEW HAMPSHIRE. U.S. Bureau of Education, Circular of Information, no. 3, 1898. Washington, D.C.: Government Printing Office, 1898. 170 p.

> Common schools, academies, and Dartmouth College.

New Jersey

Burr, Nelson R. EDUCATION IN NEW JERSEY, 1630-1871. Princeton, N.J.: Princeton University Press, 1942. 355 p. Illus.

> A model work for a state's educational history. The year 1871 marked the beginning of free public schools in New Jersey.

Murray, David. HISTORY OF EDUCATION IN NEW JERSEY. U.S. Bureau of Education, Circular of Information, no. 1, 1899. Washington, D.C.: Government Printing Office, 1899. 344 p. Illus.

> One half of the monograph deals with common and secondary education; the remaining half with higher education.

New Mexico

Wiley, Tom. PUBLIC SCHOOL EDUCATION IN NEW MEXICO. Albuquerque: University of New Mexico, 1965. x, 158 p.

> Much on control of schools and fiscal matters from the nineteenth-century territorial days to 1965.

New York

Abbott, Frank C. GOVERNMENT POLICY AND HIGHER EDUCATION: A STUDY OF THE REGENTS OF THE UNIVERSITY OF THE STATE OF NEW YORK, 1784-1949. Ithaca, N.Y.: Cornell University Press, 1958. xi, 417 p.

> A study of the governance of the New York state education de-

partment, especially as it pertains to higher education in the state.

Boese, Thomas. PUBLIC EDUCATION IN THE CITY OF NEW YORK: ITS HISTORY, CONDITION, AND STATISTICS. New York: Harper and Brothers, 1869. 228 p.

   History of schooling in New York traced from 1614 to 1868 by the clerk of the city's board of education.

Bourne, William O. HISTORY OF THE PUBLIC SCHOOL SOCIETY OF THE CITY OF NEW YORK. New York: William Wood, 1870. xxxii, 768 p.

   The Public School Society commissioned the author to write a history of the organization which had begun as the Free School Society in 1805.

Draper, Andrew S. ORIGIN AND DEVELOPMENT OF THE COMMON SCHOOL SYSTEM OF NEW YORK STATE. Albany, N.Y.: J.B. Lyon, 1890. 48 p.

   An address given before the New York State Teachers Association by a former superintendent of public instruction.

Finegan, Thomas B. FREE SCHOOLS: A DOCUMENTARY HISTORY OF THE FREE SCHOOL MOVEMENT IN NEW YORK STATE. Albany: University of the State of New York, 1921. 682 p. Illus.

   Development of free public schooling with roots going back to the colonial period. Much on legislation and people involved. Essentially a collection of source materials.

Hough, Franklin B. HISTORICAL AND STATISTICAL RECORD OF THE UNIVERSITY OF THE STATE OF NEW YORK. Albany, N.Y.: Weed, Parsons and Co., 1885. viii, 867 p.

   History of the Board of Regents, the governing board of public education in the state of New York. The work also includes histories of academies, the College of the City of New York, normal schools, and private colleges.

Kilpatrick, William H. THE DUTCH SCHOOLS OF NEW NETHERLAND AND COLONIAL NEW YORK. U.S. Bureau of Education, Bulletin no. 12, 1912. Washington, D.C.: Government Printing Office, 1912. 239 p.

   The definitive work on the earliest schooling in New York, especially of the Collegiate School, the oldest institution.

Maxwell, William H. A QUARTER CENTURY OF PUBLIC SCHOOL DEVELOPMENT. Introduction by Nicholas Murray Butler. New York: American Book Co., 1912. xii, 417 p. Illus.

   A collection of the author's writings after he had completed twenty-five years as superintendent of schools in New York.

Miller, George F. THE ACADEMY SYSTEM OF THE STATE OF NEW YORK.
Albany, N.Y.: J.B. Lyon, 1922. 180 p. Reprint. New York: Arno Press,
1969.

> Academy movement in New York began in 1787 with De Witt
> Clinton Academy in Easthampton and Erasmus Hall Academy in
> Brooklyn. This work examines the several hundred such institutions
> established through the nineteenth century.

Palmer, A. Emerson. THE NEW YORK PUBLIC SCHOOL: BEING A HISTORY
OF FREE EDUCATION IN THE CITY OF NEW YORK. New York: Macmillan,
1905. xxx, 440 p.

> Accounts of the colonial schools, the Manumission Society (early
> society concerned with freeing slaves), the Free School Society,
> and the New York City Board of Education.

Randall, Samuel S. HISTORY OF THE COMMON SCHOOL SYSTEM OF THE
STATE OF NEW YORK. New York: Ivison, Blakeman, Taylor, 1871. xiv,
477 p.

> An important source on public education from 1795 to the 1870s.
> The religious controversies of 1821, 1832, and 1840 are covered.

Ravitch, Diane. THE GREAT SCHOOL WARS: NEW YORK CITY, 1805-1973.
New York: Basic Books, 1974. xviii, 449 p. Illus.

> From the incorporation of the Free School Society in 1805, through
> the battle on school decentralization in the early 1970s, the po-
> litical-religious struggles that confronted New York City's schools
> are set forth.

Rogers, David. 110 LIVINGSTON STREET: POLITICS AND BUREAUCRACY
IN THE NEW YORK CITY SCHOOLS. New York: Random House, 1968.
xii, 585 p.

> A critical report of the administration of the public schools of
> New York especially important for the volatile years of the 1960s.

Sherwood, Sidney. THE UNIVERSITY OF THE STATE OF NEW YORK. U.S.
Bureau of Education, Circular of Information, no. 3. Washington, D.C.:
Government Printing Office, 1900. 538 p. Illus.

> Monograph deals essentially with the colleges and universities in
> New York, but the first part presents the history and structure of
> the Board of Regents.

North Carolina

Coon, Charles L. THE BEGINNINGS OF PUBLIC EDUCATION IN NORTH
CAROLINA: A DOCUMENTARY HISTORY, 1790-1840. 2 vols. Raleigh:
Edwards and Broughton, 1908.

> The significant school documents to the pre-Civil War period.

Knight, Edgar W. PUBLIC EDUCATION IN NORTH CAROLINA. Boston: Houghton Mifflin, 1916. viii, 384 p.

A work by a distinguished educational historian on a state which has been a leader in southern educational progress.

Smith, Charles L. THE HISTORY OF EDUCATION IN NORTH CAROLINA. U.S. Bureau of Education, Circular of Information, no. 2. Washington, D.C.: Government Printing Office, 1888. 180 p. Illus.

A general survey with one chapter devoted to secondary education, from the Province of North Carolina through the 1880s.

Ohio

Burns, James J. EDUCATIONAL HISTORY OF OHIO. Columbus: Historical Publishing Co., 1905. ix, 756 p. Illus.

The educational history since Ohio became a state. Biographies and portraits of state officers are included.

Freese, Andrew. EARLY HISTORY OF THE CLEVELAND PUBLIC SCHOOLS. Cleveland: Robinson, Savage and Co., 1876. 128 p.

An early history of a city school system.

Ohio State Centennial Education Committee. HISTORICAL SKETCHES OF PUBLIC SCHOOLS IN CITIES, VILLAGES, AND TOWNSHIPS OF THE STATE OF OHIO. N.p.: n.p., 1876. Illus.

Individual histories were locally prepared and compiled into this rather large volume which is not paged. A valuable source of information on Ohio public schools in mid-nineteenth century.

Pennsylvania

Custis, John T. THE PUBLIC SCHOOLS OF PHILADELPHIA. Philadelphia: Burk and McFetridge, 1897. 680 p. Illus.

A large and well-illustrated volume beginning with the formation of the city's first school district in 1818. The schools of each subsequent district are described and pictured.

Riddle, William. ONE HUNDRED AND FIFTY YEARS OF SCHOOL HISTORY IN LANCASTER, PENNSYLVANIA. Lancaster, Pa.: By the author, 1905. xix, 442 p. Illus.

One of the most thorough early educational histories of a city school system. Early church and private schools are included.

Wickersham, James P. HISTORY OF EDUCATION IN PENNSYLVANIA. Lancaster, Pa.: Inquirer Publishing, 1886. xxiii, 683 p. Illus.

One of the classic state histories of education. The scope is
from the settlement of the Swedes to the third quarter of the nineteenth century.

Rhode Island

Carroll, Charles. PUBLIC EDUCATION IN RHODE ISLAND. Providence:
E.L. Freeman Co., 1918. 500 p.

By a Providence lawyer and sometime professor of education, law,
and government at Rhode Island College of Education.

Stockwell, Thomas B., ed. A HISTORY OF PUBLIC EDUCATION IN RHODE
ISLAND FROM 1636 TO 1876. Providence: Providence Press Co., 1876.
v, 458 p.

Papers on the history of schooling in Providence as well as in
other places in the state.

Stone, Edwin M. A CENTURY OF EDUCATION: BEING A CONCISE HIS-
TORY OF THE RISE AND PROGRESS OF THE PUBLIC SCHOOLS IN THE CITY
OF PROVIDENCE. Providence: Providence Press Co., 1876. 84 p.

A monograph that chronicles the city's early school history in five
epochs from 1776 to 1876.

South Carolina

Meriwether, Colyer. HISTORY OF HIGHER EDUCATION IN SOUTH CAROLINA
WITH A SKETCH OF THE FREE SCHOOL SYSTEM. Washington, D.C.: Government Printing Office, 1889. 247 p. Illus.

Common schools and academies are included along with the colleges.

Tennessee

Holt, Andrew D. THE STRUGGLE FOR A STATE SYSTEM OF PUBLIC
SCHOOLS IN TENNESSEE, 1903-1936. New York: Teachers College, Columbia University, 1938. xvi, 502 p.

Forces promoting and retarding educational growth prior to 1902
are dealt with in part 1. The years after 1903 saw much legislation on public education.

Texas

Eby, Frederick. THD DEVELOPMENT OF EDUCATION IN TEXAS. New York:
Macmillan, 1925. xv, 354 p.

From the Spanish regime to the early 1920s. There is a chapter
on Negro education.

Lane, John J. HISTORY OF EDUCATION IN TEXAS. U.S. Bureau of Education, Circular of Information, no. 2. Washington, D.C.: Government Printing Office, 1903. 334 p. Illus.

One chapter of public schools with others on church schools, normal schools, the University of Texas, and the A & M College.

Utah

Moffitt, John C. THE HISTORY OF EDUCATION IN UTAH. N.p.: n.p., 1946. xvi, 375 p.

The work of the Mormon Church in establishing schools.

Vermont

Bush, George G. HISTORY OF EDUCATION IN VERMONT. U.S. Bureau of Education, Circular of Information, no. 4. Washington, D.C.: Government Printing Office, 1900. 216 p. Illus.

There is a lengthy treatment of common and secondary schools.

Virginia

Bell, Sadie. THE CHURCH, THE STATE, AND EDUCATION IN VIRGINIA. Philadelphia: Science Press Printing Co., 1930. xi, 796 p. Reprint. New York: Arno Press, 1969.

Important for the early close ties between church and schooling in Virginia.

Washington

Bolton, Frederick E., and Bibb, Thomas W. HISTORY OF EDUCATION IN WASHINGTON. Washington, D.C.: Government Printing Office, 1935. xxi, 448 p.

Includes general historical background of the region. Educational history is comprehensive and includes legislation, developments at all levels and in all counties.

Bowden, Angie B. THE EARLY SCHOOLS OF WASHINGTON TERRITORY. Seattle: Lowman and Hanford, 1935. xiv, 631 p. Illus.

Each county's provisions for schooling are chronicled up to the date of statehood in 1889.

West Virginia

Ambler, Charles H. A HISTORY OF EDUCATION IN WEST VIRGINIA FROM EARLY COLONIAL TIMES TO 1949. Huntington, W. Va.: Standard Printing and Publishing Co., 1951. x, 1,010 p. Illus.

Chapters on academies and higher education, and the new education of the early twentieth century. Three chapters are devoted to the Depression.

Whitehill, Alexander R. HISTORY OF EDUCATION IN WEST VIRGINIA. U.S. Bureau of Education, Circular of Information, no. 1. Washington, D.C.: Government Printing Office, 1902. 163 p. Illus.

Development of public schools, normal schools, denominational schools, and higher education.

Wisconsin

Jorgenson, Lloyd P. THE FOUNDING OF PUBLIC EDUCATION IN WISCONSIN. Madison: State Historical Society of Wisconsin, 1956. ix, 252 p.

The book's mandate is the "founding," thus the treatment of the several themes (teachers, support, district schools, etc.) does not reach much beyond the 1860s.

Wyoming

Monahan, A.C., and Cook, Katherine M. EDUCATION SURVEY OF WYOMING. Washington, D.C.: Government Printing Office, 1917. 120 p. Illus.

First part of monograph gives a sketch of the early history of schooling in Wyoming beginning in 1860.

STUDENT DISSENT AND REVOLT

Altbach, Philip G., and Kelly, David H. AMERICAN STUDENTS: A SELECTED BIBLIOGRAPHY ON STUDENT ACTIVISM AND RELATED TOPICS. Lexington, Mass.: Lexington Books, 1973. xiv, 537 p.

An updating of a 1967 work. Includes references to the activism of the 1960s and early 1970s.

Avorn, Jerry L. UP AGAINST THE IVY WALL: A HISTORY OF THE COLUMBIA CRISIS. New York: Atheneum Press, 1968. vi, 307 p. Illus.

A detailed account of the events of April and May 1968 in the student revolt on the Columbia University campus. A defense of the action: "By seizing the buildings, we took back our university."

Brickman, William W., and Lehrer, Stanley, eds. CONFLICT AND CHANGE ON THE CAMPUS: THE RESPONSE TO STUDENT HYPERACTIVISM. New York: School and Society Books, 1970. 528 p.

A collection of writings, from the early 1960s to the end of that decade, on student activism. Parts 1 and 3 cover the situation in the United States.

Califano, Joseph A., Jr. THE STUDENT REVOLUTION: A GLOBAL CONFRONTATION. New York: W.W. Norton, 1970. 96 p.

An interpretation of student dissent from 1965 in selected countries of Europe (Britain, France, West Germany, and Italy), Japan, and briefly, Israel, from a trip to those places by the author. Chapters 5 and 6 deal with the United States.

Carnegie Commission on Higher Education. DISSENT AND DISRUPTION: PROPOSALS FOR A CONSIDERATION BY THE CAMPUS. New York: McGraw-Hill, 1971. viii, 312 p. Appendix.

How dissent on campus may be protected and how disruption may be prevented. Considerable appendix material with statements of policy from several institutions.

Cohen, Mitchell, and Hale, Dennis, eds. THE NEW STUDENT LEFT: AN ANTHOLOGY. Boston: Beacon Press, 1966. xxxi, 288 p.

Writings on issues of political activity involving race, poverty, and free speech. The early 1960s Berkeley troubles are included.

Ehrenreich, Barbara, and Ehrenreich, John. LONG MARCH, SHORT SPRING: THE STUDENT UPRISING AT HOME AND ABROAD. New York: Monthly Review Press, 1969. 189 p.

Revolt among college students in Germany, Italy, France, England, and in the United States (at Columbia), by two former graduate students who made visits in spring of 1968.

Erlich, John, and Erlich, Susan, eds. STUDENT POWER, PARTICIPATION AND REVOLUTION. New York: Association Press, 1970. 254 p.

Excerpts from a variety of activist sources from 1960 to 1970, arranged in five parts (e.g., rise of student power, confrontation, etc.) on student dissent and revolution.

Flacks, Richard. YOUTH AND SOCIAL CHANGE. Chicago: Markham Publishing Co., 1971. xi, 147 p.

Source material from author's involvement at the University of California at Santa Barbara. How a generation of youth transformed the placid campus of the 1950s into the turbulence of the 1960s.

Frankel, Charles. EDUCATION AND THE BARRICADES. New York: W.W. Norton, 1968. 90 p.

States the issues involved in the student protest movement. Author is unhappy with tactics of protesting students, but he is also unhappy with the inadequacies of higher education.

Harris, Janet. STUDENTS IN REVOLT. New York: McGraw-Hill, 1970. 176 p.

The 1960s student troubles at Berkeley, San Francisco State, and Columbia are covered. Other chapters cover Paris, Mexico, Prague, and West Germany.

Henrick, Irving G., and Jones, Reginald L. STUDENT DISSENT IN THE SCHOOLS. Boston: Houghton Mifflin, 1970. x, 400 p. Illus.

Limited to public secondary schools. Dress codes, student rights, drugs, and other themes, with much material taken from contemporary sources. Practical suggestions from the schools themselves for coping.

Kenniston, Kenneth. RADICALS AND MILITANTS: AN ANNOTATED BIBLIOGRAPHY OF EMPIRICAL RESEARCH ON CAMPUS UNREST. Lexington, Mass.: D.C. Heath, 1973. xxi, 219 p.

The "campus unrest" here is that of the 1960s and early 1970s.

Lipset, Seymour Martin, and Wolin, Sheldon S., eds. THE BERKELEY STUDENTS REVOLT. Garden City, N.Y.: Doubleday, 1965. xiv, 585 p.

An early look at what was to become a much larger social phenomenon. Facts and interpretation presented.

Menashe, Louis, and Radosh, Ronald, eds. TEACH-INS: U.S.A. New York: F.A. Praeger, 1967. xv, 349 p.

A collection of reports, opinions, and documents on campus political activity.

Sampson, Edward E., and Korn, Harold A., eds. STUDENT ACTIVISM AND PROTEST. San Francisco: Jossey-Bass, 1970. xviii, 265 p.

Chapters by the editors and several others on the decade of protest, 1960-70. The sources and the psychology of dissent are among the topics covered.

STUDENT FRATERNITIES AND SOCIETIES

Baird, William R. AMERICAN COLLEGE FRATERNITIES: A DESCRIPTIVE ANALYSIS OF THE SOCIETY SYSTEM IN THE COLLEGES OF THE UNITED STATES, WITH A DETAILED ACCOUNT OF EACH FRATERNITY. Philadelphia: L.B. Lippincott, 1879. 212 p.

The first descriptive listing of college fraternities. The work has gone through subsequent editions known as BAIRD'S MANUAL OF AMERICAN COLLEGE FRATERNITIES.

Scott, William A. VALUES AND ORGANIZATIONS: A STUDY OF FRATERNITIES AND SORORITIES. Chicago: Rand McNally, 1965. 290 p.

> A sociological study of college Greek-letter societies.

Sheldon, Henry D. THE HISTORY OF PEDAGOGY OF AMERICAN STUDENT SOCIETIES. New York: D. Appleton, 1901. xxii, 366 p.

> European backgrounds of student life. Student life in American colleges from colonial days to 1900.

Voorhees, Oscar M. THE HISTORY OF PHI BETA KAPPA. New York: Crown Publishers, 1945. xi, 372 p. Illus.

> Study of the oldest college fraternity, founded in 1776 at the college of William and Mary.

SUPERVISION OF SCHOOLS

Barr, A.S., et al. SUPERVISION: DEMOCRATIC LEADERSHIP IN THE IMPROVEMENT OF LEARNING. 2d ed. New York: A. Appleton-Century, 1947. viii, 879 p. Illus.

> This work is a revision and expansion of William H. Burton's first book on supervision, SUPERVISION AND THE IMPROVEMENT OF TEACHING, published in 1922, and of one by Barr and Burton, THE SUPERVISION OF INSTRUCTION, in 1926. It was a popular text in graduate courses on school supervision.

Goldhammer, Robert. CLINICAL SUPERVISION: SPECIAL METHODS FOR THE SUPERVISION OF TEACHERS. New York: Holt, Rinehart and Winston, 1969. xiv, 370 p.

> A five-state sequence model of supervision of educational leaders which grew from the Harvard-Lexington Summer Program.

Gwynn, J. Minor. THEORY AND PRACTICE OF SUPERVISION. New York: Dodd, Mead, 1968. 473 p. Illus.

> Treats both elementary and secondary supervising practices. A modern analysis suitable for a graduate course in the field or for reference use of supervisors at work.

Lucio, William H., and McNeill, John D. SUPERVISION: A SYNTHESIS OF THOUGHT AND ACTION. New York: McGraw-Hill, 1969. x, 329 p.

> A text for graduate students of educational supervision. Both human skills (behavior) and technical skills (evaluation) are featured.

Wiles, Kimball, and Lovell, John T. SUPERVISION FOR BETTER SCHOOLS. 4th ed. Englewood Cliffs, N.J.: Prentice-Hall, 1975. viii, 328 p.

> Supervision at district and individual school level. Especially helpful guidelines for a new supervisor.

TEACHER EDUCATION

History of Teacher Education

Barnard, Henry. NORMAL SCHOOLS, AND OTHER INSTITUTIONS, AGENCIES, AND MEANS DESIGNED FOR THE PROFESSIONAL EDUCATION OF TEACHERS. Hartford, Conn.: Case, Tiffany and Co., 1851. 435 p.

> Normal schools in Europe, Canada, and the United States.

Borrowman, Merle L., ed. TEACHER EDUCATION IN AMERICA: A DOCUMENTARY HISTORY. New York: Teachers College Press, 1965. x, 251 p.

> Addresses, essays, and lectures comprising a history of teacher education.

Fowle, William B. THE TEACHERS' INSTITUTE. Boston: W.B. Fowle, 1847. iv, 258 p.

> Especially written for young and beginning teachers, many of whom would have had little or no training. Fowle was a Massachusetts teacher, book publisher, and prolific author of schoolbooks.

Harper, Charles A. A CENTURY OF PUBLIC TEACHER EDUCATION: THE STORY OF THE STATE TEACHERS COLLEGES AS THEY EVOLVED FROM THE NORMAL SCHOOLS. Washington, D.C.: National Education Association, 1939. 175 p.

> The story of the normal school movement brought up to the development of the twentieth-century teachers college.

Hinsdale, Burke A. THE TRAINING OF TEACHERS. Albany, N.Y.: J.B. Lyon Co., 1899. 49 p.

> A monography by a former president of Hiram College and superintendent of schools in Cleveland, Ohio, prepared for the U.S. educational exhibit at the Paris Exposition of 1900.

Mattingly, Paul H. THE CLASSLESS PROFESSION: AMERICAN SCHOOLMEN IN THE NINETEENTH CENTURY. New York: New York University Press, 1975. xxiii, 235 p. Illus.

> History of the public school teacher as a professional in America. Piety and virtue were themes for a good part of this history.

Norton, Arthur O., ed. THE FIRST STATE NORMAL SCHOOL IN AMERICA:

THE JOURNAL OF CYRUS PIERCE AND MARY SWIFT. Cambridge, Mass.: Harvard University Press, 1926. lvi, 299 p. Reprint. New York: Arno Press, 1969.

> Documentary history of the first state normal school at Lexington, Massachusetts (later moved to Framingham), at its opening in 1839.

Pangburn, Jessie M. THE EVOLUTION OF THE AMERICAN TEACHERS COLLEGE. New York: Teachers College, Columbia University, 1932. vi, 140 p.

> The transformation of the nineteenth-century normal school into the twentieth-century teachers college. The work begins with the normal school situation in 1890.

Issues of Teacher Education

Conant, James B. THE EDUCATION OF AMERICAN TEACHERS. New York: McGraw-Hill, 1963. ix, 275 p.

> Results of a two-year study of seventy teacher-training programs. Some radical alterations suggested.

Haberman, Martin. TEACHER EDUCATION AND THE NEW PROFESSION OF TEACHING. Berkeley, Calif.: McCutchan, 1973. vi, 257 p.

> Some introductory chapters on the history of teacher training. Most of book concerns selection of students, content, newer practices, and competency-based programs.

Koerner, James D. THE MISEDUCATION OF AMERICAN TEACHERS. Boston: Houghton Mifflin, 1963. xiv, 360 p.

> A critical assessment of the preparation of teachers (at baccalaureate, master, and doctoral levels). Twenty case studies of individual degree programs are examined and generally found wanting.

McCarthy, Donald J., et al. NEW PERSPECTIVES ON TEACHER EDUCATION. San Francisco: Jossey-Bass, 1973. xiv, 255 p.

> Several leaders in teacher education analyze problems in teacher preparation and suggest reforms.

Rosner, Benjamin. THE POWER OF COMPETENCY-BASED TEACHER EDUCATION. Boston: Allyn and Bacon, 1972. ix, 260 p.

> The report of the Committee on National Priorities in Teacher Education of the U.S. Office of Education. Competency-based teacher education was a new departure beginning in the 1970s.

Rugg, Harold O. THE TEACHER OF TEACHERS: FRONTIERS OF THEORY AND PRACTICE IN TEACHER EDUCATION. New York: Harper, 1952. x, 308 p.

> Emerging designs in teacher education from the 1920s into the 1950s.

Ryan, Kevin, ed. TEACHER EDUCATION. 74th Yearbook, National Society for the Study of Education. Chicago: University of Chicago Press, 1975. xiv, 464 p.

> A collection of essays brought together by the Committee on Teacher Education of the National Society for the Study of Education. There is a chapter on performance-based teacher education.

TEAM TEACHING

Bair, Medill, and Woodward, Richard G. TEAM TEACHING IN ACTION. Boston: Houghton Mifflin, 1964. x, 229 p. Illus.

> Rationale, space requirements, small and large group instruction, and an assessment of team teaching.

Beggs, David W., ed. TEAM TEACHING: BOLD NEW VENTURE. Bloomington: Indiana University Press, 1964. 192 p. Illus.

> A discussion by a number of authorities on what happens when team teaching is practiced.

Chamberlin, Leslie J. TEAM TEACHING: ORGANIZATION AND ADMINISTRATION. Columbus: Charles E. Merrill, 1969. vii, 152 p. Illus..

> Several patterns of team teaching are presented.

Shaplin, Judson T., and Olds, Henry F., Jr., eds. TEAM TEACHING. New York: Harper and Row, 1964. xv, 430 p.

> A discussion of team teaching from many perspectives: psychological, sociological, architectural planning, curriculum, and administration.

TEXTBOOKS, HISTORY OF

Carpenter, Charles H. HISTORY OF AMERICAN SCHOOLBOOKS. Philadelphia: University of Pennsylvania Press, 1963. 322 p. Illus.

> Elementary and secondary schoolbooks through the nineteenth century.

Elson, Ruth M. GUARDIANS OF TRADITION: AMERICAN SCHOOLBOOKS OF THE NINETEENTH CENTURY. Lincoln: University of Nebraska Press, 1964. xiii, 424 p. Illus.

> A study of one thousand schoolbooks showing how the white Protestant value system was reflected in these books.

Ford, Paul L., ed. THE NEW-ENGLAND PRIMER: A HISTORY OF ITS ORIGIN AND DEVELOPMENT. New York: Teachers College, Columbia University, 1962. 78 p. Illus.

A reprint of an 1897 work on the 1727 edition of the NEW ENGLAND PRIMER.

Johnson, Clifton. OLD-TIME SCHOOLS AND SCHOOL-BOOKS. New York: Macmillan, 1904. xxi, 381 p. Illus.

The kinds of schools found in America to the middle of the nineteenth century, and a presentation of the best-known textbooks used in these schools.

Littlefield, George E. EARLY SCHOOLS AND SCHOOL-BOOKS OF NEW ENGLAND. New York: Russell and Russell, 1965. 354 p. Illus.

A reissue of a 1904 edition. Two-thirds of the book deals with the textbooks used in New England schools during the eighteenth and nineteenth centuries.

Mosier, Richard D. MAKING THE AMERICAN MIND: SOCIAL AND MORAL IDEAS IN THE McGUFFEY READERS. New York: Russell and Russell, 1965. vi, 207 p.

The reading books of McGuffey, beginning 1836, had great influence in forming the moral concepts of American children. A reissue of a 1947 edition.

Nietz, John A. OLD TEXTBOOKS. Pittsburgh: University of Pittsburgh Press, 1961. x, 364 p. Illus.

An analysis of American schoolbooks, essentially those used in common schools before 1900.

UNIONIZATION OF TEACHERS

Braun, Robert J. TEACHERS AND POWER: THE STORY OF THE AMERICAN FEDERATION OF TEACHERS. New York: Simon and Schuster, 1972. 287 p.

History of the AFT from its establishment in 1916, as a part of the American Federation of Labor. The 1970 Newark teachers' strike, and the 1968 Ocean Hill-Brownsville episode, in New York City, are discussed in detail.

Donley, Marshall O. POWER TO THE TEACHER: HOW AMERICA'S EDUCATORS BECAME MILITANT. Bloomington: Indiana University Press, 1976. xii, 242 p. Illus.

Development and power of the National Education Association, American Federation of Teachers, and the issue of teacher strikes, are among the topics.

Garbarino, Joseph W. FACULTY BARGAINING: CHANGE AND CONFLICT. New York: McGraw-Hill, 1975. ix, 278 p.

Collective bargaining in institutions of higher learning. A report prepared for the Carnegie Commission on Higher Education and the Ford Foundation.

Shils, Edward B., and Whittier, C. Taylor. TEACHERS, ADMINISTRATORS AND COLLECTIVE BARGAINING. New York: Thomas Y. Crowell, 1968. xi, 580 p.

Several items of state legislation on collective negotiations are summarized. Work grew out of the 1968 Philadelphia School District negotiations with the American Federation of Teachers.

U.S. OFFICE OF EDUCATION, DEPARTMENT OF EDUCATION

Johnson, Julia E., ed. SELECTED ARTICLES ON A FEDERAL DEPARTMENT OF EDUCATION. New York: H.W. Wilson Co., 1927. lxxii, 359 p. Bibliog.

A collection of articles from periodicals with a bibliography on the subject through 1926. A precursor of a development to come over fifty years later.

Kursh, Harry. THE UNITED STATES OFFICE OF EDUCATION: A CENTURY OF SERVICE. New York: Chilton Books, 1965. xvi, 192 p. Illus.

A historical evaluation of the former U.S. Bureau of Education, created in 1867, and its subsequent growth as the Office of Education.

Warren, Donald R. TO ENFORCE EDUCATION: A HISTORY OF THE FOUND-ING YEARS OF THE U.S. OFFICE OF EDUCATION. Detroit: Wayne State University Press, 1974. 239 p. Illus.

Essentially on the early days of the OE, ending with a chapter on "Barnard's Bureau in the 1970's."

URBAN EDUCATON

Booth, Robert E., et al. CULTURALLY DISADVANTAGED: A BIBLIOGRAPHY AND KEYWORD-OUT-OF-CONTEXT INDEX. Detroit: Wayne State University Press, 1967. viii, 803 p.

The term "culturally disadvantaged" came into use in the 1960s and books, monographs, and articles appeared in profusion. This work is helpful because of the many keywords under which information is likely to be found.

Chandler, B.J., et al., eds. EDUCATION IN URBAN SOCIETY. New York: Dodd, Mead, 1962. viii, 279 p.

Problems of schooling children in the cities are stated in essays by administrators, sociologists, political scientists, and professors of education.

Conant, James B. SLUMS AND SUBURBS: A COMMENTARY ON SCHOOLS IN METROPOLITAN AREAS. New York: McGraw-Hill, 1961. 147 p.

> An early work on urban education. An argument is made against token racial integration across school district boundaries.

Fantini, Mario, et al. COMMUNITY CONTROL AND THE URBAN SCHOOL. New York: Praeger, 1970. xix, 268 p.

> The struggle for community control of public schools in New York during the late 1960s.

Gittell, Marilyn, ed. EDUCATING AN URBAN POPULATION. Beverly Hills, Calif.: Sage Publications, 1967. 320 p. Illus.

> Considers the demands on school policy from several sources and suggests ways for achieving change in an urban school system.

Miller, Harry L. SOCIAL FOUNDATIONS OF EDUCATION: AN URBAN FOCUS. 3d ed. New York: Holt, Rinehart and Winston, 1978. vii, 407 p.

> A college text on urban education. Book is divided into two parts: (1) the social and economic influences on schools in cities, and (2) the schools themselves (curriculum, teachers, desegregation, governance).

Morine, Harold, and Morine, Greta. PRIMER FOR THE INNER-CITY SCHOOL. New York: McGraw-Hill, 1970. 169 p. Illus.

> Describes a curriculum based upon cognitive development and behavior modification for the inner-city school student.

Rudman, Herbert C., and Featherstone, Richard L., eds. URBAN SCHOOLING. New York: Harcourt, Brace and World, 1968. xii, 296 p. Illus.

> Twelve essays on socioeconomic and racial problems in urban schools.

Spear, George E., and Mocker, Donald W., eds. URBAN EDUCATION: A GUIDE TO INFORMATION SOURCES. Urban Studies Information Guide Series, vol. 3. Detroit: Gale Research Co., 1978. x, 203 p.

> Annotated listing of books, monographs, and articles in periodicals. Most sources are from the 1960s on as the topic, as such, did not appear as a separate category much before then.

Tyack, David B. THE ONE BEST SYSTEM: A HISTORY OF AMERICAN URBAN EDUCATION. Cambridge, Mass.: Harvard University Press, 1974. xii, 353 p. Illus.

> The first comprehensive history of American urban education. A look at some modern departures in the field with the conclusion that there is no "one best system" for all.

VOCATIONAL EDUCATION

Barlow, Melvin L., ed. VOCATIONAL EDUCATION. 64th Yearbook, National Society for the Study of Education. Chicago: University of Chicago Press, 1965. x, 310 p., vi.

Thirteen chapters on topics current at the time.

Hawkins, Layton S., et al. DEVELOPMENT OF VOCATIONAL EDUCATION. 2d ed. Chicago: American Technical Society, 1962. ix, 656 p. Illus.

Contains text of Smith-Hughes Act of 1917 and much on the history of vocational education.

Lapp, John A., and Mote, Carl H. LEARNING TO EARN: A PLEA AND A PLAN FOR VOCATIONAL EDUCATION. Indianapolis: Bobbs-Merrill, 1915. 421 p.

An early call for vocational education in the schools.

McMahon, Gordon G. CURRICULUM DEVELOPMENT IN TRADE AND INDUSTRIAL AND TECHNICAL EDUCATION. Columbus: Charles E. Merrill, 1972. x, 134 p.

A treatment of the individuals, factors, and practices involved in preparing curriculums in vocational education.

Thompson, John F. FOUNDATIONS OF VOCATIONAL EDUCATION: SOCIETAL AND PHILOSOPHICAL CONCEPTS. Englewood Cliffs, N.J.: Prentice-Hall, 1973. xvii, 260 p. Illus.

Historical development, legislation, underlying assumptions, and contemporary programs in vocational education.

VOUCHER PLAN

Fantini, Mario D. PUBLIC SCHOOLS OF CHOICE. New York: Simon and Schuster, 1973. 256 p.

A rationale for the voucher plan. Alternative schools in Berkeley, California, are cited as an example of public schools of choice.

LaNoue, George R., ed. EDUCATIONAL VOUCHERS: CONCEPTS AND CONTROVERSIES. New York: Teachers College Press, 1972. viii, 176 p.

A collection of writings on the economic, legal, and educational aspects of the voucher plan.

Mecklenburger, James A., and Hostrap, Richard W. EDUCATIONAL VOUCHERS: FROM THEORY TO ALUM ROCK. Homewook, Ill.: ETC Publications, 1972. 412 p. Illus.

The movement toward the voucher proposal began about 1967. This work carries the thinking and events up to 1972 as reported in periodicals and other sources.

WOMEN, EDUCATION OF

Emerson, George B. A LECTURE ON THE EDUCATION OF FEMALES. Boston: Hilliard, Gray, Little and Wilkins, 1831. 27 p.

A lecture given before the American Institute of Instruction. Author had opened a school for girls in Boston in 1823.

Frankfort, Roberta. COLLEGIATE WOMEN: DOMESTICITY AND CAREERS IN TURN-OF-THE-CENTURY AMERICA. New York: New York University Press, 1977. xix, 121 p. Illus.

Focuses on Bryn Mawr and Wellesley at turn of the century and examines the lives of Elizabeth Peabody, Alice Palmer, Martha Thomas, and Ellen Richards.

Goodsell, Willystine. PIONEERS OF WOMEN'S EDUCATION IN THE UNITED STATES. New York: McGraw-Hill, 1931. viii, 311 p. Illus.

Emma Willard, Catherine Beecher, and Mary Lyon are featured.

Kendall, Elaine. PECULIAR INSTITUTIONS: AN INFORMAL HISTORY OF THE SEVEN SISTER COLLEGES. New York: G.P. Putnam's Sons, 1976. 272 p. Illus.

Mount Holyoke, Smith, Vassar, Bryn Mawr, Radcliffe, Barnard, and Wellesley are the "peculiar" institutions, all established for women in the nineteenth century. The work presents how these colleges nurtured an intellectual and professional leadership.

Newcomer, Mabel. A CENTURY OF HIGHER EDUCATION FOR AMERICAN WOMEN. New York: Harper, 1959. 266 p.

The struggle for women's higher education with a treatment of the curriculum.

Rush, Benjamin. THOUGHTS UPON FEMALE EDUCATION. Philadelphia: Prichard and Hall, 1787. 32 p.

An address given at the Young Ladies Academy in Philadelphia. Rush was an advocate of female education.

Talbot, Marion. THE EDUCATION OF WOMEN. Chicago: University of Chicago Press, 1910. ix, 255 p.

Discusses changes which have taken place in education of women since the nineteenth century. Author, dean of women at University of Chicago, urges physical training, some new courses, and more recognition of women in academic and intellectual fields.

Thomas, Martha C. EDUCATION OF WOMEN. Albany, N.Y.: J.B. Lyon, 1900. 40 p.

> A monograph prepared for the Paris Exhibition of 1900 by the first president of Bryn Mawr. Thomas established the first graduate school at a college for women.

Thwing, Charles F. THE COLLEGE WOMAN. New York: Baker and Taylor, 1894. 169 p.

> By the president of Western Reserve University, a prolific nineteenth-century writer on education, and an advocate of higher education for women.

Willard, Emma H. A PLAN FOR IMPROVING FEMALE EDUCATION. Middlebury, Vt.: Middlebury College, 1918. 35 p.

> First published in Albany in 1819 under title AN ADDRESS TO THE PUBLIC . . . PROPOSING A PLAN FOR IMPROVING FEMALE EDUCATION. Willard was one of the earliest leaders in the movement for the education of women.

Woody, Thomas. A HISTORY OF WOMEN'S EDUCATION IN THE UNITED STATES. 2 vols. Lancaster, Pa.: Science Press, 1921. Illus.

> The definitive work on female education in the United States.

NAME INDEX

This index includes all persons covered as subjects and all authors, editors, compilers, and other contributors to works cited in the text. Alphabetization is letter by letter and references are to page numbers.

Name Index

Name Index

Name Index

Hutchins, Robert M. 20, 21, 47, 94
Hutt, Max L. 204

I

Illich, Ivan D. 22, 49
Inglis, Alexander J. 187
Irby, Richard 140

J

James, Henry 62
James, May H. 208
James, William 55, 65
Janeway, James 3
Jantz, Richard K. 26
Jarolimek, John 199
Jefferson, Thomas 10, 11, 66
Jencks, Christopher 23, 97, 201
Jenkins, John 85
Jenkinson, Edward B. 25
Jensen, Arthur R. 79
Jewell, James P. 29
Johanningmeier, Erwin V. 112
Johnson, Alvin S. 66
Johnson, Clifton 227
Johnson, Doris J. 203
Johnson, Edna 40
Johnson, Henry 66, 151
Johnson, Henry C., Jr. 112
Johnson, Jack T. 152
Johnson, Julia E. 228
Johnson, Laurence B. 194
Johnson, Russell 28
Johnson, Samuel 4, 66
Johnson, William R. 159
Johnston, Herbert 172
Joncich, Geraldine M. 71
Jones, Barbara 138
Jones, Charles E. 209
Jones, Edward A. 111
Jones, James J. 28, 179
Jones, Reginald L. 222
Jones, Rufus M. 134
Jones, Theodore F. 127
Jones, Thomas E. 136
Jordan, David S. 66, 94
Jorgenson, Lloyd P. 220
Joyce, Bruce 165
Joyce, William W. 77, 199

K

Kaestle, Carl F. 212
Kandel, Isaac L. 15, 58, 148, 189
Katz, Michael B. 49
Kaufman, Martin 161
Kayser, Elmer L. 108
Keep, Rosalind A. 105
Kelly, Brooks M. 107
Kelly, David H. 220
Kelner, Bernard G. 165
Kelsey, Rayner W. 198
Kendall, Elaine 231
Kennedy, Millard F. 185
Kennett, White 1
Kenniston, Kenneth 222
Kerr, Clark 97
Keyes, Ralph 188
Kiddle, Henry 76
Kiefer, Monica 40
Kilpatrick, William H. 19, 67, 163, 167, 173, 178, 215
Kimball, Solon T. 49
Kindred, Leslie 165
Kinnear, Duncan L. 140
Kinsolving, Arthur B. 198
Kirk, Russell 25
Klapperman, Gilbert 128
Kleibard, Herbert M. 182
Klein, Frederic S. 134
Klein, H.M.J. 197
Kluger, Richard 38
Knauss, James O. 213
Knight, Edgar W. 14, 15, 148, 217
Knight, George W. 102
Knowles, Asa 43
Knowles, Malcolm S. 29
Knox, Samuel 10
Koerner, James D. 34, 225
Kohl, Herbert R. 32, 169, 181
Koos, Leonard V. 19, 42, 157
Korn, Harold A. 222
Korpalski, Adam 190
Kozol, Jonathan 81, 212
Kraft, Leonard E. 28
Kraus, John 158
Kraus-Boelte, Maria 158
Kraushaar, Otto F. 153
Krepel, Wayne J. 170
Kropp, Simon F. 124

Name Index

Popper, Samuel H. 74, 165
Porter, Earl W. 129
Porter, Noah 16, 93
Postman, Neil 50
Potter, Alonzo 12, 162
Potter, Norris W. 191
Potter, Robert E. 149
Poulus, Kathleen 61
Powell, Arthur G. 118
Powell, Lyman P. 209
Powell, William S. 129
Power, Edward J. 184
Powers, Joseph F. 30
Pratt, Sally B. 87
Prescott, Peter S. 154
Prescott, Samuel C. 118
Price, Carl F. 107
Prince, Nathan 4
Proctor, Samuel 110
Pronovost, Wilbert 206
Pulliam, John D. 150
Pusey, Nathan M. 98
Pyburn, Nita K. 209

R

Radosh, Ronald 222
Ragan, William B. 74
Ragle, John W. 192
Rambusch, Nancy M. 167
Ramsey, Marjorie E. 158
Randall, Prudence B. 75
Randall, Samuel S. 216
Rarig, Emory 41
Raub, Albert N. 163
Rauh, Morton A. 87
Ravitch, Diane 22, 50, 216
Raywid, Mary A. 50
Read, Donald A. 152
Read, Herbert 31
Read, Katherine H. 54
Reeder, Ward G. 179
Reischauer, Robert D. 81
Reisner, Edward H. 75
Rezneck, Samuel 127
Rice, Joseph M. 16, 45, 164
Rice, Joseph P. 83
Rich, John M. 155
Richards, Laura E. 65
Richardson, Joe E. 136

Richardson, Leon B. 123
Richel, William C. 197
Richey, Herman G. 147
Rickover, Hyman G. 21, 47
Ridd, Merrill K. 82
Riddle, William 217
Ridgeway, James 98
Riesenberg, Felix 117
Riesman, David 97
Rigg, Edward 8
Rippa, S. Alexander 150
Risley, James H. 208
Rist, Ray C. 179
Rivera, Geraldo 205
Rivlin, Harry N. 76, 165
Roa, Lynn 204
Roberts, Gene, Jr. 26
Robinson, Nancy M. 205
Rochmis, Lyda N. 206
Rockcastle, Verne N. 186
Rogers, David 216
Rogers, Dorothy M. 53
Root, Nathaniel W.T. 175
Rosenberger, Jesse L. 127
Rosner, Benjamin 225
Ross, Alan O. 204
Ross, Dorothy 65
Ross, Earle D. 113
Roswell, Florence G. 181
Roubinek, Darrel L. 168
Roucek, Joseph S. 151
Rouse, Parke 59
Ruddiman, Thomas 7
Rudman, Herbert C. 229
Rudman, Masha K. 41
Rudolph, Frederick 91, 150
Rudolph, Marguerita 157
Rudy, S. Willis 89, 125
Rugg, Harold O. 19, 179, 225
Rulon, Philip R. 132
Rush, Benjamin 9, 10, 231
Russell, James E. 154
Russell, William 13
Ryan, Kevin 226

S

Sabaroff, Rose 169
Sachar, Abram L. 117
Sack, Saul 102

Name Index